work

spheres

Design and Contemporary Work Styles

Edited by **Paola Antonelli**

THE MUSEUM OF MODERN ART, NEW YORK

Distributed by Harry N. Abrams, Inc., New York

Published on the occasion of the exhibition *Workspheres*, organized by Paola Antonelli,
Curator, Department of Architecture and Design, The Museum of Modern Art, New York,
February 8–April 22, 2001.
(www.moma.org/workspheres)

This exhibition is made possible by Haworth, Inc., Herman Miller Inc., Knoll, Inc.,
Steelcase Inc., and the Xerox Foundation.

Additional support is provided by Peter Norton, Norton Family Foundation,
The Norman and Rosita Winston Foundation, and The Junior Associates of
The Museum of Modern Art.

Produced by the Department of Publications
The Museum of Modern Art, New York

Edited by Joanne Greenspun
Designed by Antony Drobinski, Emsworth Design, Inc.
Cover design by Ed Pusz
Production by Christina Grillo
Color separation by Barry Siddall, MR Reproduktionen, Munich
Printed and bound by Dr. Cantz'sche Druckerei, Ostfildern, Germany
Printed on 150 gsm Luxo Art Silk
Typeface: ITC Stone Sans

Library of Congress Catalogue Card Number: 00-136719
ISBN: 0-87070-013-8 (MoMA, T&H)
ISBN: 0-8109-6217-9 (Abrams)

Published by The Museum of Modern Art, New York
11 West 53 Street, New York, New York 10019
(www.moma.org)

Distributed in the United States and Canada by Harry N. Abrams, Inc., New York (www.abramsbooks.com)

Distributed outside the United States and Canada by Thames & Hudson Ltd., London

Printed in Germany

Front and back cover:
Bart Hendriks. "Frederique," from *If/Then Design: Implications in New Media,* no. l. Netherlands Design Institute /BIS publishers, Amsterdam, 1999. William Gaver, Heather Martin, and Andy Boucher.Double Deck Desk 2, version B. Concept, 2000

Contents

	6	FOREWORD
	7	PREFACE
Paola Antonelli	8	WORKSPHERES
Larry Keeley	18	WORK WAVES
Christopher Budd	26	THE OFFICE: 1950 TO THE PRESENT
John Thackara	36	DESIGNING THE SPACE OF FLOWS
Aura Oslapas	44	TIME: CHANGE: BOUNDARIES
Kayoko Ota, Jim-hee Chang, Hui-Chi Chou, and Rachaporn Chouchouey	46	TOKYO, SEOUL, TAIPEI, AND BANGKOK
Paola Antonelli	52	*Interview with* BRUCE MAU
Sarah Robins	57	*Interview with* MICHAEL BRILL
Paola Antonelli	61	*Interview with* FRANCIS DUFFY
	64	TESTIMONIALS
		PLATES
	70	THE OFFICIAL OFFICE
	96	THE INDIVIDUAL WORKSTATION
	108	CHAIRS, TABLES, AND OTHER FURNITURE
	132	THE NOMADIC OFFICE
	170	DESKTOP OBJECTS
	198	THE DOMESTIC OFFICE
	211	WORKSPHERES: SIX COMMISSIONED PROJECTS
	218	ACKNOWLEDGMENTS
	220	PHOTOGRAPH CREDITS
	221	INDEX
	224	TRUSTEES OF THE MUSEUM OF MODERN ART

Foreword

During the past two years, curators at The Museum of Modern Art have focused on the Museum's collection, organizing a series of extensive exhibitions that included major holdings from the six curatorial departments. These exhibitions have examined the Museum's history and reflected on the role it has played in interpreting modern art. *Workspheres*, the first exhibition to follow this celebration, acknowledges the present while projecting the future. It is both timely and poignant in that it continues the Museum's energetic tradition of observing contemporary practices while encouraging artists and designers to think in new and innovative ways.

Workspheres is a design exhibition and thus, by definition, it is an exhibition about the intersection of aesthetic values and practical realities. Its primary concern is the workplace today, and it offers numerous design solutions to help us balance work and life. *Workspheres* recognizes the growing importance of work in our lives, and it has specific relevance to the Museum's staff as we commence our move to MoMAQNS, in Queens, New York, and the expansion of our present building on 53 Street in Manhattan.

This provocative exhibition explores the individual worksphere in the context of an official office, a home office, and in a travel setting. Its scope is international and includes examples of work styles from around the world. By highlighting innovative solutions by designers and manufacturers, it empowers the public to understand design quality in their everyday surroundings.

Included in *Workspheres* are newly commissioned projects by six teams of architects, designers, and engineers; there are also many other new works, prototypes, and objects. The displayed design paragons range from the ubiquitous Post-it® note and Bic pens to a giant SUV and trailer equipped to allow one to live and work on the road. *Workspheres* is groundbreaking not only in its embrace of the subject of work in relation to good design, but in the many satellite activities it has undertaken and will undertake: video interviews commissioned by the Museum; questionnaires asking people all over the world about their workstyles; an online survey, which similarly asks for work-related anecdotes; and a forthcoming symposium.

Paola Antonelli, a talented curator in the Department of Architecture and Design at the Museum, conceived both the exhibition and the accompanying publication. She was joined by a distinguished group of advisors, including Larry Keeley, Bruce Mau, Aura Oslapas, and John Thackara. Together, they have developed an exhibition and project that extend and transform our understanding of the working environment.

Glenn D. Lowry, Director
The Museum of Modern Art

Preface

One of the leitmotifs of *Workspheres* is "soft and fuzzy," from software to fuzzy logic. If soft and fuzzy sound more like a blanket than a place, it isn't such a bad metaphor. Being "wrapped up with your work" is a phrase that has an all new meaning in *Workspheres.*

A comparison of the environments and products in this book and their ancestors is notable. The grandparents of *Workspheres* can be seen, for example, in Frank Lloyd Wright's 1906 design for the Larkin Company, a mail-order soap business in Buffalo, New York. Incoming mail and outgoing orders moved through the assembly line of clerical workers' desks, chairs, lamps, and file cabinets like chassis through a Ford Motor plant. Photographs of the Larkin Company's employees at work show a humming mill of activity in and around a skylit atrium. The precise brickwork and machinelike quality of the steel desks and chairs are only slightly mediated by the hand-carved detail, edifying inscriptions, and potted plants crowning the atrium, and the Gibson Girl look of the women, whose clerical work kept the mail-order business running.

Workspheres' parents are less likely to be found in steel and iron cities like Buffalo than in the outlying areas around them. The big-city vertical axis of the Larkin building gave way to the horizontal axis of the suburbs. Skidmore, Owings & Merrill's 1957–61 design for the IBM headquarters in Armonk, New York, epitomized the emergence of a corporate culture built on the lessons derived from the war effort in terms of scale, organization, and discipline. While no less paternalistic and certainly no less competitive than the Larkin Company, the architects and designers commissioned by IBM and other emergent multinational companies framed the new managerial culture in an environment of suburban ease that belied the self-effacement required to achieve it.

If the working world of *Workspheres'* grandparents and parents is easily evoked, so are their domestic counterparts. The industrial energies that produced the Larkin Company were the same that dreamed of and often built the "company town," paternalist utopias where workers' lives would be integrated in an orderly physical environment of work, recreation, and socializing. In the next generation, the town company often built itself on the relatively open suburban landscape, creating entire white-collar communities based on the corporate values of their employers.

The real inheritance left to *Workspheres* by its grandparents and parents is not the soap or Selectric typewriters they produced, but the working systems that they created and developed in response to the emergence of larger local, then national, then international, systems of communication and transport. As sophisticated as they had become, however, those communication and transport systems were fairly rigid in their application, and the effect could be seen throughout the working environment of the 1960s and 1970s. The continuing emphasis on standardization and Taylorized tasks was reflected in the spaces and equipment in which they were performed: acres of cubicles and offices lined with file cabinets, and punctuated by the ubiquitous typewriter, telephone, postage meter, and photocopier.

The explosive emergence of digital technologies in the 1980s produced the wild child that is *Workspheres.* Its hallmark is not the abolishment of standardized systems but the development of systems that are so vast, flexible, and fast that they no longer appear to be systems. Where *Workspheres'* parents and grandparents adapted themselves to fit their technologies, *Workspheres* is an ocean of technology navigated in infinite ways. While driven by the same culture of capital and materialism as its forbears, *Workspheres* strives to be less paternalistic and more fraternalistic, which can be taken to include the promise of less hierarchy as well as the threat of "Big Brother."

The placelessness of the cyberworld is a principal definer of the nature of *Workspheres.* In an ideal world, it heals the gap that arose in the nineteenth century between the public world of men at work and the private world of women at home, between the gritty urban world of factories and the over-compensating domestic fantasia of suburban culture.

Terence Riley
Chief Curator, Department of Architecture and Design

Workspheres
Paola Antonelli

Bart Hendriks. "Frederique," from *If/Then Design: Implications in New Media,* no. 1. Amsterdam: Netherlands Design Institute/BIS publishers, 1999

Design is about life. When historical revolutions happen that shake the world and ultimately affect the way we live, design can provide the power, grace, clarity, and balance necessary to accommodate these stressful circumstances. Today, major changes are happening in the workplace, brought about by the rapid evolution of information technology. If well directed, they could affect not only economic and technological progress, but also, and more importantly, improvements in the way we treat our families, ourselves, and the environment. Better than an information revolution, they could become a knowledge revolution. Good design can act as the mediator between technology and human beings and is always an advocate of the latter.

Workspheres is an exhibition devoted to the way we work and the role of design in creating effective solutions for future work environments and tools. Its emphasis is on those work areas that could benefit from the efforts of designers to provide creative ideas and thus make real contributions. It is an exhibition that focuses on developed world regions or those undergoing rapid development. In other words, it deals with a condition that stems from abundance. It does not address the work environments of agriculture, mining, manufacturing, and other industries because these areas are more the task of economists, politicians, unions, and engineers than of designers.

The exhibition presumes that while our work has determined our lives and will continue to do so in the future, our lives will also shape the way we work or, at the very least, these two spheres will better inform each other. To achieve this new balance, which is considered economically significant at all levels of employment, new work tools and environments must be designed for flexibility and customization.

Background on the Exhibition
This is not the first time that The Museum of Modern Art has addressed current design issues and solicited new responses. The Low-Cost Furniture competition of 1948 was conceived to accommodate the booming lower middle class supported by the GI Bill and by the robust economy; in the exhibitions *Useful Objects of American Design under $10* (1939) and *Useful Objects in Wartime under $10* (1942),

Museum curators chose and exhibited the best-designed functional items; in the Good Design program (1950–55) the curators, in collaboration with the Merchandise Mart in Chicago, singled out functional objects from the current production, from hairbrushes to chairs, and awarded them a "Good Design" label; and the *Taxi Project* of 1976 was an occasion to ask designers to rethink New York taxicabs. These competitions and exhibitions, initiated by The Museum of Modern Art, were fertile ground for many successful products, such as the furniture of Charles Eames and Eero Saarinen that is still manufactured by Herman Miller, which was first developed for a 1940 competition at the Museum before becoming an American design icon.

With these precedents in mind, the workplace became the target of the Museum's next design exhibition. Slowly but surely in the past decade, work has lost its immediate identification with the office as a room or space in a designated building, where all work tasks are carried out, from writing and faxing to attending meetings. Work has become transportable and ubiquitous, almost a state of mind. Like a bubble of pure concentration that one can turn on and off with or without the help of tangible tools, work is where you are.

Wary of the cacophonous neologisms that are one of the dark sides of the recent work-style revolution, we tested a myriad of titles for the exhibition, among them the meaningful, yet unpronounceable *Workdom,*[1] before settling on *Workspheres*. This title comes from the concept of the individual workspace as a halo, a private and personal space, that better defines and enables interaction.

Workspheres features built models of newly conceived tools and environments for knowledge workers produced by design teams from around the world. Some of the models were already under development; others were proposed for the exhibition. Six of them were commissioned by the Museum on this occasion. These models are complemented by a display of products already on the market, selected according to curatorial criteria.

Although many of the design solutions presented are intended for the Western world, we looked everywhere for suggestions. Japan, which has undergone the deepest internal cultural shift in the workplace, was instrumental in the study of rapid change. Some parts of Europe provided several suggestions in balance, lifestyle, and workspace. Brazil was an inspiration in alternative office solutions, while India showed the power of contrasts, between tradition and innovation, wealth and poverty, and the efforts to overcome it by means of design.

the commute

Guru.com advertisement:
The Commute. 1999

In addition to the models and environments, this exhibition also sheds light on the many theories about our working future, for there have been dramatic innovations devoted to the management of time and priorities and to the balance between private and professional life. For example, there is one theory that has us all working from home in our pajamas; another holds that a separate office away from home is still viable and desirable; a third suggests ways that we can work as effectively in transit as in a designated workspace. Moreover, the exhibition also takes interfaces into consideration as virtual work environments.

To delineate the commissions and prepare the exhibition, we embarked on extensive research and, more importantly, chose excellent partners with a vast knowledge of design, economics, planning, and overall logical thinking. The official advisory board includes Larry Keeley, president of Doblin Group, Chicago, and a known expert on design strategy and innovation; Bruce Mau, a philosopher and designer, from Toronto, Canada; Aura Oslapas, designer and an expert on behavioral design, from San Francisco; and John Thackara, director of Doors of Perception design futures conference in Amsterdam.

With their help and that of many unofficial advisors, ranging from creative entrepreneur Jay Chiat to Indian designer Satyendra Pakhale, we compiled a *cahier des doléances* of sorts, outlining the foremost frustrations and desires in the contemporary workplace.

We asked ourselves the following questions: What does the contemporary workplace look like? What is wrong with the way we work? What could be improved? How do we measure work today? Is it still a matter of productivity? What can design do about it? The briefs for the commissions come from these discussions; the designers were selected on the basis of their responses to the perceived problems.

The Role of Design
Labeled by some "the discipline of problem-solving," design finds itself in a crucial position, as it is often expected to take total control of the fast and fractal evolution, in this case, of the workplace. However, designers and architects will not steer the world. Instead, they will design its new configurations based on human needs and requirements. We agree with Bill Joy, the lucid co-founder and current vice president for research at Sun Microsystems, who said, "Redesign [of the workplace to accommodate the possibilities of digital technology] begins by designing individual objects to be part of these spaces, without trying to dictate in advance exactly how the people who use the spaces will ultimately put them to use; as engineers we call this style 'bottom-up design.'"[2]

Our work activity occupies many different physical and virtual spheres. A portable computer integrated with a cellular phone and operated from a seat on a train to Boston, for instance, is enough to generate an invisible and efficient bubble of workspace. With a little design help—such as a foldable handkerchief screen and keyboard—this accommodation can become as efficient as an office desk in New York, and may be more conducive to inspiration.

Larry Keeley pointed out that in a diagram with a worker in the center, surrounded by the various scales of a work environment—an office building, office equipment, and supplies—the worker is only the apparent center of the universe. In reality, the effort of reaching out to achieve an understanding of how things work is a burden on his or her shoulders. The opposite should instead be true; everything should be conceived and explained to function for the worker, and to be commensurate with him or her. Making this diagram centripetal, as opposed to centrifugal, is the long-term design ideal.

Work Tools

Compiling a list of the work tools most knowledge workers use daily, and the locations where they use them, was an interesting exercise. Computers, the center of our contemporary working world, are set on a dematerialization path. So much has happened since the Mac 128K appeared on our desks in 1984. Most laptops today are as powerful and fast as desktop computers. Soon all of our applications will be available from a network, and most of our interactivity will be absorbed by cell phones; these applications will become even lighter and, hopefully, simpler and more reliable than they are now.

In some countries, cell phones now allow people to make payments and purchases, not to mention connecting to the Internet and storing a scheduling program and an address book. In the most advanced markets, more than sixty percent of the population carry cell phones.[3] After the analog and digital series, the third generation will be even more efficient, transforming cell phones into control panels for our lives.

One can also mention other recent products and systems, such as Real-Time Digital Video, teleconferencing systems, Personal Digital Assistants, digital secretaries, pagers, Bluetooth, Global Positioning System devices, and web cameras. Other fresh innovations just delivered to the market include keyboards embedded in textiles, voice recognition, and large-capacity Dictaphones, cell phones that take a picture and send it via the Internet, cell phones with real-time video, Ultra-Wide Band radio, smart devices connected to a network that can signal their malfunction, and high-speed and wireless connectivity. The list is dizzying and often so is the experience. "In this era of amazing change we will face a huge challenge of design: how to humanize our digital devices, our homes and offices, and our public places; how we will make them serve our needs; and how we will make the digitally enhanced places beautiful," says Bill Joy. "The design style I am advocating is one in which each device and service is simple and directly reflects its use."[4] So are we.

Design is concerned with building our relationship with these tools and with the environments and workstations. It is also bound to ensure that these devices help us to be more creative and efficient by making them easier and more comfortable to use. A great past example of this role of design is the Graphic User Interface conceived by the members of Xerox PARC in 1981. The GUI, the interface with a desktop, files, and folders that became the Macintosh's official work environment and was later adopted by Windows, helped us accept our new simulated parallel office and facilitate the daily transit from our habitual physical office. By keeping the simulacra of our past life, the files and folders, it eased even the most romantic lovers of manual typewriters into a new way of thinking. Personal computers changed the way we conceive our daily tasks and organize our thoughts.

However, we must not forget that old tools and habits remain important in our lives. Even the most technologically advanced individuals need to see accomplished tasks crossed out with a red pen to feel satisfied or need to scribble out ideas and think aloud on paper to align their thoughts. The future will move in this direction: while technological devices will be scaled down and linked to a network, we will maintain our structural attachment to some traditional tools such as a pen, pencil, eraser, paper, and Post-it® notes. This should be the paradigm for design at all levels.

Telework: Nomadic and Domestic Offices

Presence in an office is no longer mandatory, and in some cases it could even be considered redundant. The possibility of working at home or at a remote location, once the good fortune of a few conceptual work categories, such as writers and freelance professionals,

Financial Times. British Press Campaign. October 1999

Motorola advertisement, c. 1995

Screen shot from Kaliber 10000 (*www.k10k.net*), showing a collection of personal desktop screen shots sent in by viewers

and the curse of traveling salesmen, has become more viable across the board. It has also shown considerable positive social and economic relevance. In a traditional employment situation, telework responds to the employee's need to improve the balance between home and work by eliminating or cutting down the commute time; by reducing costs; by providing increased mobility and flexibility; by making for a healthier personal and family life by leaving more room for serious recreation. On the employer's side, it helps the company maintain loyalty and well-being among its employees; it allows for a better use of the existing facilities; and it ultimately increases productivity. The benefits continue at a larger scale, as workers spending more time at home improve the safety and liveliness of their neighborhoods, reduce air pollution and traffic, and conserve energy.

Last but not least, telework allows the most important fuel for human creativity: freedom. "For all the new tools of the workplace, for all its electronic appliances and communication apparatuses, for all its human-engineered desks and ergonomically correct chairs,

why do so many of us do our best thinking when we're some place else? And does the thinking that we do in our beds, showers, gardens and cars lead to a different wisdom than the thinking we do in our workplace?"[5] In other words, when the workplace can be everywhere, so can inspiration.

According to the Bureau of Labor Statistics, about 12 million out of 131 million workers in the United States fit the description of "workers with alternative arrangements."[6] In the forest of new terms coined to describe this aspect of our new work style, "telesprawl" defines this type of decentralization of work activities that has initially been made possible by faxes, E-mail, and FedEx. While some urban-studies scholars at first felt that telework would threaten the life of city centers, so far it has merely revitalized the suburbs. The social side of work has proven to be an important aspect for people's well-being. Workspheres need to collide and interact to be effective. In response to this and to the need to share some costlier technological equipment, many telework centers, also called "hoteling"

The world's hottest new financial headquarters.

Check stock quotes. Research companies. Get up-to-the-minute financial news. Then go to the kitchen and make an omelette. www.yahoo.com

Yahoo! Finance

Do You YAHOO!?

Yahoo! advertisement. 1991

centers, have been set up in the suburbs, where desks, telephones, office equipment, meeting rooms, and especially watercoolers are provided, in the guise of a Kinko's or an airline club.[7]

The role that design should assume is obvious, as this new typology of the workplace has to be conceived from scratch and needs to accommodate new human behavior. The tenets of telework are applied in the exhibition to the projects that deal with nomadic and domestic offices, which aim at helping the transition and designing the new archetypes.

The Official Office

What will happen to the spaces in dedicated buildings away from home, devoted both to individual work and to physical interaction and meetings? If people are learning to be free, how can employers avoid restraining them by means of design, while still providing the necessary infrastructures? These are some of the major questions that are continually being explored by architects and scholars. As Michael Brill, president of BOSTI Associates, a multidisciplinary

workplace analysis firm, says, "Most companies now recognize that their people are their primary asset (their 'intellectual capital') and recognize that the workplace is a tool that can be shaped and managed to purposefully increase performance; enhance creativity, teamwork and learning; and give pleasure in work. . . . While the workplace is not a dominant contributor, it always makes a significant contribution to performance and satisfaction, and enough to justify investments in shaping workplaces to be more supportive."[8]

While *Workspheres* focuses on the individual workspace, it is clearly influenced by its aggregation in offices and buildings, which could and should be the subject of another—or many other—architectural exhibition. In terms of a progressive approach to the individual worker, the first scale is the geographic one: the location of the official office is of paramount importance. One of the workspaces in the exhibition is a partial replica of Hiroaki Kitano's Symbiotic Systems Project office, located in a former residential building facing Omotesando, one of the busiest day- and nighttime streets in Tokyo. Kitano, whose team designed and engineered AIBO pet robots produced by Sony, says that the area is beneficial and necessary to the creativity that his team's job demands. The office is open twenty-four hours a day, and life is constantly buzzing around it. According to Kitano, there is a relationship between the different scales of the office building and creativity. The space must let ideas flow comfortably, while the location stimulates ideas.

Very revealing is the comparison between the United States and Europe delineated by Francis Duffy, a renowned office buildings architect and thinker. According to him, while the U.S. has a high gross national product and, overall, can rely on cheap real estate, Europe has to make do with much less money and has higher real-estate costs. That is why the investment in sustainability and durability is of much greater concern in Europe, where designers and architects have to compensate for the built-in inefficiencies of the system. For these reasons, offices in Europe tend to be designed to have more enclosed rooms and to be environmentally more sophisticated, while American offices can count on a lower density but also on a lower specificity of design.

During his career at the helm of Chiat/Day, Jay Chiat built at least two famous office spaces: the Venice headquarters, designed

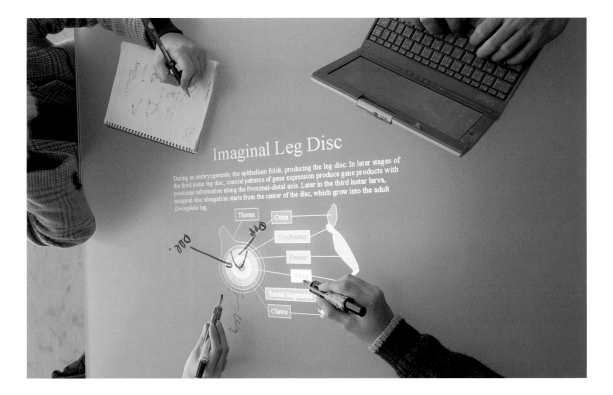

Hiroaki Kitano and others. Kitano Symbiotic Systems Project office, Tokyo. 1999

by Frank Gehry, and the New York City ones, designed by Gaetano Pesce. These spaces were revolutionary experiments that marked milestones in the evolution of office configurations. In his new incarnation at ScreamingMedia, an Internet content company, Chiat is once again setting the archetype for a particular type of contemporary workspace. As the ScreamingMedia website explains, Chiat commissioned partners Jane Sachs and Thomas Hut of Hut Sachs Studio to transform the 25,000-square-foot interior "to be a second home and social hub for its young staff members, whose average age is 26. . . . Organization was to be open and non-hierarchical. Moves typical of early experiments in hotelling and virtual officing were to be avoided. Each of the 160 employees would have a permanent place." The latter is a clear reference to the bygone, fabulous, yet unlikely Chiat/Day offices in New York, where 140 employees had no dedicated office, and worked at docking desks with laptops, communicated by cell phone, and put their personal belongings in lockers.

The office as a home is one of the most repeated paradigms. Employers use comfort as a way to build loyalty in a high-turnover market. USAA in San Antonio, an insurance and financial services company, provides its employees with child-care centers, great cafeterias, beautiful facilities, vanpools, health clubs, children's playgrounds, dry-cleaning service, and a bank. ScreamingMedia offers its younger employees a sense of belonging: a cool location (the Starrett-Lehigh Building in Chelsea), a buzzing activity, social oppor-

tunities—the office as a studio. All over, a new sense of hierarchy is having an impact on architecture, and dress codes have moved in a casual direction. In the exhibition, one of the commissions, realized by LOT/EK, is devoted to providing even more homey character to the workplace by inserting private spaces to take a nap, relax, concentrate, or simply be elsewhere and get some of the best thoughts of the day, as if under the shower.

Design can do much to establish corporate culture, and the interior space should be seamlessly the subject of equal attention. There are thousands of different standard office systems available on the market, from the barest cubicle to the most imaginative tree structure. As in architecture, the biggest design effort today appears to be devoted to the improvement of the revolutionary modernist Action Office of the 1960s by Robert Propst for Herman Miller, whose innovative panels, as many say, "gave designers power over walls." That great leap forward sadly led to the AO's corruption into the much-hated cubicle. Designers and manufacturers are now trying to substitute screens and membranes for walls, replace orthogonal rationality with a more cellular and organic disposition, and move away from muted corporate colors toward more freedom of choice and customization. More importantly, they are trying to make all this affordable and sensible. Many of these examples are reflected in the products and the commissions in the exhibition.

Descending one more degree in scale, furniture has gained

higher status, thanks to a new mode of production and composition. The 1960s and 1970s were the years of the ergonomics breakthroughs, when designers like Henry Dreyfuss and Niels Diffrient set the scientific parameters of comfort with their studies on ergonomics. The past thirty years have seen tremendous progress, resulting in exceptionally comfortable chairs, accessories such as footrests, handrests, and lumbar supports, new and better surfaces, and modulated lighting. Relaxation and physical well-being are universally considered very important for optimum productivity. There even exists on the market an "ergonomic stretching program" for Windows computers called Stretch Break Pro, produced by Para Technologies. Repetitive strain injuries, like the infamous carpal tunnel syndrome, are being addressed by better design and a more thoughtful work style, aided by the innovations in manufacturing techniques and in the technology of materials.

The Commissions

The preliminary research in the preparation of *Workspheres* attempted to achieve a deeper understanding of contemporary work practices and needs, to set limits, to create categories, and to delineate the tasks for the designers. Time and pressure seem to be the most recurrent concerns, as they are the summation of all the other defects in our work styles. The pressure generated by the difficulty of juggling work and family, of keeping up with technology, of changing pace so often, of simply having so much work to do and so little inner and outer guidance is responsible for many personal and collective dysfunctions. "Nearly half of workers engaged in unethical or illegal acts in the last year, according to a survey. . . . Faced with demands of overtime, balancing work and family, and downsizing, workers said they feel more stress than five years ago, as well as more pressure to act unethically. . . .The most common behavior involved cutting corners on quality (16 percent), covering up incidents (14 percent), abusing or lying about sick days (11 percent) and lying to or deceiving customers (9 percent)."[9] This is, of course, one of the most dramatic consequences of pressure malaise and stress.

There are consultants who specialize in teaching how to manage priorities, allot time, and organize information. Yukio Noguchi, an expert in information organization, invented the "squeeze-out"

Delaney Lund Knox Warren, London: Alan Burles, art director, and Paul Evans, copywriter. Financial Times. British Press Campaign. October 1999

method to store information in a computer: "Human memory is such that when we are presented with information it is organized in temporal order. Information is classified according to its meaning to the individual, and then stored as long-term memory. With the 'squeeze-out' method unused envelopes are gradually pushed to one side, where they remain if there is space. Envelopes are not discarded even if untouched for years. This is not out of desire but fear. . . . It's Murphy's law: 'a document thrown away will be needed the next .'"[10] This statement is an example of how very often the best solutions are the most commonsensical ones, the ones dictated by our natural way of thinking and acting.

Thanks to their familiarity with the practice of synthesis and projection and to their closeness to human nature, designers are often able to anticipate future needs and provide realistic and reliable suggestions without being carried away by science fiction or ideology. We asked six teams to work on diverse aspects of stress, pressure, pleasure, and satisfaction by addressing those aspects that could help the whole workplace be a better, more suitable place. Architects, designers, and companies have been selected from different countries and cultures to highlight the fluctuating relationship between pluralism and individualism, and national and global concerns, that will characterize the present century.

The full-size models are designed to represent solutions to specific needs and desires that are apparent among contemporary knowledge workers from all over the world. They are real and effective concepts for new design objects that not only address all the requirements indicated, but also suggest possible improvements in the use of technologies and materials either currently available, or available in the near future. In other words, *Workspheres* is a staged presentation of sensible, well-designed tools and environments for the workplace in the early twenty-first century. This catalogue is a tool that represents our notes in the preparation of the exhibition. At the time this catalogue went to press, the models and the exhibition were not yet completed. We invite you to visit the exhibition website to learn more about them.[11] Nonetheless, the most important part of any design project, the study of its field of action and the setting of goals and means, is here to be shared. In life, there is never just one solution to a given problem. The work compiled in this volume, we hope, will open up many more solutions than we can possibly imagine.

Felderman and Keatinge Design. Interface Americas Corporate Headquarters, Cartersville, Georgia. 1999

Notes

1 *Workdom* is the contribution of designer and friend Lisa Krohn.

2 Bill Joy, "Design for the Digital Revolution," *Fortune* 141, no. 5 (March 6, 2000), special 70th anniversary issue, p. F-10+special section, "The Capitalist."

3 Telecommunications survey in *The Economist*, October 9, 1999, pp. 5–36.

4 See note 2.

5 Akiko Busch, ed., "The Ways We Work," *Metropolis,* October 1993, p. 62.

6 Michael Lewis, "The Artist in the Gray Flannel Pajamas," *The New York Times Magazine,* March 5, 2000.

7 Karrie Jacobs, "Waiting for the Millennium, Part III," *Metropolis,* October 1994, pp. 86–97.

8 Michael Brill, E-mail message to the author, July 12, 2000.

9 "Cutting Corners: Workplace Stress and the Breakdown of Ethics," *International Herald Tribune*, April 7, 1997, p. 10.

10 Yukio Noguchi interviewed by Noriko Takiguchi on Axis, July-August 1995, p. 23

11 http://www.moma.org/workspheres

Work Waves
Larry Keeley

The Perils of Prediction

About forty years ago, Joe Barbera and his team at Hanna Barbera treated us to an entertaining vision of work in our time with *The Jetsons* cartoon. Although only twenty-four episodes were produced for the original 1962–63 series—remarkably it ran at prime time on ABC—*The Jetsons* show has been with us ever since and can still be seen routinely on the Cartoon Network. As with most visions of the future, by and large they got it wrong. Work at Spacely Sprockets, George Jetson's job, was factory life—George thought very little, had virtually no authority, pushed lots of buttons, hated his work, was obsessed with his title and his career ladder, and was engaged in continuous class warfare with his autocratic and domineering boss.

George Jetson did have a remarkable home life. He lived in a condo at Skypad Apartments. His travel was made easy and completely "automagical" by a personal aircraft. Rosie, the family robot, did all the cleaning. Unseen systems in the home prepared all the

Steven Guarnaccia. *New Uses for Old Technology: The Pencil.* 1999

meals. Teenage daughter Judy loved to shop, but no one else ever had any need to. Every bit of daily life was automated, sanitized, and stripped of ritual and any warmth. Even Bill Gates doesn't live like this!

Knowledge Work at the Turn of a Century

What has *actually* occurred in that forty-year span has been far more remarkable than anything anticipated by these superficial projections. What *The Jetsons* got right is the omnipresence of computing power; they missed the true fabric of how this shift would change everything: nothing less than a change in the fundamental nature of work.

As the social scientist Peter Drucker noted in 1980, the center of gravity in the world of work has sharply shifted from manual work to "knowledge work." Regardless of the amount of knowledge, skill, or tools required, manual work converts material from one form to another. As a result this work produces a tangible output. By contrast, knowledge work involves converting information from one form to another. The results of a knowledge-work process are frequently intangible. Although it is true that both the manual worker and the knowledge worker deal with knowledge and information, only the knowledge worker works on them. Consequently, the nature of working is very different for a knowledge worker than it is for a manual worker.

In 1920 the ratio of manual workers to knowledge workers was 2:1. John Naisbitt noted a midpoint in this shift around 1956, the year white-collar workers first outnumbered blue-collar workers. By 1980 this ratio had completely flipped to twice as many knowledge workers as manual workers. Some industries are more knowledge intensive than others, of course. The percentage of knowledge workers in the computer industry is estimated to be seventy-two percent and in the legal profession it would be close to ninety-five percent. But the pace of the shift from manual work to knowledge work seems to be slowing considerably, if census data can be trusted. Now the percentage of the employed workforce engaged in actual manufacturing operations is estimated at thirteen percent and seems unlikely to decline below, say seven percent, even if we give it another couple of decades.

Knowledge work is not only ascendant; it is truly weird. Many leading social scientists from Drucker to Zuboff, Nickols, Toffler, Zand, and others have written about the odd ways that knowledge

Felderman and
Keatinge Design.
Fabergé Corporate
Headquarters, New
York. 1971. Stanley
Felderman on
stairwell

work differs from manual work. Knowledge work is less visible, more abstract, nonlinear, and often controlled largely by the worker.

But these mere descriptive factors may miss a larger point. Somewhere along the way knowledge workers have come to harbor a truly audacious expectation. It now seems that we are supposed to care about our work. (Shocking!) Indeed, many young people see it as an element of personal expression. (The nerve!) Some even expect it to have an impact on the world. (How arrogant!) Rarely if ever before in human history has this been a common or credible aspiration. Yet today we mint young people with huge ambitions, little patience, and no discernible sense that what they expect is totally out of line with anything people could reasonably expect in the history of human toil. This is such a profound change that it's worth examining just how little the modern nature of work reflects life at Spacely Sprockets and what these tectonic shifts portend.

Let's be fair. For the huge majority of people, work life is still many steps removed from self-actualization. A crew person at a fast-food restaurant, a flight attendant on a commercial airline, a call-center operator at a catalogue company, a house painter, a drill-press operator, a road-construction-crew member, a retail clerk can all be expected to mutter more than a little as they read this text. Army recruits may find themselves a bit shocked at the huge gap between the ads that promise they will "be all that they can be" and the real nature of life in basic training and the infantry. Given the profound, problematic, and worsening gulf between knowledge work and other forms of work, such people can be forgiven for their "Die Yuppie Scum!" bumper stickers. But, as ever, the future is already here; it is just not evenly distributed. In the extreme nature of knowledge work, this wide gap and its greater rate of change make it the part of work from which we can most learn. So we will focus here disproportionately on the kind of work where people are given lots of tools, the freedom to exercise their own judgment, and are expected to work in intense and driven project teams. This is where we get a sense of what is truly new, modern, and deeply strange.

Successive Waves of Work

As long ago as 1651, in his book *The Leviathan,* the English philosopher Thomas Hobbes observed that "in a state of nature, men are equal in their self-seeking and live out lives that are nasty, brutish, and short." It took three hundred and fifty years, but now all aspects of this observation have been insulated and buffered in modern life. Today's knowledge workers love to return to this state of nature, of course, wherever it may still be found. When we do it now though it's in the form of extreme sports—parasailing, base-jumping, rock-climbing, mountain-biking, sky-boarding—whatever will provide an intense thrill and sufficient challenge. To make nature less nasty, we haul along thousands of dollars of exotic gear. Teams climb Everest, K2, or Annapurna, all the while posting photos on the Internet as the climb unfolds. Similarly, the conventions of modern commerce have insulated us from what is brutish. Competition is fierce, businesses can and do routinely fail, but little of this conflict is physically dangerous. What's more, with modern genetic sciences, we face the tantalizing prospect that life need no longer be short.

With these hostilities buffered, the conditions have been set for a revolution. A graduate of any of today's advanced professions—business, engineering, medicine, or law, for example—can count on having many options for work. This phenomenon is both recent and rare. Even today, in an era of relative peace and prosperity, the largesse is not widespread. Fewer than two percent of the world's workforce actually enjoys the sense that they can choose among many jobs and can then select, in part, what would please them most. But it fundamentally changes many basic aspects of life. Suddenly, those of us fortunate enough to participate in this knowledge-work revolution are faced with two big questions: What choices should we make to earn a living? And how ought we live once we make that living?

LIFE IS A LITTLE WORK, A LITTLE SLEEP, A LITTLE LOVE AND IT IS ALL OVER.
Mary Roberts Rinehart

Wave 1: Subsistence

Going back thousands of years, the social construct we call work has occurred purely out of necessity. We worked to produce our food or to produce sufficient funds to buy food, housing, and necessities. Work was broadly seen as drudgery: difficult tasks out of our control done at the behest of others.

From its earliest incarnation, there were clear, often paternalistic, class distinctions in office work, with sharp boundaries between the workplace and home. For the average person, work was role-oriented more than goal-oriented, and people tended to know and keep their place.

Facilities and organizational styles tended to mimic this structural norm. Consider even beautiful sites like the Johnson Wax headquarters so comprehensively designed by Frank Lloyd Wright in the 1930s. It clearly reflects a world of supervisors in elevated positions, where they could watch over a sea of clerical workers. This is not an environment that anticipated any significant degree of worker autonomy or individual initiative. Like George Jetson's world, this is factory work, and it seems shockingly anachronistic today.

Plenty of exceptions to this general pattern occurred, of course. As ever, artists, writers, some farmers and fisherman, craftspeople, actors, inventors, scientists, and other creative workers enjoyed a higher degree of control over their work than did unskilled laborers. Doctors also had an unusually high degree of personal autonomy in their work. Neither their patients—whom they usually knew personally—nor their nursing staffers would question them. House calls were common, specialization was comparatively rare, and it was not unusual for medical doctors to be paid with food or some other form of barter.

Rooted in social patterns that had existed for thousands of

years, this basic model for office work was very slow to change. Businesses were generally proprietorships until the late 1800s and tended to be small in scale. From frontier-town general stores, blacksmiths, and millinery shops evolved somewhat larger retailers, hardware stores, farmworkers, meatpacking plants, and service firms. But with owners and supervisors managing businesses with ironclad control, the pervasive sense that workers needed to be told what to do, then were watched as they did it, forced businesses to be small.

The industrial revolution changed this, of course: a time when scaling up became imperative for efficient use of capital and category leadership. Henry Ford did not really change the level of trust and esteem in the way he viewed his workforce; he just changed the number of employees he needed for a single enterprise. This set up workplace conflicts that became embittered and dangerous. But Henry Ford did want to pay workers well enough so that they could afford to buy a car of the type they were making. Only incidentally did this manage to change everything.

BY WORKING FAITHFULLY EIGHT HOURS A DAY YOU MAY EVENTUALLY GET TO BE BOSS AND WORK TWELVE HOURS A DAY. *Robert Frost*

Wave 2: Ambition and Achievement

Perhaps the most pervasive American invention since participatory democracy is the very notion of mass markets. In this country the cultural expectation is that we would have a few poor people, a few wealthy people, and a great many others in between. Tax codes were set accordingly. The great invention of mass markets set the conditions to make thousands of products always with an emphasis on volume and efficiency, with resulting low prices. It also unleashed a business evolution that changed the strength of America relative to all other economies, a pattern that has not changed since.

A key mechanism that emerged in this wave was *entrepreneurialism*. Although the word derives from French, the behavior is quintessentially American. It gave rise to a huge panoply of risk-taking and personal initiative, producing innovations large and small. This is what birthed electrification, convenience devices of all sorts, media devices ranging from radios to telephones and televisions, and eventually to the Popeil's Kitchen Magician and Pocket Fisherman, then to George Foreman's Grilling Machine.

Piercy Conner. Full Pod. 1999. Project for Concept House competition, England, 1999. Computer rendering

It is particularly fascinating to look at the epitome of technology during World War II. This is easily possible if one goes to the Museum of Science and Industry in Chicago and looks at the captured Nazi U-boat, the submarine they designate as U-571. This is an extraordinary achievement in mechanical hydraulics with beautiful plumbing that is packed as densely and precisely as possible. Indeed, just glancing at the complexity causes a certain wonder: are there any engineers and mechanics still alive who could design and build such a system today without resorting to electronics of any kind to do so?

Contrast this with the epitome of technology today. Modern Intel Pentium semiconductors are the most complex commonplace chips, but they are by no means the most powerful. Some are so complex that they operate at speeds of up to two billion instructions per second (2GHz) and would offer millions of times more power than the original IBM personal computer. The circuit diagram in this case, just like the hydraulic lines in World War II submarines, uses plumbing so daunting that very few individuals in the world can be expected to understand it. More to the point, this latest chip design is just another in a string of relentless increases in processing power over the last quarter century. Collectively, these improvements have forced a literal revolution in the norms of how we communicate, share information and ideas, and work today.

Importantly though, the revolution is happening from the bottom up. The reinvention of work was first technological, then, more slowly, sociological. There has not yet been a concomitant political reinvention of work. For many prior decades the principal effect of economic "progress" was to periodically shorten the normal workweek—but with little change in its true nature. From a period when it was reasonable to work sixty or seventy hours per week, productivity enhancements coming out of the industrial revolution shortened this to fifty hours, then forty-eight, then forty.

Many experts think it would have been wise to cut this significantly again in the mid-1980s, but due to a wide variety of political factors this shift in workweek norms has been untenable in the United States. Various countries have dealt with the increase in worker productivity in different ways. In Germany a prevailing socialist polity has insisted that virtually all employees be paid for thirteen months per year, workers are guaranteed three-weeks annual paid vacation, and it is nearly impossible to fire anyone.

By contrast here in America we have maintained forty-hour workweeks, while tolerating a huge divide in the skills expected for knowledge workers versus skilled and especially unskilled laborers. Even admission into America's volunteer armed forces has become very daunting. During the Vietnam War, the government was content with taking the bottom performers in high schools; today it is the top half of the class that they recruit and the top twenty percent whom they develop as officers.

Medicine once again epitomizes both aspects of this shift. Routine medical practice is now scrutinized relentlessly and second-guessed continuously by managed care companies. But the frontiers of medicine, genetic research, and pharmacology are hyperspecialized and are producing innovations at an unprecedented pace. The huge gulf in specialization, skills, and personal control is echoed in careers in every walk of modern life.

It's obvious that this affects the quality of an individual's career. Part of the reason for the massive influx of immigrants into the American medical profession is that the life of a doctor is far less pleasant than it used to be even a decade ago. As a career it is now less attractive to talented Americans, though still lucrative enough to attract talented individuals from countries where the practice of medicine is less advanced and less lucrative. Similarly, the intense scrutiny and low pay norms for government officials, teachers, and others have made it harder to attract motivated and talented individuals. Naturally, this is causing knowledge workers to expand their expectations for what a career should reasonably provide. It seems that instead of quietly dying, the "Yuppie Scum" so many love to resent are intent on fundamentally reshaping the workplace, their jobs, and the nature of work.

A MAN AT WORK, MAKING SOMETHING WHICH HE FEELS WILL EXIST BECAUSE HE IS WORKING AT IT AND WILLS IT, IS EXERCISING THE ENERGIES OF HIS MIND AND SOUL AS WELL AS OF HIS BODY. MEMORY AND IMAGINATION HELP HIM AS HE WORKS.   *William Morris*

Wave 3: Self-Expression and Impact

As far back as 1954, in his book *Motivation and Personality,* sociologist Abraham Maslow published a five-stage "Hierarchy of Human Needs." At the bottom, usually associated with money, are *physiological needs*—food, water, oxygen, stable temperatures, and the like. The second level is *safety*—the need to be in shelters or environments that have low potential for physical or mental harm. The third level is *social*—the need for friends and companionship, perhaps a spouse and children. The fourth level is *esteem*—the need to achieve self-respect and gain the respect of others. Attaining this is key to self-confidence. The fifth and highest level, rarely attained, he called *self-actualization*, wherein men and women become what they need to be for their own reasons.

Maslow applied this hierarchy to individuals. Half a century later it is possible that a similar scale is now being used, albeit subcon-

sciously, to sort out great jobs from those that are merely stepping-stones along the way to ones we would love. In such a world, talent and celebrity are vital forms of currency, and the recruiting burden has shifted from one where the employer holds all the cards to another where talented individuals want to believe that what they will work on is truly vital. Importantly, this is not only an ability to generate levels of earnings that many find obscene, but often an additional sense that the work is truly important, that it can change the world, and that the team members and colleagues will provide some fulfillment. It is no longer enough that work fulfill low-level needs; it is now supposed to provide a sense of mission and spirituality.

Savvy employers are learning to manage this level of needs with great dexterity. Greeters at Wal-Mart, product demonstrators at Home Depot, call-center operators at the Pleasant Company dealing with kids spending their allowance on the wildly popular American Girls doll collection, and UPS delivery people who are greeted like family on their daily routes are often refugees from other jobs that they didn't enjoy. Many of them cite feelings of great satisfaction and fulfillment. Their employers select them in part because of their personal style as individuals and their ambitions in the world. Then they manage these individuals so that they feel appreciated and respected.

In a similar way, one can witness true human dedication among elite teams everywhere. Army Rangers, Navy Seals, the Marine Delta Force, Coast Guard rescue teams, the firefighters that protect our nation's National Parks, surgical teams that work together on transplants (or, sadly, cosmetic surgeons), etc., talk about their work with intensity, affection, and zeal. In many similar cases when age pulls individuals like these from their jobs, it is often hard to ever achieve a similar sense of camaraderie or esprit in "normal" work. What is fascinating is that all the project work today that people truly enjoy may be converging on a similar sense of importance, intensity, and accomplishment.

This base trend has also occurred alongside a demographic revolution. Women have been steadily more integrated into the workforce, and given much more meaningful roles. So have minorities and, lately, the elderly. This has humanized the workplace and made it more truly emotionally resonant and a more complete mirror of the rest of life. As this occurs, the job per se is less important than

Felderman and Keatinge Design. MTV
Network West Coast Headquarters, Santa
Monica, California. 1997

Gaetano Pesce. Chiat/Day Offices, New York. 1994–95

the work output and the team. Naturally this makes our careers more fungible and volatile. If we are fortunate enough to have skills and relevant training, we move from a job to projects; from employers to colleagues; from a career to a mission; from a paycheck to a sense of fulfillment.

But it is a grave mistake to be too Panglossian here: there is a dark side to thinking your work is vital and then centering your life around it. American workers average two thousand hours of work every year—the highest in the world. This is seventy hours more than the hard-working Japanese, for instance, and nearly three hundred and fifty hours more per year than Europeans average. What may be worse is that the boundaries between work and the rest of life have become porous, wiggly, and unclear. The concept of working nine to five now rarely applies. High-powered portable computers, cell phones, and even Palm Pilot-like devices with integral modems ensure that work can intrude on us wherever we are. FedEx and other courier services guarantee that no vacation spot is out of the reach of our colleagues.

For many of us this creates a low-level anxiety that we are mismanaging everything. At work it is easy to be obsessed about the children we leave at home. Go home and we worry about all the work we left unfinished. Amid this struggle we become chronically sleep-deprived and feel deeply inadequate. Or we may get unbearably self-important and impatient with others. Welsh philosopher

Bertrand Russell wrote, "One of the symptoms of an approaching nervous breakdown is the belief that one's work is terribly important." And social scientist Arnold Lazarus said, "Too many people who faithfully follow the prescription to work hard, sacrifice, achieve, accomplish, create and get ahead either 'crack up' in the process or find an emotional vacuum at the end of it all."

This precise phenomenon is clearly evident in Silicon Valley and most other sites where the increase in wealth has been extraordinary for more than twenty years. An astonishing number of people who make it find that the goals they sought so obsessively were surprisingly hollow. In the Valley the psychotherapy business is enjoying unprecedented growth rates. The most common diagnosis is now nicknamed Affluenza. Now and then we catch a public glimpse of how over the top we may be. Recently, in Nantucket, a businessman was glimpsed jogging *while* smoking, carrying a cappuccino, and talking on a cell phone. Oh, good golly!

HELL, THERE ARE NO RULES HERE—WE'RE TRYING TO ACCOMPLISH SOMETHING.
Thomas Alva Edison

Future Waves: Extreme Autonomy and Project Work?
How can these extreme conditions evolve and what indignities should we prepare ourselves for next? Strategy-consulting firm McKinsey & Company (among others) has characterized the current commercial landscape as a "war for talent." This is not only advice

McKinsey sells to its clients but a painful lesson it has had to learn for itself. For thirty years McKinsey could count on routinely attracting the top ten percent of graduating classes at the world's leading business schools. Within the last three years the tables have turned: now the top talent goes to technology start-up firms or others with lots of Internet leverage. To battle this trend McKinsey has had to pledge to fund the start-up firms that students conceive while in graduate school, and they have created an internal incubation network for managing these ideas.

Just possibly Hollywood may be showing us a peek at what lies ahead. The act of producing any movie entails scores, even thousands, of specialists toiling away for a year or so, many of them in remote places or exotic locations. The talent in this case comes in many forms, from directors to special-effects wizards, cinematographers, musicians, animators, computer programmers, stunt people, etc. But the data about wages for actors tells a story that's crystal clear. Fifteen years ago, movie stars used to be paid about a thousand times the wage scale that the unions set as a floor. Now this difference is extremely pronounced and easily exceeds three thousand times scale. As they say in Hollywood, this is a preview of coming attractions.

An unresolved question is how such intense project-centric work can become more routine and commonplace. Distributed but highly functional work environments like Kinko's, Laptop Lane, and airline clubs are likely to become even more vital and more lushly appointed. Modes of transport—cars, planes, trains, ships, buses—will become far more Internet leveraged, taking some of the burden off commuting stress and possibly reducing what we lug along with us. But these are minor changes on the margins. What is very likely is that any individual with useful skills will find many more efficient systems emerge to match talent with tasks. This will occur not only with full-time job postings and recruitment firms, but increasingly with projects that offer a lively challenge with an amazing team for short periods.

Fast Company, Business 2.0, and other journals have commented extensively on this trend toward a "Free Agent Nation." But few have detailed what it will take for governments to close the gaps they have inadvertently created by allowing the technology and sociology of the workplace to outstrip political change. This is likely to become a frontier for those regions savvy enough to build ahead of current trends.

One way to imagine this is to think of working in a resortlike locale, one that you would be thrilled to visit on vacation. Perhaps you might elect to work in the beautiful mountains of Montana or Idaho, the Canadian Rockies, the tip of Patagonia, Australia's Great Barrier Reef, an island in the Indian Ocean, a village in Tuscany, or the charming white dwellings on the island of Santorini.

What we can expect is that entire systems will emerge with all the necessary infrastructure and support, so that you and your family can go for whatever duration required. When you arrive, a concierge will show you to your family home, already appointed with the food, furnishings, and items listed as your preferences. Even the education for your children will be bundled in so that their studies continue as before, even enhanced with some great local geography, language, and culture lessons. This same level of support will occur for everyone on your team, wherever they may have come from in the world. This will allow switched-on firms to get precisely the knowledge work talent they need to focus intently on a tough project. They will then pay these workers well enough so that a month or two of vacation between projects can become routine. Naturally, a world like this will break down many of the remaining thin ties between employees and companies, but it would do so in ways that benefit both enormously.

What this does not solve is the huge and frightening gap in earnings across the U.S. talent pool. This income polarization has been the prelude to class war every time it has occurred in history, and usually with devastating and violent consequences. Top American earners have found their wages increasing thirty to fifty percent in recent years, while the bottom level has eked out a meager one percent real rise in earnings. The solution to this problem is very unclear, but at a minimum it demands far better educational systems and much more routine access to technology.

In the meantime we can all learn from Albert Einstein's Three Rules of Work: out of clutter find simplicity; from discord find harmony; in the middle of difficulty lies opportunity.

The Office: 1950 to the Present
Christopher Budd

I n 1959 film director Billy Wilder built a 25,000-square-foot replica of an insurance office for *The Apartment*, a motion picture about a young man's choice between a lofty rung on the corporate ladder and the girl he loves. The set conveyed a potent visual language that reflected the values of the organization and its workers. Clerks seated at rows of identical desks, newly minted executives in glazed offices, secretaries positioned outside offices guarding senior executives, and signs of restricted restrooms and eating venues were implicitly understood by audiences then, as they are now. The main character's final reward at the end of his corporate success was a "paneled office with three windows," representing a familiar model, tenacious in its ability to linger.

The social and power structures depicted in *The Apartment* reflect a number of realities about white-collar environments at the time. All professionals were white men. Women were either secretaries, shop girls, nonworking wives, elevator attendants, or barflies. Power and self-preservation between the sexes were purchased to some degree with favors, both sexual and informational. The only minorities depicted in the film either cleaned the facility or shined shoes. In the soulless mass of conformity, the distinct lack of individ-

Jack Lemmon in *The Apartment*. Directed by Billy Wilder. United Artists. 1960. The Museum of Modern Art, New York/Film Stills Archive. Courtesy of United Artists

ual expression among the white-collar proletariat is in stark contrast to the privilege and distinction of the corporate elite. It is implicit that there are many ceilings that deter access to this privileged world. Walls, doors, and restricted facilities become visual representations of these barriers. For most workers there is a universal, bland sameness to individuality: one is a discrete unit, a cog. He or she is quantifiable, trackable, observable, and contained but not distinct. This environment is passively accepted by the workforce. Work is time specific, geographically fixed, and task oriented.

One must question where the roots of these organizational values originated. When did individual expression become divorced from the corporate environment? Why did forms of paternalism, groupthink, and group control become a tacit objective of the built environment? The roots of this tenacious model are most likely the manifestation of management theory, education, economic and social changes, technological advances, and architectural assumptions of the time. Yet the model is still pervasive and insidious. Forty years after *The Apartment,* issues of control, assimilation, the warehousing of individuals, and the use of workplace tools to underscore privilege and rank remain strong. That is why we understand commercials that appeal to our affiliation with power, and why we assume particular environments are associated with a particular corporate class. Though we laugh at the familiar world of Scott Adams's cartoon character Dilbert, do we not also find it pathetic that any worker would put up with such an environment? Is the bonding among contemporary office workers over this negative humor an effective means of avoiding personal responsibility for change?

1950 to 1960
An exact contemporary of the fictional *Apartment* set was the Union Carbide Building in New York City, designed by Gordon Bunshaft of Skidmore, Owings & Merrill. At the time, SOM's new interior-design department was creating interiors that were a study in precision. Union Carbide was a highly successful culmination of SOM's efforts to design and detail a rational approach to corporate architecture. The interior elements worked within a rigid planning module. The suspended, luminous ceiling, movable partitions, and partial-height privacy partitions achieved a level of integration that set a standard

Left:
Skidmore, Owings & Merrill. Union Carbide Building, New York. 1960

Below:
Manufacturers Hanover Building (originally Union Carbide Building)

and were highly influential in the development of interior systems and conventions. Many of these had appeared earlier in other SOM projects such as Lever House (1952), the Connecticut General Life Insurance Company (1957), and the Pepsi-Cola Building (1960). Though certainly Frank Lloyd Wright's Johnson Wax Buildings of 1935–39 had an impact on the modern office, SOM is largely credited with developing the vocabulary and approach to designing the modern office.

In addition to Bunshaft, the contributions of SOM's Davis Allen in defining the modern office are enormous. Allen, a one-time designer with Hans and Florence Knoll's postwar company, was hired by Bunshaft and while at SOM contributed to many of the most notable interior projects of the time. Many of the people working with SOM to invent the modern office vocabulary went on to form design houses and furniture companies that created a virtual "Who's Who" among office-furniture designers.

The configuration of Union Carbide's office space was a physical expression of hierarchy that is recognizable and pervasive today. Status or rank was indicated by the size and location of one's office, the number of windows in that office, and the refinement of its furnishings. Clerical staff worked in open areas. The aesthetic was undeniably rational, a hallmark of the International Style that dominated American architecture. Individuality was subordinate to an overall exquisitely detailed expression of utility, efficiency, and modernity. To put the role of architecture and the individual in perspective, one might consider what Bunshaft once said: that social welfare workers were wonderful,

Herman Miller Design. Action Office.
1964–70

but they shouldn't be called architects. At the same time, his commitment to using architecture to expose employees to public art, amenities, and light on a grand social level is indicative of his desire to have a
positive impact on people on a larger level.

The language of the modern office has roots not solely in architecture but in such things as the rise of management theory, technological innovation, and economic shifts. For instance, the ordered,
rational, precision-obsessed office designs with their expressions of
hierarchy mirror classic management theories. These theories date
from the late nineteenth to the early twentieth centuries. The French
engineer Henri Fayol, for example, focused on the division of work,
authority, and the unity of command. American efficiency engineer
Frederick Taylor developed a scientific management theory empha-
sizing the individual, performance, and output. And the work of the
German sociologist and theorist Max Weber centered on rules, prescription, and a defined hierarchy. Among these theorists, there was
an emphasis on controlling, monitoring, and commanding of
personnel. Communication and information technologies of the day
supported a linear approach to organization in order to record,
send, isolate, and protect hard-copy information. As the economy
became more focused on a white-collar workforce, the human effort
to organize, record, retrieve, and create information became the
dominant task of a majority of the workers. Between telephones,

adding machines, intercom systems, and typewriters, technology
was kept fairly simple. Still, as early as SOM's Lever House, IBM
machine rooms were beginning to be designed and a fascination
with automation was starting to occur.

At the same time that *The Apartment* was being filmed and
Union Carbide was being constructed, a German management consulting firm, Quickbourner Group, was proposing work environments not as a systematized, rational organization of boxes but as
more fluid, organic facilities. These environments, besides being
influenced by more modern management theorists, were based on
analyses of communication, work processes, and paper flow. The
resulting floorplans were extraordinarily free-flowing and emphasized work areas for groups, lack of barriers between management
and staff, and efficiency. Developed in Germany, this open, free-
flowing concept, known as *Bürolandschaft,* counteracted what many
viewed as the sterile anonymity of rectilinear International Style
plans. Special lightweight furniture products had to be developed to
respond to the organic floorplans. Plants and freestanding screens
provided only minimal visual separation and boundary markers.

Though one may view these environments as democratic,
Bürolandschaft did not necessarily provide equality. Close scrutiny of
the floorplans indicates that hierarchy was still expressed to some
degree in terms of furnishings, location, and screening. Also

Herman Miller Design. Action Office 2.
1968–76

manager/staff relationships were not necessarily altered from a control and supervision model. These new spaces made it more difficult for individuals to escape the scrutiny of their managers than did the standard, cellular approach. Ironically, many of the issues that contemporary open offices grapple with—acoustics, lack of privacy, lack of individual control, and lack of status—contributed to *Büroland-schaft*'s failure to gain widespread acceptance.

1960 to 1970

The next decade would begin to cement the definition of the late-twentieth-century office. In an eerie case of art predicting life, the director Jacques Tati created an impersonal, cellular environment in 1967 for his film *Playtime* that mirrors the uniformity of cubical applications so prevalent for the next thirty years. This film debuted a year before the introduction of the original panel system of office furniture (forerunner of the modern cubicle) and only seven years after the filming of *The Apartment.*

The 1960s saw a proliferation of International Style offices. The acceptance of the SOM model (Union Carbide) and its adherence to planning grids provided an opportunity for interior systems such as suspended ceilings, cable and wire ducts, lighting, and partitions to be standardized and mass-produced. Nothing has had a more profound impact on the office environment than the advent of modern

systems furniture, a now ubiquitous solution that gave rise to the cubicle. In the 1960s Robert Propst, then with the Herman Miller Furniture Company, wrote the seminal book *The Office: A Facility Based on Change.* A reaction to the International Style, this book was a summation of Propst's research and a comprehensive description of future officing from a social, technological, and process viewpoint. With the assistance of the influential designer George Nelson, whose office furniture is legendary, Propst developed Action Office 2, the first open-plan system, which was marketed in 1968 (a 1964 non-panel-based system had preceded it). The system was modular; it lessened the need for tailored or customized design so prevalent in Union Carbide, and allowed the physical environment to accept change and be far less static. Propst's objectives supported a new degree of human dignity and control at an individual level, foresaw huge changes in technology, and, most importantly, underscored the relevance of individual motivation, work patterns, and expression.

Supposedly, Propst was influenced by modern management theorists such as Douglas McGregor, whose X and Y management styles were a study in contrast. Management style X was largely dictatorial and punishment oriented, discouraging individual freedom and expression. Management style Y trusted that people have a basic propensity to seek challenge, and it worked to develop high performance through encouragement and increased opportunity. Rather than support an either/or model of cellular office or open work area, Propst looked at balancing the ability to achieve privacy, control acoustics, and create open access. Learning lessons from both International Style offices and *Bürolandschaft,* Action Office 2 tried to develop an approach to supporting a very different type of management. Sadly, the approach also allowed for extreme cellularization, standardization, anonymity, and conformity, which ran counter to its goals. In the years to follow, blanket approaches to literal warehousing of people and universal applications again would ignore the individual in terms of differences and de-emphasize group communication. The cubicle would come to represent a form of individual housing that neither provided privacy nor fostered interaction.

1970 to 1980

The notion of corporate control and a passive acceptance of the work environment by employees continued to influence work environments in the United States in the 1970s. The model of individual contribution and a balance of privacy, open communication, and adequate work tools may have been overshadowed by the size of large corporations and the ease of implementing and maintaining facilities that were more homogeneous in terms of workspaces. Highly detailed space standards were developed and implemented hierarchically. The visual language was as important as social control. Individuals did not modify their assigned piece of real estate; it was prescribed to them based on their value to the company.

Perhaps the most important work environment of the 1970s was Herman Hertzberger's Centraal Beheer Office Building in Apeldoorn, The Netherlands. Breaking with prevailing models of hierarchy and control, he introduced a democratic approach to the work environment. Rank was not expressed in the physical vocabulary, and individual and group control and expression of work settings were highly encouraged. Architecturally, there were several significant departures from the furniture systems model being developed in the United States. The basic planning module centered on group spaces rather than on the individual. Because the environment was to be democratic, the notion of providing a range of status-related standards for the individual was eliminated. While the American model was adding complexity to furniture-based solutions by incorporat-

ing utilities, the architectural solution of Centraal Beheer reduced the process of space-making by incorporating utilities into the architecture and allowing a vocabulary of simple furniture to be rearranged according to the taste of the occupants.

In the United States, several key design firms were highly influential in defining interior design as a discipline and business in its own right during the 1970s and early 1980s. Among the leaders and pioneers of this phenomenon were Margo Grant, former SOM designer and colleague of Davis Allen, and Orlando Diaz of Gensler and Associates, along with their counterparts at ISD, Caudill Rowlett Scott, and Environmental Planning and Research. Each of these firms focused on interior design, largely corporate entities, as a core business process. The acknowledgment and organization of corporate interiors as a stand-alone business proposition by this new generation of design firms led to many of the standard practices in place today.

An interesting blip on the office-furniture market, at a time when numerous panel systems were being developed, almost indistinguishable from one another, was the work of the Canadian industrial designer Douglas Ball for the innovative company Sunar. The Race System, as it was called (now owned by Haworth), was ahead of its time in solving issues of the technological infrastructure and reducing the complexity of office-furniture systems. It redefined the notion of privacy, allowing strategic screening while maintaining a high degree of visual communication. Its most important contribution may be that it broke with the fascination for modularity and puzzlelike precision that had so dominated the industry. For the first time, ambiguity and elasticity were introduced in an office-systems product that questioned the value of rigid standards and dimensional specificity.

The American movie *Nine to Five*, released in 1980, involved a backlash against the rigidly controlled model of the workplace that had become ubiquitous in the States. Glass ceilings, extreme supervision, and hierarchy were challenged in a coup by the working classes. Dream imagery included shackles being broken and sunlight spilling into a dark prison cell, no doubt representing the emancipation for which workers yearned. The "proletarians" were successful, and by the end of the film an enormous amount of diversity in terms of job sharing, personal expression, personalized

Jane Fonda in *Nine to Five*. Directed by Colin Higgins. Twentieth Century Fox. 1980. The Museum of Modern Art, New York/Film Stills Archive. Courtesy of Twentieth Century Fox

Herman Miller Design. Ethospace. c. 1990

schedules, and the advancement of women to leadership positions had taken place. Oddly, these changes were completely overlaid on the original environment so that no physical changes to the office were made. The new multigendered leadership continued to be represented by large offices, and the clerical staff remained in an open, albeit highly self-expressive, workspace.

1980 to 1990

In the 1988 film *Working Girl* the theme was class struggle and discrimination against women in terms of climbing the corporate ladder. Though the young heroine ultimately succeeds, her reward is the very model of corporate America that dates back to 1960. She merely assimilates after breaking through the glass ceiling. Her rewards are a private office and an assistant, two conventional achievements that were perceived as an unconventional success story. Sadly, very little changed in the working culture; in fact, far less than in *Nine to Five,* filmed eight years earlier. The movie represented the decade in terms of greed, hierarchical focus, and ambition at all costs.

In 1985 Phillip Stone and Robert Luchetti published an article in the *Harvard Business Review* entitled "Your Office Is Where You Are," which became a mantra for innovation and forward thinking among those challenging conventional office environments. It may well be the single most influential document of its kind. Its premise was that

office spaces can support a working philosophy but cannot actually create it. The office environment that they proposed presumes that management "has a democratic attitude toward the workplace and creates an atmosphere of trust and shared responsibility." In this scenario, the emphasis on employees went from an extracted degree of productivity to a fostered and supported contribution. Furthermore, the article questioned the validity of the cubicle and the type of efficiency it represented. It advocated activity-based planning, a concept where individuals and groups would select the appropriate setting for specific tasks rather than expect a single space, such as the cubicle, to be effective for every task. This called for a high degree of mobility, supportive technology, and far less ownership of space and management controls. Like Propst's *The Office: A Facility Based on Change,* Stone's and Luchetti's article anticipated technology that did not yet exist. Another important text was Cecil B. Williams's *The Negotiable Environment,* based in part on Jungian principles and Myers-Briggs concepts. It began to question the notion of control and conformity, focusing more on the individual and personal choice.

In the early 1980s the personal computer became widely accepted, and soon most white-collar workers had them. These new machines necessitated a complex system of utilities, which had an impact on building infrastructures. This new challenge to the workplace was solved by the increased capability of office-furniture systems. Perhaps the most influential of these systems of the 1980s was

Herman Miller Design. Ethospace. 1999

Herman Miller's Ethospace, designed by William Stumpf, which became much more architectural in its construction and ability to be modified. At the same time that the system could be modified to a degree by the user, it offered a more-traditional approach to closure and a less-temporary aesthetic than did panel systems. Perhaps most importantly it may have been intended to bring back into the office environment more personal meaning and context, which had been eliminated by the prevailing corporate aesthetic.

One of the first and largest users of Ethospace was the American Express headquarters in New York, designed in 1983 by Swanke Hayden Connell. This project represented the state-of-the-art in corporate headquarters: sophisticated ambient light, modular carpet, an impressive amenities package, a signature building, well-appointed individual work areas, and a strong art program. It was the ultimate project in terms of the application of products that are now being designed for the corporate environment, and its complex aesthetic was revelatory.

It was designed to be far more meaningful and relevant to individuals than the early offices of the 1960s; yet, in many ways, it reflected the hierarchical language of early SOM designed headquarters in that it was organized to reflect status and individual space. Modularity was its basic notion, though in contrast to the early SOM pure design rationale, the modularity designed into American Express was aimed at a broader degree of change and reconfiguration.

Despite the ability to reconfigure, systems furniture was to become so difficult to change and so expensive to reconfigure because of dimensional, structural, and technological dependencies overcomplicating the systems that universal plans began to be adapted by many organizations. This lessened even further the degree of diversity among work settings. It was commonly defended with the phrase "move people not furniture." Though there typically was some variation based on worker type, the idea was to create as much uniformity as possible.

1990 to 2000

A number of other important consultants emerged in the 1980s who have become catalysts in changing the concept of the workplace. They include Francis Duffy, Franklin Becker, Fritz Steel, and Michael Brill. As a group, the combination of architecture, research, and environmental psychology made a critical impact on what was later to be termed Alternative Officing. Of particular influence was Brill's *BOSTI Studies* and Becker's numerous publications and research on the workplace. The concept of alternative work environments was a total rethinking of how work gets done and what adds value to the organization. Within this mix, time and geography are far more blurred than in traditional environments, allowing work to be done almost anywhere at any time. Much of this would be achievable with technological advances to be realized throughout the decade, such as wireless capabilities, mobile technology, and the Internet. An emphasis was placed on less-hierarchical, more-nimble organizations that focused on interaction and communication, and on the increasing importance of social connections. Unfortunately, many companies employed alternative officing merely to cut real-estate costs, and its continuing evaluation is clouded by insensitivity, poor change management, and cost-driven priorities.

Perfectly reflecting this cost-driven trend toward impractical densification, the 1999 film *Being John Malkovich* depicts clerical workers inhabiting a bizarre "half" floor in an office building, a peculiar low-ceilinged space wedged between the eighth and ninth floors, where employees walked about bent over to avoid hitting their heads. The space, comically reflecting downsizing and the disassociation of the human being from physical space, emphasized the lack of connection we make between work and the environment. Entirely focused on maintaining a highly favorable rent structure in downtown Manhattan, the situation mirrors the bias of much of the corporate world toward real-estate metrics and away from support of the work being done. This commonly held position is an insult to the innovations the workplace consultants mentioned above.

As an example, a popular notion to emerge in the late 1980s was the concept of hoteling, where space was used on an as-needed basis rather than daily by one individual. This concept was adapted early on by a number of consulting firms such as Ernst and Young, Andersen Consulting, and Price-Waterhouse Coopers. Often it has been applied narrowly to achieve real-estate savings rather than purposefully to support the behaviors and activities of its occupants. Though hoteling has attained mixed success at many types of organizations, it has become a controversial, emotion-driven issue for many workers. It represents the overall concept of alternative officing rather than being an option under the alternative officing umbrella with extreme variability in application.

Perhaps the most publicized case of alternative officing has been the multiple facilities of Chiat/Day. Though many other projects exist, such as the activities-settings-based Corning Glass in Toledo, Ohio (on which Robert Luchetti consulted), none caught the imagination and interest of the late-twentieth-century public more than Chiat/Day. Its New York office, designed in 1995 by Gaetano Pesce,

provided maximum opportunity for individuals to connect and work together. State-of-the-art mobile technology was employed; there were no individual space assignments; and the notion of hierarchy was stripped from the visual language. The design and aesthetic had no parallel model. It was the antithesis of Union Carbide in 1960. A value was clearly placed on high motivation, teamwork, diversity of ideas, and value-laden communication. Casual dress and television breaks were an accepted part of the workplace. Entitlements were transferred from space to other tools necessary to survive in such an environment. It was all about contribution, not some mechanical notion of productivity.

Despite the grand experiment, the environment may not have been wholly successful for Chiat/Day, considered by many to be the most extreme adapter of this concept. Whether this was due to unsuccessful change management, a mismatch between the concept and type of work being produced, or lack of fulfillment of some basic human needs is not really understood. What is known is that the Los Angeles office of Chiat/Day, opened in 1998, has made a number of modifications that diverge from the New York office.

Masterfully designed by Clive Wilkinsen, the Los Angeles facility provided an individual space for every employee based less on hierarchy and more on function, an enormous variety of work settings, and an aesthetic that has a sense of fun and a sense of humor. Wilkinsen managed to knit together concepts of privacy, ownership, image, motivation, control, and efficiency that have been the source of contrast and controversy between classic and alternative work environments. In doing so, he may very well have left a design legacy that will begin to define corporate environments.

Interestingly enough, "incubator space" has emerged in the last few years as a space type geared toward innovation and idea generation. It is being built for young, dynamic entities to use, yet traditional corporations are creating similar spaces distinct from their typical work environments to grow ideas and "incubate" innovation. Traditional corporations seem to be saying that innovation and change take place in a different work environment than a typical office space.

2000 and the Future

The work environment model of 1960 is still with us, and it remains potent today. The American office continues in many ways to expose the irony of American individualism in which everybody desires to be the same but expresses that desire in maverick terms. The dream of a corner office, of achieving status, etc., is as pervasive as it was forty years ago. A pattern has developed in the last fifty years; there is a tension between control and freedom, productivity and contribution, status and function, privacy and accessibility, and the individual and management. Much of the contrast between what SOM produced and what influenced the Quickbourner Group is alive today.

Still, it is a hopeful time to be involved in workplace making. We are seeing changes in how people who have never known life without the personal computer, the Internet, or cell phones, and who have strong interests in opportunities for personal success and quality of life are affecting the workspace. It will take changes in values and self-esteem to truly revolutionize the work environment; architects cannot do these things.

Despite the tenacious lingering of the traditional office, many of us are visualizing a new physical model that eliminates inappropriate class and power structures from the architectural language. We are dreaming of environments that send messages about opportunity, the synergy of multiple minds, the value of people, the inherent strength of diversity, and, most importantly, that emphasize contribution rather than archaic notions of individual productivity. Some psychologists suggest that learning new behaviors or adapting new beliefs are most likely to occur in the context of models that are unique, unfamiliar, and novel. Important historical blips like the Quickbourner experiments, Hertzberger's Centraal Beheer Office Building, Luchetti's landmark article, and Wilkinsen's Chiat/Day offices represent departures from prevailing models and what has been a quiet, constant protest and tension against uniform, authoritarian models over the last fifty years.

Considering this, the role of design as a meaningful and influential agent for positive change should keep our hearts beating faster, our expectations high, and our belief in the power of a renewed built environment. In the century to come we will have incredible opportunities for design to empower an entire workforce, greatly improve the quality of our lives, and reflect our basic humanity. In *The Apartment*, it was the promise of this humanity that spurred Jack Lemmon, the disillusioned young executive, to leave the vulgarity of the corporate world for Shirley MacLaine, a casualty of the corporate system. In the future, this promise may even be realized.

Note

Numerous publications were consulted and an interview conducted in the preparation of this essay. I wish to acknowledge especially the following authors, whose texts or oral communication provided important background information on specific subjects, as noted in parenthesis: Lance Knobel, Donald Albrecht, and, most notably, Élisabeth Pélegrin-Genel (*The Apartment* and/or *Playtime* compared with contemporary architecture and design); Pélegrin-Genel, Knobel, and John Pile (*Bürolandschaft*); Carol Herselle Krinsky and Maeve Slavin (Skidmore, Owings & Merrill, Gordon Bunschaft, and Davis Allen); Todd DeGarmo (interview: SOM and Swanke's American Express headquarters); Péligren-Genel (Central Beheer Office Building); Robert Propst, Leslie Piña, and Knobel (Herman Miller's products and influence); James L. Bowditch and Anthony F. Buono (key management theories); Robert Propst (influence of X and Y management theory on his work); Michael Brill, Professor Franklin Becker, and Robert Luchetti (key perspectives on contemporary shifts in office environment). The author owes particular debt, academically and professionally, to Dr. Becker.

Designing the Space of Flows
John Thackara

In May 1993 I arrived in Amsterdam to begin work at the Netherlands Design Institute, where I had been appointed its first director. Builders were already on site at the former Fodor Museum, on Keizersgracht, which was to be our home, so I cannot claim to have been involved in the project from the very beginning. But when I first met the architects, Jan Benthem and Mels Crouwel, most of the internal space and infrastructure had still to be designed. A full year remained before we were due to open. Between that first site visit and leaving the job at the end of 1999, I had six and a half years of on-the-job training in the design, commissioning, and use of a workplace building. During that same period, we designed and built a new knowledge-based organization, also from scratch. We created a think-and-do tank whose objective was to reframe the way we perceive and use design. During those years, the building and the organization interacted in powerful ways—most of them positive, some negative. It is not often that a design critic brings first-hand experience to a subject, so I jumped at this opportunity to reflect on the relationship between work, space, and design.

The eminent Spanish economist Manuel Castells, whose first lecture in Amsterdam was by invitation of the Design Institute, has written about the networked economy as "the space of flows"—a brilliant metaphor that helps us understand the changing nature of the workplace. Castells observes that while connections between people can indeed be multiplied by information and communication technologies, understanding still requires space, place, and time. Our dilemma is this: we have fashioned an urban, networked, complex, and constantly mobile society in which the qualities of space, place, and time are given too little attention.

Airports, where many of us in the kinetic elite now work, exemplify the problem. Besides being thresholds between land and air, modern airports are gateways to complexity. Through them we enter the operating environment of global aviation, surely mankind's most complicated creation. But in airports, although we are isolated from the rhythms of the natural world, we remain ignorant of how this artificial world works. The result is to reinforce what philosophers call our ontological alienation: a sense of rootlessness and anxiety; of not quite being real; of being lost in space. In many respects, aviation is typical of the way the whole world is going:

Above:
Jan Benthem and Mels Crouwel. Netherlands Design Institute, Amsterdam. 1993

Opposite:
Benthem and Crouwel. Netherlands Design Institute, Amsterdam. John Thackara's office

saturated with information and systems; complex but incomprehensible. Our workspace is an exhilarating human achievement, and a terrifying prospect at the same time.

We move to work, but moving is hard work. We are going farther and faster, but without much efficiency. In the olden days, when airports were planned and operated as transport utilities, if only for an elite, engineers and operations people would have regarded an idle passenger as evidence of system inefficiency. Not today. Mobility is just one of the products on sale at a modern airport. So much so that to commercial managers, passenger discretionary time, or dwell time—the time spent by passengers between flights—is a sales opportunity. Why else ask people to check in up to three hours before takeoff? The management of dwell time to optimize commercial yield is one reason—traffic jams are another—that between 1950 and 1990 the proportion of time spent in the air by passengers on a journey has steadily decreased. As the transport economist John Whitelegg has observed, the amount of time each person devotes to travel is roughly the same regardless of how far or how fast they travel. Facilities are sited farther apart, and people have to travel farther to reach them than they did seventy years ago. "Time is money, we are told, and increasing mobility is a way of saving time," says Whitelegg. "But how successful are modern transport systems at saving time?" If air travel is any guide, the answer appears to be: not very successful.

In fact, the faster we go the less time we feel we have. Following up on the work of Ivan Illich in the 1970s, the German sociologist D Seifried has coined the term "social speed" to signify the average speed of a vehicle (and its passengers) after all sorts of hidden time costs are added in. So in addition to getting-to-the-airport time—and dwell time once you get there—Seifried reminds us about the time spent earning the money to make the journey in the first place. That is, work.

Catatonic Space

The word catatonic is horribly apt as a description of the way these great modern workspaces make us feel. What happens is that any space, including artificial space, affects our minds and our bodies. But artificial environments shield us from phenomena like climate, and particularly daylight, whose cycles in the natural world expose us physically to the reality of constant change. In an optically static environment, such as a mall, airport, or open-plan office, the body is physically desensitized from its sense of time.

In an essay titled "The Poetics of Light," the American architect Henry Plummer observed that "our very sense of being is based on an experience of process, activity, and movement. We seem to find an image of our own existence in the changing lights of the natural world." Moment-to-moment mutations of light also provide what the philosopher Henry Bergson called "lived time," and Ernst Cassirer "a consciousness of sequence." According to the psychologist David Winnicott, loss of temporality is a feature of the psychotic and deprived individual, in which a person "loses the ability to connect the past with the present." The bridging of the present into the past and into the future is, says Winnicott, "a crucial dimension of psychic integration and health." So there you have it. Complex modern spaces, by scrambling your mind-and-body clock, create the preconditions for psychosis. Small wonder that modern life feels strange!

People have tried really hard to design alternative ways to meet and communicate. Unfortunately, the capacity of information and communication technology to re-create what it's like to be in a meeting with people somewhere else is a long way off. Besides, if the aim of travel were simply to exchange information, then we wouldn't bother doing it. The trouble is, to state the obvious, that's not why we do it. It's that mind-body business again: experientially, there never will be an alternative to actually being there. Now I know that, and you know that, but the terrifying thing is that the world's telecommunications companies do not appear to know that. On the contrary, they continue to spend vast amounts of money, and gobble ludicrous quantities of bandwidth, in the search for systems and networks that will reproduce as closely as possible the sensation of being there. They are missing the point.

Modern mobility affords us the illusion of compressing space and time, but moving faster does not, per se, improve the creation of knowledge. We tend to scoff nowadays at nineteenth-century medical experts who warned that the acceleration of life, and use of the telephone, would cause "serious mental degeneration"; we think it quaint to discover that the word phony should derive from early descriptions of the communicative quality of telephones. But how sophisticated are we really today? We seldom step back and think critically about qualitative aspects of the complex work situations we have made.

That may now be changing. Management of the work environment as a combination of space, place, time, and interaction is moving center stage. Many discussions about innovation, learning, and the knowledge economy properly focus on these multiple dimensions of the work environment. Hard questions are being asked about all the physical assets owned by businesses, with buildings being singled out as an albatross hanging around their necks. In the extreme view, ownership of any kind of asset other than information is becoming a liability. You gain flexibility not by owning physical assets, the argument goes, but by concentrating on ownership of intellectual property.

But even albatrosses—and buildings—have their uses. If it is indeed the quality of interactions among people, communities, and customers that determines the success of a knowledge-nurturing organization, then buildings can still deliver value. In an economic world dealing in knowledge, the secret of success is the combination of different types of expertise in a productive manner, continuously. I am skeptical about the claims being made against place, and for web-based work and learning. Most of it strikes me as old wine in new bottles. The potential of the Internet is not understood—let alone exploited—by much of the virtual, distant, or online education that is out there now. Most of it focuses on just one aspect of the learning process: the delivery of text or media from one place to another. This scenario is often accompanied by fantasy images of privileged individuals surrounded by all the world's knowledge— "streaming learning" for the high-tech elite.

Learning Geographies

There are two problems with this picture. First, it is technically not yet feasible. The tools and infrastructure for multichannel broadband communications on a large scale are simply not there yet. Second, a much bigger problem is that any service that restricts itself to the delivery of prepackaged content ignores the social and collaborative nature of learning and the cultural qualities of time and place that add depth and texture to the process. I call these key ingredients the

geographies of learning. Visions of a vast, semiautomated learning machine remind me of the joke about the factory of the future: it will have only two employees, a man and a dog. The man will be there to feed the dog; the dog will be there to stop the man from touching the equipment.

Our dilemma is that although the Internet and new media technologies can do amazing things, they cannot support important soft and wet aspects of learning that are crucial if a modern organization is to succeed. Learning is understood—if it is understood at all—as a one-way, point-to-mass distribution system. Delivering content down a pipe, like water, is not teaching. And receiving content—like an empty bucket under a tap—is not learning. The English writer Charles Hampden-Turner has put it better than I can: "Knowledge is becoming too complex to be carried in the individual heads of itinerant experts. Knowledge as it grows and grows is necessarily social, the shared property of extended groups and networks." The distribute-then-learn model cannot embrace these more complex geographies of learning. Learning, at all levels, relies ultimately on personal interaction and, in particular, on a range of implicit and peripheral forms of communication. Technology is still very far from being able to handle these liminal communications efficiently. But buildings can. So real-world spaces remain useful in knowledge work.

But not static space. The criticism that products and buildings are frozen software is a powerful one. Anything that blocks complex interactions among individuals, communities of practice, and customers, hinders innovation. The criticism leveled at the Design Institute's building was that it isolated and separated the people in it from the real world outside it. It was so beautiful that the outside world paled by comparison. Most buildings are dumb and inflexible. The Design Institute was not that. But neither was it an easy space to change to suit circumstances: the spaces determined the interactions that occur within them and could therefore be a problem.

Fostering complex interactions—the constantly changing flows of people and ideas that characterize a dynamic organization— means designing the context of innovation and learning—our workspaces and places—in a new way. In the words of Nobel laureate Murray Gell Mann, innovation is an emergent phenomenon that happens when an organization fosters interaction between different kinds of people and disparate forms of knowledge. A new task for design is to increase the flow of information within and between communities. This design process does not deliver finished space or fixed equipment. Rather, it asks: What inputs need to be plumbed into a particular context? Which people should be there and when? What kinds of experiences should they have? In what kind of space?

Smart Space Is Hybrid

The concept of emergence is changing the way our products, systems, organizations, and buildings are designed, the way we use them, and how they relate to us. Everything about us is now a combination of hardware and software. The world is already filled with thirty-five computer chips for every man, woman, and child on the planet. A growing proportion of these chips talk to each other, thanks to another revolution: wide-area computer networking. Ubiquitous computing spreads new forms of intelligence and connectivity everywhere, from the bottom of the sea to the bottom of our shoes. As connected computing suffuses the environment, the notion of designing particular behaviors and qualities into that environment becomes a realistic proposition. When combined with the explosive growth of mobile telephony, the result is a transformation—that we are experiencing right now—in the way we use time and space.

When new multimedia technologies and the Internet first appeared, there was excited talk of "parallel worlds" and escape into a "virtual reality." That fuss has now died down and here we still are, in the same old bodies, on the same old planet. Things have changed, but in subtle and more interesting ways: the real and the virtual, the artificial and the natural, the mental and the material, coexist in a new kind of hybrid space.

We tend to think of products and buildings as lumps of dead matter: inert, passive, dumb. But buildings are becoming lively, active, and intelligent. Objects that are sensitive to their environment, act with some intelligence, and talk to each other, are changing the basic phenomenology of buildings—the way they exist in the world. The result is to undermine long-standing design principles. "Form follows function" made sense when products were designed for a specific task, but not when responsive materials that modify

their shape or behavior are available. Another nostrum, "truth to materials," was a moral imperative of the modern movement in design; it made sense when products were made of "found" or natural materials whose properties were predetermined. But "truth" is less helpful as a design principle when the performance and behavior of materials can be specified in advance.

Once workspaces become suffused with unfrozen software, their designers will encounter another revolution—this one in the way software is designed. Every day, computer designers at companies like Netscape receive thousands of messages directly from the users of their products. These products are never finished, but evolve continuously in response to the to-and-fro of messages between users and designers.

Software-suffused work environments may soon be subject to similar online redesign twenty-four hours a day. What's more, it may be done for free, thanks to yet another revolution: open source. Open source describes the tradition of open standards, shared source codes, and collaborative development behind software operating systems and languages such as Linux and Perl. Some of the most significant advances in computing—ones that are shaping our economy and our culture—are the product of little-understood hacker and file-sharing culture that delivers more innovation and better quality than conventional innovation processes. Open source is one symptom of a powerful worldwide trend toward networked collaboration that companies and specialist knowledge workers, isolated in their professional and institutional ghettos, have been slow to pick up. The faint outline of such a world was already visible at the Netherlands Design Institute. The task of tweaking our telephone and computer networks never really stopped, and, more and more, expert people traded their time spent fixing our systems for benefits we could give them, such as participation in events or introductions to interesting people.

Amsterdam: Strange Attractor

The transformation of business processes means that a good geographical location does not always carry as much weight as it once did, as the distance between the producers of goods or services and their users shrinks. Sophisticated distribution and logistics systems,

Benthem and Crouwel. Netherlands Design Institute, Amsterdam.
"The Collector" (library)

computer-integrated manufacturing and design, new materials, and direct marketing have changed fundamentally what it means to design, produce, distribute, or sell a product or service.

But place still matters—a lot. Location is one more edge that smart entrepreneurs capitalize on. The value of location can be seen in Amsterdam, where the Design Institute's building was located. Amsterdam's harbor, its position in Europe, and its connections with the great rivers of Europe give the city a gateway status. An advanced physical infrastructure for the smooth movement of goods adds to its value. Now a new infrastructure of wired and wireless networks is adding to the city's potency, to quote the writer Manuel de Landa, as an "attractor." These cumulative investments in physical and information connectivity have led many international information-technology companies to view Amsterdam as the ideal European base.

In her influential book *World Class,* Harvard University professor Elizabeth Moss Kantor analyzed what makes a city competitive. She talked about a "golden triumvirate of world class resources: concepts, competence, and connections." Cities and organizations alike, she argued, should develop these three assets to link their local population to the global economy: to be a place where new ideas are generated by interactions among a variety of disciplines and cultures; to be a place where some production skills are concentrated; and, above all, to be a place which, if it does not possess a skill or competency itself, has links to a place that does.

Workspace and organizational designers need to learn now how to map the way communications flow in different kinds of communities at different scales. These maps will not just focus on so-called purposive communication—letters to the bank, calls for a taxi, project meetings—but also embrace social and cultural communications: the many ways people build relationships, articulate their needs and fears, and interact informally with friends, family, officials, and so on. Such projects should focus on the people themselves, their needs, their habits, their frustrations, their daily lives.

Knowledge management is the new imperative, driven by the shift away from a world of goods and services toward one of information and relationships. The key word here is "minds" in the plural, and in particular the capabilities of *groups*. Traditional workplace design emphasized the individual worker; space and equipment for teams have more recently been given attention. Workplace design that fosters continuously changing and complex knowledge relationships and flows is the new priority.

Speed Is God, Time Is the Devil

Space and place are important to the way an economic entity manages time. "Speed is God, Time is the Devil" goes Hitachi's fatuous company slogan. But it's hard to accelerate, or change direction, when you suffer from too much dispersal of places and people. "Mobility is starting to backfire," says Lufthansa, without a blush. The relationship between workspace design and mobility is a paradoxical one. Nothing would appear to be more immobile than a building, but new workplaces can adapt themselves to cope with constantly changing configurations.

An important new book, *The Social Life of Information*, by Paul Duguid and John Seely Brown, reminds us that we learn not only by

Benthem and Crouwel. Netherlands Design Institute, Amsterdam. Meeting space

the acquisition of facts and rules, but also through participation in collaborative human activities. The most valuable learning takes place among social networks, not at the end of a pipe filled with prepackaged content. The fact that one author of this book, Seely Brown, is chief scientist at Xerox, suggests that big companies may be moving away from a technology-led approach.

New technology has worked best when helping people interact across time, rather than across space. When worker-students can access web documents at different times, they can escape the temporal confines of the classroom, say experts like Seely Brown. The best of such Internet tools are usually an extension of—not a replacement for—face-to-face exchanges.

The concept of a death of distance made great headlines a couple of years ago. It was nonsense then, and it is nonsense now. Its grandchild is the concept of anytime, anywhere learning. The idea sounds attractive and uncontroversial, but when based on a point-to-mass distribution model it overlooks the significance of place and local knowledge. Cities, for example, are unique learning ecologies. So too are offices. The danger we face is a combination of death of distance ideology and the sheer pressure of money and technology behind global Internet scenarios that could marginalize local forms of knowledge regardless of their importance.

A lot of learning takes place in offices, research labs, hospitals, design offices, web studios—anywhere, indeed, that people gather to work. The way we organize education and work today hinders integration among communities. The Internet makes it easier to connect parts together in a technical sense, but breaking down the walls between school, work, and home will involve cultural and institutional changes that will be harder to achieve.

We need to consider how new electronic forms of experience might enable real, novel, social interaction. This is necessary from the commercial perspective of creating new markets for entertainment applications, and also from the sociopolitical perspective of countering the negative social impacts of current media and entertainment technologies. A specific goal is to make inhabited information spaces available, useful, and enjoyable for groups of worker-citizens with heterogeneous access to the network, in bandwidth as well as presentation and interaction devices. The use of large-scale display technologies, such as projection systems, domes, and immersive virtual environments, may enable the provision of public interfaces to social computer systems. Such interfaces may eventually allow users to be immersed without being encumbered by equipment. They will also be inherently shareable—several people may use the same interface at the same time. Present technologies fail to support meaningful interaction between the crowd of observers and the shared display: typically, one person drives and the others merely watch. Research is required into techniques whereby groups of people can meaningfully interact with a shared display in a relatively easy, flexible, and unencumbered manner. Theater people are getting in on the act: the Walt Disney Company employs "imagineers" to ensure that its supremely artificial environments do not become catatonic. We are beginning to see something similar emerge in the offices of knowledge-based companies, where the job of office clowns, animateurs, show-business impresarios, and other people is to liven up the place.

Interactive communication networks linking public and private spaces will have a considerable impact on the future of urban functions, local communications, and lifestyles. Ultimately, however, work is not just about earning money to buy products. "We work not just to produce," said the artist Eugène Delacroix, "but to give value to time." Work has social, cultural, and personal, as well as economic, meaning. It was that meaning that the Design Institute's building so powerfully fostered. It was intensively used by more than twenty thousand people each year as a knowledge and activity center. The building hugely impressed every visitor, and contributed to the institute's standing as a leading-edge organization. The building stimulated innovation mainly because it worked well as a meeting place. Workspheres don't have to be much more complicated than that.

Time: Change: Boundaries
Aura Oslapas

Time is an enigma. We want to control it, rule it, own it, but time just keeps going by. In fact, the more fun we're having, the faster time advances. We believe that we all suffer from having "no time," but perhaps we have just raised our expectations of what it is we can accomplish over time.

In the business world the speed of change has increased dramatically. Today, the lifespan of a business is unpredictable, and there is no guarantee that it will outlive the majority of its employees. Annual restructuring of a company is the norm, and changing jobs, employers, or locations is expected. Alvin Toffler, in his book *Future Shock*, called this phenomenon "psychic disruption": too much change in too short a time. But is the tension about time or is it about managing change? We talk a lot about managing time, but aren't we really talking about managing change as time rushes by?

American culture thrives on work: this is the heartland of Calvinism, Franklinism, the industrial revolution, Taylorism, and the current, second digital Gold Rush. The industrial revolution spurred people like the efficiency expert Frederick Taylor, at the end of the nineteenth century, to study the workforce and very scientifically increase human productivity. By the 1960s most people's work was compartmentalized, departmentalized, and both blue- and white-collar workers were packaged into tidy squares of human efficiency. The twentieth century will be looked upon as the century that symbolized the evolution of humans into efficiency machines. Our preoccupation with work means that we have effectively given up leisure as an activity. We work hard, then pay lots of money to go somewhere far away to "do" leisure in short bursts of time, only to return to work hard again.

We have moved beyond a work ethic to dependence on work for identity, self-esteem, and happiness. Our culture celebrates work, yet continually strives to eliminate it. Time-saving devices fill our world, yet most of these devices merely give us the opportunity to do more work, to accomplish more during the course of a day. Once again, we have raised our expectations as to how productive we can be.

During the past century, thanks to people like Taylor, work has been engineered in a linear manner: start an activity, complete it, clean up, and move on to the next activity. Thus we exist in a highly monochronic time culture, planned and linear. The traditional American corporation impressed that upon us, and therefore the shape of the workplace as we know it has come to reflect clear hierarchies, job tasks, and paths toward success.

If large corporations have evolved into hierarchical, monochronic machines that focus on developing linear paths of productivity and work flow, then the current rush of small, new companies, particularly those launching products and services on the Internet, tend toward a more chaotic, polychronic work mode that is task-based, not clock-based. These small companies tend to be people-focused, chaotic, and nonlinear and are built on constant change.

The emergence of the computer as an everyday work tool first began to push us beyond the linear way of working. The perception was that the computer would save or organize time better, and it has enabled work to be more enjoyable through speeding up tedious tasks and allowing a broader range of work per individual. The computer has enabled workers to shift into a multimodal way of working, akin to the way farmwork is carried out: a combination of daily, seasonal, unexpected, and planned tasks moving forward simultaneously. With the computer, one can more easily navigate around the desktop, both physically and digitally. Think how that has evolved: concurrently opened computer files, paper reference materials, E-mail, and calendaring. We naturally move back and forth trying to manage the range of communications, new information, and ongoing efforts. We are able to either engage laterally across many activities or close out everything in order to focus on one task for a period of time.

True to our inventive culture, we are overly focused on creating more and more devices that assist us in managing our time. These devices, we think, will help us set boundaries that enable us to balance life and work. Although the boundaries between work and home have been unclear for centuries, they became quite rigid during the past century. Given the proliferation of services and devices that allow those boundaries to overlap, we must manage the boundaries between work and life more overtly.

People manage work and life very differently. Some thrive on the overlap, some try desperately to separate the two completely. Telephones, personal digital assistants (PDAs), pagers, and many of the new connected devices allow us to manage those moments of

Paul Schudel. Wall Clock DK.
1980. Mfr.: Designum,
Holland, 1980. The Museum of
Modern Art, New York

transition and overlap. If we feel that we have too much to do at work, we probably have constructed a lifestyle that demands too much of us all around.

As work can follow us anywhere, we desperately try to manage the boundaries between work and play. We feel better about getting to the office late if we have put in a few calls in between home and the office. We enjoy cutting off work as soon as we leave the office by shifting into a private call on our cell phones. We call from "on the road" because we can: hierarchies in these new nonstructured organizations unfold through waiting games and strategic contact. In new, nonhierarchical organizations, hierarchies are often played out over devices. For example, getting the corner office has shifted to the question of who gets the newest, coolest connected appliance; there is also the waiting game and the games of considerate calling. For example, middle managers will call subordinates while sitting in a loud airport setting, yet they will wait for a quiet location to call their superiors.

A paper calendar fundamentally works as well as a PDA does for much of the working population. However, PDA users can leverage the device to manage their boundaries between work and home. It is easier to keep multiple calendars on a PDA. There are games to play, chimes to remind us of transition times. Files for play that can reside next to files for work. One can readily flip between one's personal life and work. Similarly with a PDA, one may be sitting on a bus, perhaps checking a schedule. This device serves more as a reflection on the day; one can prepare for the next day, perhaps play a game for a while to take one's mind off work, or checking what movies are playing this week. In perusing websites full of software for palm-based devices, it is apparent that at least half of the programs are for personal use.

We are fascinated with the technology behind the machines around us. The manufacturers try to hide them behind facades, packaging them into tidy, neat, little devices that alternate between being very contained, very opaque, businesslike, anonymous, or conservative. These predetermined fairly decorative solutions either work for us or they do not. There is not much choice or option in personalizing them.

This exhibition prompts me to ask some questions about recently designed and manufactured devices. Why not design devices that celebrate what it is they were invented to do? If these devices are not really there to save time, why do they have to look the way they do? Notice how fascinated people are with see-through timepieces, clear covers for phones, drive-through car washes. Why not allow our tools to celebrate what it is they actually do? Cell phones have eliminated the need for receptionists. Who will give us that warm greeting, "How are you feeling?" anymore? What are we doing to actually make devices behave this way?

Since we celebrate work, perhaps we should celebrate the environments and devices with which we work more than we currently do. Buildings are erected to stand for decades. Entire floors within a building are changed on a much shorter cycle to reflect either a change in occupancy or to better support the current condition of the same occupant: growth, culture change, a change in direction of the company's vision, industry, offerings. It is always intriguing to ride up and down elevators and be able to peek in to see how different companies have shaped and dressed their workplace environments.

Similarly, it would be great if people were able to hang on to the core technology of their devices, while updating systems. Why not be able to dress and update other aspects of our devices according to our personal preference? For example, why not take the personalization of cell phones and PDAs beyond "fashion faceplates" and treat them more like hot rods—adding, replacing, and decorating both the internal workings and the shell over time. The Smart car (currently available in Europe) is the first vehicle to experiment with a deeper concept of customization. Now imagine buying the equivalent of a T-shirt for the seats, washing them, replacing them, trading them.

Many companies, such as Palm, Handspring, and the like, come out with an entirely new product every six to twelve months. Why not sever the imposition of culture, spirit, and character from an object that would be more temporary, personal, transparent, changeable? This would allow us to humanize and personalize the tools we use day to day.

Tokyo
Kayoko Ota

Workaholic

The Japanese are known to be workaholics, and indeed we are. I can think of two main reasons why: we are all trained to act in a regimented order as members of a group, which places productivity and achievement of the group over personal concerns; we also pay a lot of attention to formality and order, both in behavior and physical appearance. These require time and effort that lead to the extension of working hours. Yet at the same time we criticize ourselves for being workaholics. A few months ago, the parents of a young businessman who died of excessive work (karoshi) brought a lawsuit against his company, the leading advertising firm in Japan. The court ruled in favor of the parents. In a country where working hard has been taken for granted, it was a brave move to prove that the company was at fault. Yet there is a growing tendency to disapprove of "workaholism."

Young people in general are becoming more and more easy-going about work, to the extent that fewer and fewer consider a full-time job absolutely necessary, but prefer "swinging" with part-time jobs. But those in their forties and fifties, who came through the bullet-train-like economic-growth period of the 1970s and 1980s, who actually used to feel proud of dedicating their life to work, do not know how to slow down. Men especially are said to be isolated from their families because they are never at home, which directly and indirectly has triggered various social problems.

Economic Crisis

The glory days are over, and the current economic downturn is giving us more time to think about ourselves as individuals. Companies can no longer maintain the lifetime employment system and have been restructuring themselves. The restructuring of the market with the deregulation of foreign and/or venture capital is also encouraging a change in the employment system. Although this is hard on employees, I think it is a good shift as we are beginning to value individual productivity and profit-making abilities over just being a responsible member of a group. Our sense of loyalty and attachment to one company has changed drastically over the last decade.

Conditions for female workers are changing as well. Women used to stay in a company until they were about twenty-seven years old, just serving tea and doing the simplest tasks. Then they retired to get married. But this is becoming a thing of the past. No longer do they feel obliged to quit their jobs to get married. More and more women have become part of the competitive workforce.

Ringi—A Decision-Making Process

One thing that has not changed is the way we process jobs. For example, we make decisions by the *ringi* system, which is to pass proposals from the bottom up. Most items that need consensus go along this route. Quite recently, NTT Communications, a major telecommunications company in Japan, started a new *ringi* system using the "i-mode," a mobile-phone technology connected to the Internet. They have some six thousand items a year to process by this system, and have already transferred it to their LAN domestic computer connections. Now with i-mode, everybody can access and get updated on the latest *ringi* proposals twenty-four hours a day. The company says it implemented this new technology to speed up its decision-making process, maximize everyone's time, and economize on paper. But will it? My guess is that it will just accelerate the company's compulsive mobile-phone syndrome, which will only help it catch up with the speed and aggression of the market competition.

Nemawashi: Laying the Groundwork

Meetings are carried out in such a way as to avoid confrontation and conflict. Especially in the higher ranks, some coordination is usually done prior to meetings to ensure that the meeting will progress as desired. This practice is called *nemawashi,* originally a horticultural word that means to "turn the roots" prior to replanting or, by implication, "carefully laying the groundwork."

Why do we bother spending a lot of energy doing *nemawashi*? Why don't we just discuss things straight out in meetings? Remember, the company or group always comes first, the individual last. One is always speaking for what he or she represents, that is, the company or group, and the opinion or reaction that he or she presents is supposed to have been decided upon by consensus. Another reason is that we have a strong sense of position, and try to ensure that no one loses face in public. Formality and order must be well maintained, especially in meetings.

Kyoichi Tsuzuki. Office space from *Tokyo Style*. Kyoto: Kyoto Shoin, 1997

Office Furniture

For a long time it was thought morally indefensible to spend more than the minimum for office furniture or create lavish interior décor. In the 1960s and 1970s, when Japan was focused on productivity and growth, amenities in the working environment were the last thing to consider. In those decades, gray-colored steel desks and chairs were prevalent. But with the economic boom in the 1980s and early 1990s, this tendency started to change. New construction and renovation of office buildings introduced partitioning systems, better-quality chairs, and filing systems.

A public relations director of an office-furniture manufacturer told me: "Generally, executives in their forties and fifties still hold on to their old values that investing in office furniture is not important. But when they are gone and replaced with younger generations, we imagine they'll all start getting new furniture that is much more tuned in to their way of work. Mobile or easily readjustable furniture, for example. Today, it's only intelligent technology companies that buy them." Even in major corporations occupying state-of-the-art high-rise buildings, most office interiors and furniture are very generic, gray, and conservative.

The Café as Extended Office

I'm writing this in a café in a downtown office tower in Tokyo. It's eleven o'clock in the morning and more than a third of the people here are businessmen. Of course, they are not just relaxing. They are meeting with clients or discussing issues with colleagues over a cup of coffee. I've also seen a section meeting of some ten people carried out here. In fact, the café is very much a part of our daily life. For businessmen, the café is an extended office space where they can work in a more relaxed mood; they may also not have enough space in their offices to hold a meeting. So, by day, the café is a place for workers to escape. By night, pubs and karaoke bars are where they go to release work pressure.

The following three texts are transcriptions of interviews conducted by Kayoko Ota in July 2000 in Tokyo. The interviewees were asked to comment on the work environment in their respective cities.

Seoul
Jin-hee Chang

TEMPERAMENT: Koreans are rather direct—one could even say short-tempered. They don't hold feelings inside too long, but respond on the spot, which can lead to arguments or even real quarrels. But this also means they don't retain negative feelings once the conflict is settled.

I think this temperament reflects the way they work. Although there is usually a clear hierarchy within a company, that doesn't change people's nature. I myself have worked in a large firm for a few years, and have occasionally seen even lower-level workers stand up and argue with their bosses. The good thing is that this is seen as professionalism, rather than just an emotional outburst. So you can imagine company meetings where lots of questions are raised and lively discussions occur.

FAMILYLIKE RELATIONSHIP: Korean companies are like big families. Once you become an employee, you begin to develop a sense of belonging to a family. The bond is so firmly established that even after you leave the company, a close relationship tends to continue. In my office, each team of six to seven employees, headed by a chief, usually juggles about five projects at a time. We work together and spend time together after work. We go out for drinks or for supper, where talk may be about almost anything, from family to love affairs. Also, it's not unusual to invite one's personal friends or "steady" to join office outings. Yet, while employers pay great attention to human relationships among office colleagues, employees are evaluated on the basis of ability and skill rather than on background or age, which may sometimes jeopardize peaceful relationships.

OFFICE LAYOUT AND POLICY: In spite of the familylike atmosphere, work is strictly ordered in a hierarchical structure. The office layout clearly reflects this. One typical layout has desks arranged in rows so that a superior can see the backs of subordinates and their computer screens as a way of keeping watch. So it's impossible to play computer games in the office. There is certainly some discrimination against women in an office. Normally, the more important

jobs go to men and the rest to women, a fact that always frustrated me. It's women's work to serve tea and make copies; it's men's to tackle the substantive issues. Perhaps that's why each section has at least one female.

Women receive one extra paid day off each month. The majority of female workers still retire after marriage or pregnancy. Female employees generally wear uniforms in offices: a skirt, blouse, and jacket. I once complained to my boss that this clothing was too uncomfortable for my particular job—working on a drawing board and making models. My boss agreed, and women in my team were allowed to wear more casual clothes. Women in the rest of the company then teased us about it.

GETTING MARRIED IS AN OFFICE SCENE: Employees are treated like family, which means that the company tries to take good care of them. Of course, this nurturing is also a tactic to heighten employees' loyalty and keep them. Here are a few examples.

In large firms, there is usually an employees' dining hall where meals are free of charge. This dining hall is typically transformed and used as a wedding and banquet hall for employees on weekends. A catering company is hired to make the arrangements and organize weddings, which occur almost every Saturday and Sunday. This is a very popular venue because it's much cheaper than elsewhere. About four couples a day get married there during the high seasons, which are spring and fall. Usually two to three hundred people attend a wedding ceremony. In Korea almost anyone the couple knows is invited. The company allows employees who are working on weekends to come for drinks and fun. It is a unique way for office workers to take a break.

The company also encourages employees to develop skills such as learning English or Japanese, computer expertise, or getting a professional license. Some of the expenses for this training are paid for by the company. They also financially support employees' sports activities. There are a lot of opportunities in and out of the office for employees to meet and share private time together, fall in love, and eventually use the dining hall on the weekend for their wedding.

You may think that Korean life puts a heavy emphasis on work, but that is not how we see it. To us there is a good balance between private life and work; we don't think we are sacrificing our life for work. After all, becoming intimate with one another like a family is such a natural thing for Koreans in any group situation.

Taipei
Hui-Chi Chou

NAP: No one answers the phone in an office building during lunch hours in Taipei. Even if someone did, the voice would sound very annoyed. Office workers usually take a nap after lunch—between noon and 1:30 P.M.—and common sense tells you that you don't make phone calls during this time. The nap lasts only twenty to thirty minutes, but it recharges you so you're ready to work again. At 1:30, an alarm clock or radio that somebody has set starts to buzz. How do we sleep? Usually we just lean over our desk or a meeting table. If we're lucky, we can sleep on a sofa in a reception room. We don't find leaning over an office desk painful because we have done it since elementary school and are used to it.

RATIONALISM: Family ties are strong in Taiwan, and they have some impact on company management, but, otherwise, we value individualism and rationalism in office work. We also value private life, so we try not to work after regular hours. We love eating and drinking together, but not necessarily with office colleagues. As part of being rational, we clearly establish work parameters for our colleagues. We probably do this so that no one infringes on another's territory and causes him or her to lose face. That is considered shameful behavior. We do occasionally have conflicts between this individualism and family-controlled company management. Those who are otherwise professionally capable and promising can sometimes hit a ceiling because of family members who hold the top positions. One recent phenomenon is that there is an increasing number of people who have more than one job. They do not divide their time; they juggle different jobs at the same time. This is one sign that we value individualism more than loyalty to a company. In fact, Taiwanese workers tend to change jobs without hesitation.

GENDER: Women in Taiwan are not burdened with simple jobs such as serving tea, making copies, or sending faxes, as in some other Asian countries. Indeed, men and women perform the same tasks, and the wage difference between them is comparatively small. Women usually continue to work after marriage and children. I wonder if there is some connection to Chinese society in this regard. There are few "pure housewives." Children are usually taken care of by their grandparents while their parents work; often three generations live together helping one another.

COMPUTERS: The Taiwanese tend to think that larger is better; size is one visible measure of status. This used to hold true for computers, which are a valuable asset at the office. Thin and light laptop computers didn't attract people for some time, but this is fast disappearing as a result of American and Japanese influences. Another interesting aspect of Taiwan life is that we do not customarily use a notebook to keep track of our schedules. That's something we just keep in our heads. So electronic notebooks or "palmtops" haven't been particularly popular. Although Taiwan is manufacturing an increasingly larger amount of computer hardware and parts for export, domestic consumption is another story.

STREET VENDORS: Just outside office buildings, the streets and alleys are filled with shops and vendors selling virtually everything. Central business districts are no exception. Also, in large multi-tenant building complexes, which are typical in Southeast Asia, ground-floor corridors are filled with restaurant tables and chairs. All of these cater to the lunchtime needs of office workers. Some eat there; others take food back to the office.

In Taiwan street vendors work twenty-four hours a day, but usually they open around ten o'clock in the morning to get ready for the lunchtime rush. Popular ones are those that offer different kinds of dishes, which are put on a tray with a bowl of rice. Sometimes you are charged by weight. Some vendors also cater to your office. In the street, you would spend an average of four dollars for lunch. Around three o'clock workers go out in the street again to get sweets, which they share among colleagues. Chatting during this sweet break is a popular pastime among workers. There is no extended "tea time" during work hours; people have to wait until they are off duty to enjoy a leisurely tea break in Taiwan.

RELIGION AND FENG SHUI: Taoism, the most popular religion in Taiwan, is practiced in some offices as much as Feng Shui. It is not uncommon to find an altar in offices with a statue of the Buddha, Kuan Yin the Goddess of Mercy, or guardian deities with offerings of food and flowers. Some very religious companies burn sticks of incense on the first and fifteenth day of each month. Many businesses determine the locations of their offices and the orientations of their premises based on the principles of Feng Shui. This Chinese theory holds that a harmonious environment can be created if one follows certain guidelines that allow positive forces to enter that environment. For office interiors, this means determining the most congenial placement of office furniture, doorways, plants, and so on.

At Chinese New Year, a popular activity is to paste red paper with a lucky character on it or an icon of a god on the office front door, just as one does at home. On July 15, the day to chase evils out of buildings, people put a table with all kinds of offerings on it in front of the office. They also burn incense and "hell money." All these traditional rituals and customs are still performed in lively business premises in Taiwan.

Bangkok
Rachaporn Chouchouey

TRAFFIC JAMS: The notorious traffic jam dictates the life of office workers in Bangkok, and must be factored into whatever one does. Some workers avoid them by driving their cars to the office as early as six A.M. and sleeping in the car until nine A.M. Executives do the same, but at least they have their guest-room sofa. People normally spend a few hours a day in a car; of that time there may be only thirty minutes without traffic. One can never be sure how long travel will actually take, which makes people relatively easygoing about delays. In this city, one cannot be anxious about people not showing up on time.

After work, there are more traffic jams. Some people kill time around the office until traffic conditions improve. Some male workers play chess or watch TV together in the office. Others go shopping since most supermarkets, department stores, restaurants, and shops are open till ten P.M. Shops in the suburbs where city workers live are open till midnight or even later. It wasn't always like this. It all began about ten years ago, when the economy started to grow. The whole city is at the service of the workers, flexibly shifting its time.

Some time ago, an international newspaper ran a story about a somewhat futuristic workspace to combat Bangkok's traffic hysteria—the "mobile office station," a car complete with fax machine, telephone, and desk. I think such a station did exist before the economic crash, but as a guest service offered by luxury hotels. It isn't popular, at least not yet. But mobile phones are extremely useful, indeed practically indispensable for everybody in such traffic conditions. It's common to see drivers stuck in traffic talking on the phone.

OFFICE INSIDE AND OUTSIDE: It has only been in about the last thirty years that office space has become ubiquitous in Bangkok because of the increasing number of white-collar office workers. Economic growth meant that buildings started to mushroom. Before 1997, when the economy crashed, real-estate investment was in full swing, partly because it signified better social status and business success. Since the crash, some three to four hundred buildings under construction are on hold in Bangkok. Modernizing office space began just recently in the government sector. Before that, employers used to spend as little as possible on office amenities and managed with humble furniture. They preferred spending money on the external appearance just for the sake of investment.

The idea of the "cubicle" or independent workspace has just arrived in Thailand. Yet good office furniture, including system furniture, is still very expensive; more than half of it is imported from abroad, especially from Japan. Every building has air-conditioning nowadays. Quite often it's freezing inside while it's forty degrees centigrade outside, and office workers have to wear sweaters or jackets in this tropical country. It's difficult to adjust one's body between such drastically different climates inside and out. Funnily enough, people wearing sweaters or jackets on the streets of tropical Bangkok would be assumed to be office workers.

SNACKING: Thai people love to eat all day long, including during working hours. In the street, one sees endless chains of vendors and shops beckoning with all kinds of attractive-looking food; it is difficult to resist trying something. However, this time-honored Thai habit has recently been banned in offices where there are computers. Office workers used to bring in food and snack all day, leaving scraps for rats and cockroaches to enjoy during the night. That was when there was only paper in the office, but now with cables and computer data to damage, it's a different story. This is a serious problem in Thailand today. Snacking—not to mention chatting—used to be such a big release and favorite pastime for office workers who sit at their desks all day, but they've had to give it up for computers.

DOMESTICATED OFFICE: Personal bonds are close among Thai workers. They do things together and treat one another like family. They often call each other "auntie," "brother," "sister," or by a nickname. The company itself also tries to maintain relaxed relationships. On one's desk one puts whatever makes one feel at home and relaxed—family photos, amusements, pillows. Little things are brought in to provide comfort. This may explain why women change from high heels to slippers or sandals once they arrive at the office.

Older generations of workers—especially civil servants—are still very easygoing about work and "unprofessional" because they are employed for life. This attitude, however, began to change about a decade ago. There are two reasons for this. One is that the lifetime job system is being replaced by meritocratic skill-evaluation systems, due mainly to the privatization of firms. The second reason is the younger generation, many of whom have been educated abroad (often in the United States) and have brought back a more efficient working manner. Unfortunately, many of them have had to wait to come back until the economy in Bangkok picks up. When they do come back, I imagine this shift to more professional behavior will accelerate.

LUNCHTIME AND EVENING SHOPPING: In a central business district such as the Silom Road area, the "Wall Street of Bangkok," with its high-rise office buildings, workers eat out in the streets at lunchtime, so much so that they do not patronize cafeterias or restaurants in the office buildings, which are usually expensive and used mostly by executives. Executives have food delivered to their offices for lunch, or even for supper when they stay late to avoid heavy traffic. In fact, this has become a popular trend. By noon, streets are filled with vendors of virtually anything—from meals and sweets to cosmetics and clothes—all of which are usually good and cheap. The streets look almost like small markets. Street vendors are especially popular among working women, who go out for their fifteen-minute "lunchtime shopping." By three P.M. all these vendors are gone. Later on, different groups of vendors flood the streets again, this time serving those who stay in and around the office till around eight P.M. to avoid heavy traffic.

OFFICE AS A SMALL TRADE HUB: Offices offer a network of services for working women who have families. Women in Thailand tend to continue their careers after marriage or childbearing, especially those in academic and business fields. A variety of merchants walk into offices. Some deliver packaged food that women can bring back to their families; others sell newspapers and magazines, men's and women's clothes, or even cars. All kinds of trades come in and out of offices.

BUDDHISM AND FENG SHUI: Buddhism is generally taught up to high school in Thailand; instruction extends from the philosophy of the religion to how to pray. Some executives have Buddhist altars in their offices. Sometimes a monk is brought into the office to hold a religious ceremony to bless the place. Chinese Feng Shui is also quite popular in Thailand, where Thai and Chinese races are very much mixed. Those who follow Feng Shui insist on a particular way to arrange desks, organize space, or even design a building. Statistically, more than fifty percent of businesses in Thailand are in the hands of the "Chinese," typically the second- or third-generation Thai-Chinese. All in all, private life and professional life are not clearly divided in Bangkok. Office business goes hand-in-hand with all kinds of street business and sometimes with religion.

Interview with Bruce Mau
Paola Antonelli

PAOLA ANTONELLI: I'm curious to know what you think work has become, especially right now, for people.

BRUCE MAU: I've been thinking about this quite a bit because of the work we do [at Bruce Mau Design], and, in a way, I got involved with the question based on a personal crisis. I reached the point where I realized that the field I was working in was evolving very rapidly. There were new opportunities, and in order to take advantage of them, I had to answer some questions about how I would define work and how I would organize it in order to define it in that way. I came to a kind of dilemma between being a director and being a producer. It was the classic director/producer problem of someone directing and creating inside a work environment, on the one hand, and someone acting as a producer outside of the problem and seeing the situation from an external perspective. I realized I was a director at heart, and somebody who is inside the condition, and that I needed to work with somebody who was outside. So I began two trajectories. One was to find a producer, and the other was to look at work as a general condition and try to understand what was being transformed and what the forces that were producing the transformation were.

PA: And what did you conclude when you started looking at that?

BM: It began as an investigation that we call the Work Project. I realized, first of all, that work is a horizontal problem, and it is almost always addressed in a vertical dimension. If you look at the way we think about work, we slice it vertically and through disciplines. So we slice it through industrial design, architecture, ergonomics, or economics. We have many different vertical slices to understand work as a condition. It can be seen in the design disciplines in particular, and I think it's starting to be addressed where you have industrial designers on the one hand—furniture and product designers—coming at the problem in one scale in one dimension and the architects and the urbanists on the other hand coming at the problem from another dimension. There is always a gap between the two, architecture and product, because the problem is sliced vertically instead of horizontally. So we set about trying to develop a research project.

PA: When was that?

BM: It was about 1992 or 1993. At the time workplace malaise induced by technology wasn't such a hot issue. But as more and more people began to grapple with the effects of new technologies, it surfaced as a substantial concern. I had a discussion with Rolf [Fehlbaum, president of Vitra] recently, and he mentioned the effect that Robert Propst had when he introduced the Action Office [in the 1960s]. It did much more than simply introduce a new product; it changed the boundary between disciplines. He took the walls and pushed them into the designer's domain and out of the architect's domain. He didn't resolve the basic split between an architectural exterior and an architectural interior and the product that generates the work environment, but he changed it a lot.

PA: It was the threshold . . .

BM: Yes, and in that one gesture he changed the industry in terms of scale because, suddenly, you had businesses that were producing hundreds of millions of dollars worth of walls, whereas prior to his invention, that was all in another domain.

PA: How and when did you start your studio?

BM: I started my studio in 1985. It was just at the moment when almost everything that had to do with typographic production and communication was being transformed. It was a very volatile moment in the business, and it pushed me into an exploration of issues related to the workplace. You can credit two technologies, FedEx and fax, for an almost overnight transformation in the way design practices conducted their businesses. These technologies also had a similar impact on other fields. So, if you can imagine, when I began working, any product that I was creating would be traveling around the city [Toronto] in taxicabs. A design for an advertisement, for instance, might take ten or twelve rides in one day from client to typesetter to printer to designer and back and forth. There was no way of transmitting those visual things.

   So you had localized expertise. For instance, all the typesetters would have all the type people in the city in one place, or say, four or five places in the city. Taxicabs would line up outside those places. All day and all night, you could go there and get a cab. Businesses had accounts and would spend millions of dollars to have their proposals ferried around. When the fax machine was introduced, it decimated the taxicab business literally overnight because it meant that things no longer had to move physically. That got me interested in the urbanistic dimension of this change. When you take a business and transform it in terms of the way it communicates or is structured organizationally, that change is superimposed on the urban domain and it transforms that domain as you transform the organization. So, for instance, if you introduce something like just-in-time production, you make the infrastructure of movement part of the facility. A very large percentage of your manufacturing operation at any given moment is actually warehoused on the open road. It's a workplace concept that totally transforms the urban realm.

PA: It's about, in a way, decentralization.

BM: There's a very interesting dimension to it. You have two things happening simultaneously: decentralization in that things can be any-where, so you could have, for instance, a very high degree of mecha-nization in a very isolated domain that's serviced by infrastructure; and a concentration of a different sort that needs a new infrastructure with density to support it, as the global economist Saskia Sassen has so effectively pointed out. So you have the reemergence of centers that have to have a critical mass of intellectual capital in order to sustain themselves. For me to have a really effective design studio in Toronto, for example, Toronto itself has to have a critical mass of design culture.

PA: Yes, but it's a cultural and not a logistical problem.

BM: It's about a kind of cultural dimension.

PA: That's very interesting. You said that decentralization means that things can be anywhere. There are those who say that the next thing, with the evolution of faxes and FedEx and the Internet and so on, is that people can be anywhere. You seem not to believe that.

BM: Well, they can, but let's face it, people who come out best in the whole system are writers because they can go in the desert with their computers and do their writing. But everything else that is a collective enterprise, that is involved with a group and team dynamic, which comprises most of the workplace, is sustained by an ecology that has a critical mass of the substance that makes it up, which is intelligence. I can't have this studio anywhere. I can have *a* studio somewhere, other than a kind of nodal point in the network, but in order for people to be comfortable, they need to be in an environment where they don't feel like they're trapped. They need to have mobility, which is a function of a certain density, and that density is provided at the nodes and nowhere else. So you have a sparsely populated environment with dense nodes of activity. That produces an incredible volatility and richness in the nodes because suddenly you have brought people from all different domains into one central zone. Because of the way technology is moving toward convergence, all the design disciplines, from the technological to the communicational and cultural, are deployed simultaneously.

PA: You mean in a product?

BM: Almost any kind of activity. Take something like stock trading. It seems to be an economic activity, but actually it's a communication activity, an interface problem, a technological problem, a product-design problem. When you look at something like the Bloomberg terminal, it's actually deploying a lot of disciplines simultaneously and more and more invisibly. In order to sustain it, you need them all simultaneously.

PA So, based on that, what do you think of all those offices that try to project their own culture far away, design offices that are in many different places? Are they offering anything to the designers?

BM: I don't know. It's a very interesting dilemma actually. One of the problems we face, and I think any studio has to face, is that of scale. What's the optimum scale? What's the scale that produces the best results consistently? And how do you organize it? One thing that is changing quite dramatically in the design profession is the capital dimension of it. When I started my business, it cost me $120 to put somebody to work. I bought a drafting table for $100 and $20 worth of equipment, pencils, and erasers, and they were in business. Today, it costs me maybe $20,000 to put somebody to work. So as the design industries and the technologies converge, the technological dimension of the business increases.

You need a certain scale in order to sustain it. It's a real dilemma, of course, because the question is, how do you generate a culture that has the same cultural dimension that triggered the emergence of the studio in the first place? That's a very tough question to answer. We're grappling with it ourselves. We're now twenty-five people. How big do we get?

Pentagram [the British industrial and graphic-design firm with offices around the world] actually has a very interesting office format, which is that it is a cellular entity. It has a fairly strong resilient form because it can grow and shrink and grow and the cells can enlarge and contract and the identity of the place maintains itself. So it's actually a pretty interesting model.

PA: What is work culture? Is it something that is created by the corporation or by the individual? Who makes it?

BM: The question you have to ask in order to answer that is: "What is culture in that context?" Culture is something that exists between things more than it exists within things. It's at a higher order of organization than the individual unit. If you define culture in that way, the studio is culture. I am a person within the studio. The studio is not generated by me, but by the people in the studio. I have a responsibility. It's like an ecology, and I have a responsibility to sustain it and make it as rich and fertile as I can. In that sense, the culture exists between the people in the company, but the people in the workplace generate it. A company can't dictate culture. It can make it possible. I can make it possible for people to enrich themselves, but I can't enrich them.

PA: You say that a company cannot dictate culture. Is that always true?

BM: It can't be generated, like you can't make a plant grow. It needs to grow of its own accord. You provide the conditions for it to

grow, but it has to evolve itself.

PA: How do you provide those conditions? Do you have to work hard at being more than your normal self to provide those cultural conditions?

BM: Yes. There is a Machiavellian dimension to it, in the best possible sense. It is orchestrated. It's something you have to foster quite specifically in order for it to happen. In our case, we're very conscious of the ecosystem that we have here. But at the same time, in order for it to really work, it has to have the wildness of real life, which means you have to be somewhat reckless in order for it to be rich. That's the kind of balance that you have to navigate.

PA: Meetings have truly become one of the most time-consuming and certainly attention-consuming parts of our work time. They have become a culture of their own that differs in various geographic situations. Can you tell me what you think about meetings?

BM: Some time ago I made a rule in the studio, which is to call them "workings," not meetings. Meetings were always a kind of postponement of real production. What I need is a working, which is like a meeting only it's where things actually happen. You come to it with a different set of expectations that things will happen and that you will get results. It's probably going to last longer because you have to work through a collaborative process.

The question is, "Why meet?" There are a lot of reasons to meet that don't have anything to do with the stated outcome of the meeting. For instance, motivation, to undermine authority, to gossip, to strategize, to level hierarchies, for intimacy, for ceremony. These are social functions that have nothing to do with the meeting itself. You make a meeting ostensibly to do something. The effect of it is to put all these social functions into the process.

PA: Do you think it has always been like that?

BM: I think that our culture provides fertile ground for meetings to happen because of its egalitarian sensibility. In the past, many more decisions were made without collective input. Edicts were delivered, and whole armies were sent into production, whereas today those armies have to decide for themselves.

For instance, in London the class system is so much more powerful [than in America], and the tenor of things is quite different. To do business with Americans in England and see them mingle with the British is really fascinating. The approach to who will speak and with what authority reflects an altogether different culture. It's a powerful difference. There's a cynicism at the lower levels because they know that even if they speak, the class system will often override any kind of good sense. People of the lower classes have a cynical tone to their communication, whereas the Americans' approach is that an idea can come from anywhere.

PA: How much of our work is ritual?

BM: Well, I would go out on a limb to say that much of our work is about increasing opportunities for mating.

PA: Mating?

BM: Although it sounds outlandish, that, in a way, is what drives a lot of our cultural formations. If you think about it in those terms, it's why cities are so successful. They produce a more effective interface for mating. People in the studio buy into the ideals of the studio in a very serious way. It connects very deeply to their own identity. If you mess with that, if you begin to make changes to it, you're messing with their identity, which is a nonnegotiable issue. That's why when you make changes in the workplace, you can have a very strong response. Maybe it's just me, but I think all those things tie into status, performance, and your place in the community. When you think about what we've tried to achieve with the workplace (it's become a very big question obviously), we try to extricate sexuality from the workplace as an issue. In fact, the whole idea of the workplace is in support of sexuality. In other words, it's really crazy to think that you can put a lot of men and women, and men and men, and women and women, in an environment for a long time and expect that somehow sex is not going to be happening in the off-

hours. In terms of sexuality and social interaction, focus group work is one of the most bizarre things I've ever been involved with.

PA: Why did you do get involved with focus groups?

BM: Because we want to test certain assumptions of things that we do. We organize groups of people who are demographically related to what we're trying to achieve and show them things we're working on. It's like seeing a social dynamic without effecting it because you're behind a two-way mirror. You can actually listen and watch a social dynamic without interacting with it. It's absolutely, totally revealing. It's a great thing. I think every designer should do it. You have to be really careful because it's such a mindblower.

PA: I think the issue of extricating sexuality from the workplace, because it's a problem, is quite enormous. I also wonder what else has been extricated in some situations to eliminate problems.

BM: It's not the only social conduct that has been eliminated. For instance, when manufacturing first began, the idea of regular work was new and didn't take hold very well. The biggest problem wasn't that workers were delinquent at work, but that they would simply not show up at all. The idea that you would work a lot of hours was not thought necessary. In a subsistence environment, you worked on your patch of land, made a little extra, and traded a little. It wasn't that hard for everyone. The idea that you had to be there at a certain hour was new. In a way, we're going back to that, where people can move more freely. If you're going to have organized activity, you need to have organized presence. In order to behave properly in a workplace, you have to learn the codes of the workplace. We've internalized them so effectively that we hardly know that we've even lost anything.

PA: What is the most sensible, ideal way for you to work? What is an example of the ideal way to work?

BM: I have a few criteria that make up the ideal environment. I need a certain level of promiscuity. I'm not so good at doing one project and being focused on a single thing. For me, it's exciting to have a range of work and to allow for disciplines to lead across one another. That's part of it. I also like a cultural range, where languages and culture from other places are being mixed into new combinations. One of the basic issues is a fundamental respect for the people around you and a supportive environment, a place where people can express themselves. One of the barometers I use in the studio is how much laughter there is, how comfortable people feel laughing. They shouldn't be so pressured that they've lost their sense of humor. For me that's a basic condition. I'm very sensitive to the work issues, in other words, what it is that we're trying to achieve. I'm very professional in that sense. I need to feel confidence in the intelligence of our collaborators, in the studio, and in the people who come from outside. We've been thinking a lot about what it is that we actually do, what our product is. We have a wide range of outcomes, and the thing that is common to all of those outcomes is intelligence.

Scott Kersner, one of the founders of *Fast Company*, said that a lot of businesses with which I work have very elaborate schemes for compensating their staff because the work itself is so terrible. The companies have to jump through hoops to compensate people enough to actually make them spend time in these places. People have their own reasons for working for me. That's why I say the identity of the workplace is a critical issue now because the way people connect to a place is through its identity. It's where they live.

PA: How do you manage to have a family life?

BM: It's a hard question. I have three girls. My middle daughter wakes up at about five o'clock in the morning. I have four or five hours of family life before I come to the office, which is really brutal because I'm usually here until about 1 or 2 A.M. We're trying to work out how I'm going to spend time with them and what the long-term trajectory is going to be.

It's something I'm really grappling with because the studio is very demanding. I can't do the kind of work I do with a normal amount of focus. I need to put a lot of energy in, to produce with a kind of hyper-focus, in order to get to something new. I have to push it to a level where new things start to happen. The studio went from ten people in 1995 to twenty-five in 2000. With new projects coming in, it's looking more like fifty. That's an issue we have to work out. It goes back to the question of what is the best infrastructural scale that supports the maximum flexibility and efficiency and can allow us to do projects at the right scale.

PA: How do you go about deciding how large you want your company to grow? Do you talk to people who have similar problems?

BM: One of the benefits I've had is working really closely with people like the architect Frank Gehry. Frank has been a real mentor for me in business. In a way, if there's a model that I'm working on, it's Frank's studio. It's very humane. It supports the work at a very high level. It's super well organized and is maybe the world's leading studio. That's what I want to achieve over the long haul—to produce an environment that supports a commitment to innovation and quality. I'd like to do that and spend time with my family, and have a healthy life.

Interview with Michael Brill
Sarah Robins

SARAH ROBINS: In your research, what have you found to be the elements of a work environment that people respond to most? What has the strongest effects?

MICHAEL BRILL: The first thing that seems to have the most powerful effect is the ability to do distraction-free work, that is, to have enough acoustic privacy to concentrate. This is true even in organizations that are very team-based and interactive. The second is the ability to have easy, informal interactions with people, which is clearly the primary source of learning and problem-solving, so that any work environment has to provide for both. The idea that if you have privacy you can't have interaction is nonsense; in fact, you can easily have both. These needs have always been true and will continue to be true in the foreseeable future. If you depend on people to be thoughtful about their work, they have to have the capacity to do it. And if you want people to continue to learn about what's happening in the organization, how they can be real contributors, then the informal interactions are equally critical. Group meetings and teamwork also need to have a fairly distraction-free environment. When you have a meeting and you're working on a problem, the last thing you want to do is have it in the middle of the cafeteria.

SR: It's interesting that you should mention the cafeteria. A Dutch designer recently submitted a proposal for an office in the kitchen, based on the concept that all the best conversations at parties tend to happen in the kitchen.

MB: What we did two years ago in our office [BOSTI Associates], because we're all kind of food-oriented, and it's a group of about fifteen people so it's like family, was to put in a pretty complete kitchen, which is along one wall. On the other wall are the fax machine, the copier, and a couple of telephones. What's interesting is how much activity actually happens there. It's certainly more than "the watering hole," and it really is a center of informal activity. Also people who're doing boring things like copying materials or sending faxes have the opportunity to talk with people who're getting coffee. We installed phones there so that wherever you are, you can be reached, and you can talk to a customer or a colleague or whomever

you need to talk to. In general, I think trying to lump all of the behaviors together that aren't either formal meetings or heads-down work is a good idea, and the kitchen is not a bad model, assuming it's a pretty elaborate one. But it would never be a place to do any focused work.

SR: Could you comment on influential models of workplace schemes over the past twenty years such as hoteling, perhaps in relation to management theories, current trends, and implications for the workplace?

MB: Because you asked in relation to management theories and trends, let me start with a kind of mantra of modern business, which is that if we can satisfy our customers, that's really the predictor of long-term success and, interestingly enough, everyone has customers, even if one is a secretary.

SR: Like internal customers?

MB: Yes, you have internal and external customers, and in order to satisfy them, employees are asked to be entrepreneurial, that is, they have to do what's necessary in order to satisfy their customers. What you get is a lot less hierarchy in an organization. Many organizations no longer have pyramid organizational charts; they just don't look like that anymore. Decisions get pushed down as far as they possibly can, to individuals who, in fact, are in direct contact with their customers so you don't have to receive information, go to your manager, find out what you should do, etc., but you are both empowered to make those decisions and provided with what you need to enable you to do it. So empowerment and enablement become critical issues. Another major management trend is to use all of one's resources all of the time, so that ideas from just-in-time manufacturing have come into the office workplace—just-in-time space, just-in-time workforce, etc. Hoteling ends up being one of the outcomes of just-in-time space.

Let me talk about each of these in turn. If you want to empower employees, you obviously have to provide them with information to make the best possible decisions at the time. What that means is that essentially the job of management is to set the goals and then let people decide how to achieve them, how they should use their time, and even when they might work. Options might be working at home, in an airport lounge, at the clients'. There are a lot of sales-people, for instance, who spend the first part of their morning making all of their calls and doing their E-mails at home, before going out and meeting customers, so they're both working at home and not working at home. Some people use satellite offices rather than going downtown to an office. For example, many organizations have satellites or drop-in offices in the areas in which they do business. There's a lot of business that happens in the airline clubs and in hotels, so the location where business takes place frequently becomes the choice of the empowered individual. You can provide individuals with a lot of information, but sometimes you need a group to get the best answer. For group problem-solving, you need spaces for groups to get together. Sometimes the space is needed only for an hour, sometimes for a week, but what you need are spaces where groups can work intensely and without distraction.

In terms of enablement, that is, providing people with the right tools, obviously you need workspace types that are appropriate to the range of tasks that people do. Almost every knowledge worker does multi-tasking; very few people sit at a screen and input data anymore. In fact, those jobs are probably already automated in one way or another so that what we're beginning to see is a wider range of workspace types in the office. Another enablement is mobility so that people can work from anywhere. The implication of this is portable technology: laptops, pocket pagers, cell phones. All of these things are standard equipment for anybody who does mobile work, for anybody who goes on vacation and still has to work, as many knowledge workers do. If people are out serving customers often, if not most of the time, then what you end up with are empty workspaces. Organizations have looked around and said, "This is crazy. Our employees are out with their customers, just as we've asked them to be, using other locations, and here we have all this empty workspace."

Is there some strategy to counter this? Hoteling, which essentially uses a small number of non-owned workspaces for a larger number of people, ends up being a reasonable strategy. For those people who

are out of their offices a lot—that is, they are already in some sense gypsies—you could have a pool of shared workspaces. When workers come in, they have one; when they're out, they don't. They don't own the one that they just left; it goes back to the hotel essentially.

SR: Hoteling has been criticized for the lack of personality and ownership that people experience. How have people reacted to those aspects of it?

MB: We did the first hoteling installation in the United States in 1990 at Ernst and Young. Our research showed that employees weren't bothered by the impersonality of their work environment; nor did they feel a loss of ownership of the space. If an employee is used to having pictures in his or her workspace, they can be brought in for the length of time that person is occupying the office. When the employee is out, these personal items can be put in a locker or storage unit until he or she is in the office again. No one's performance or satisfaction seems to have been reduced by not having personal items around. I have lots of things on the walls of my office, but if you ask me what's there, I couldn't tell you. What I'm saying is that it seems not to have been a major problem. There are hoteling organizations that talk (jokingly) about the "Velcro" cat, the same way some people's name tags now have Velcro on them. Maybe the picture of the cat has Velcro on it, and if it's important enough, you'll put it up. If it's not important, you'll leave it in your storage unit. You have to remember that hoteling isn't for everybody. It is for those who are out more than they're in. That's the only time that it would make sense. To demand that everyone in an organization's workforce has to hotel is foolish. You have to have a pattern of in and out that would make hoteling sensible.

SR: Could you comment on the Chiat/Day offices in New York?

MB: Those were probably the worst offices ever designed. A couple of years ago the *Wall Street Journal* sent me six hours of videotapes of these offices and asked me to analyze them. Real hoteling offices have places for people to work; they have a distraction-free environment, but they don't own the space. In the Chiat/Day offices, now defunct as you know, nobody had any space to concentrate. You sat on a sofa or out in the middle of the room or you were in the cafeteria. There were never enough laptops to go around because people were taking them home, since that was the only place they could work! Hoteling doesn't mean you don't have a place to do heads-down, focused work. It means you have access to a space to do what you need to; you just don't own that space. The Chiat/Day offices—totally open, shared, little places where you were expected to work—drove people crazy. I watched these videotapes of people wandering around looking for a comfortable place where they could avoid other people and do work. Of course, they never found it. It was an experiment based on Jay Chiat's unique version of what he thought work should be in the late twentieth century, not on what people needed. It turns out he was terribly wrong.

SR: You have said that models of tools and environments should be based on how work is done now and in the future, in order to have a built-in reality check. What could pass your concept of a test of reasonableness?

MB: I think the best reality check is really a process. Since it's clear that the workplace affects productivity and satisfaction, what you want is a planning and design process that's based on the work people need to do and the direction of the business. The test of reasonableness for the whole design and all its parts is based on an aesthetic that comes from looking at and understanding the needs of the people, the teams, the business, and an aesthetic that grows from this analysis as opposed to being applied from without.

The workplace is a tool. It affects people's performance and satisfaction. It needs to be laid out so that it's agreeable and highly useful, with access to both distraction-free workspace and inviting places for interaction. They're not opposites. If these things really affect people at work, then it's like any other tool, whether it's a vacuum cleaner, a catcher's mitt, or something else. It is a place where jobs are performed, and its aesthetic best comes out of satisfying that need, even perhaps an enhancement and an expression of that need in visual terms. The fact is that one can't exist without the other.

SR: You spoke of the environment as a tool for work. How do you define that tool?

MB: In our surveys, we don't ask people what they need; we ask what they do. We're a research-based design house. We don't go to a business and ask people what they like, because they're experts on the work that they do. We're experts—along with others—in translating the work needs that people have into a physical form that would support those needs. It's the job of the designer to analyze the answers he or she gets and develop solutions and play them back to the organization. It isn't that employees are ignorant. They just don't understand what it is that affects their performance and satisfaction, so some kind of systematic analysis needs to be done with input from the employee, the user, the team, as to what it is they're trying to accomplish.

SR: You mentioned performance and satisfaction in relation to workplace contribution. Is there a better way to measure productivity and link it to the design of an environment?

MB: First, we need to talk about things like acoustic privacy, ease of interaction, lighting, furniture, etc., as they affect people's performance as individuals and in teams, and their job satisfaction. We do measure people's job satisfaction and performance, but we're not really interested in absolute levels. If you're contemplating making design changes, what you're really interested in is how much impact particular aspects of the workplace have on performance satisfaction after the design change. The best way that you can do things is by way of a before-and-after test. You can also do one-time measurements, and there are fairly well-known statistical methods that can predict and show you which aspects of the work environment are affecting performance and satisfaction. You can then link these to specific qualities of the workplace. You can also add them up and say all of them together equal what it is the workplace contributes to performance and satisfaction, in comparison with everything else that contributes to performance and satisfaction, like pay, good management, good colleagues. So, it isn't a mystery.

SR: How do you see corporations as less controlling and providing structure at the same time?

MB: Organizations, especially ones that are developing knowledge, are much less likely to be structured. They are more dynamic organizations. If they're going to empower and enable their staff, they have to offer them options and choices about the best way to do what they do, and if they do that, there are benefits to both the employee and the business. You've made the employee not a drone but a partner, and yet there's still a structure that the business has to impose. That is, the business sets goals and pretty much sets schedules. The employee needs to have this much done by this time and at this level of quality. The organization provides access to information and other resources. It asks employees to report on their progress and problems in a continuous manner so that situations don't get out of hand. It's a two-way street. The organization says to knowledge workers, "This is what we need to accomplish. You have the skills, the discipline, and the resources. You can structure them as needed." In the past someone might say, "It has to be done in this way." Now it doesn't *have* to be done that way. It just has to be done and done well.

This relationship between work and life—each has permeated the other's realm. For example, if you are working and you have to go out and pick up the kids, in most organizations you just do it. The employer knows, because you have goals and objectives and you're a high performer, that you'll do what needs to be done. They hire you because you're competent. Some people do need to have schedules because they have to contact customers or clients, and there are logistical issues, but with today's technology, you can be contacted just about anywhere. Almost every business is moving in this direction, even government. We're doing work for major branches of the U.S. government, and we read their mission statements and they're much the same as corporate ones—customer satisfaction, life-long learning, enablement, empowerment, more teamwork, more choices and options left to the individual.

One other side to this issue of work and life driving each other is that people who are uniquely valuable and essentially irreplaceable to an organization can do almost anything they please in most situations, so that the work will be reshaped around life, as long as they can make the contribution they need to make to the organization. I

had a call from someone who is very highly placed in my field who's being interviewed for a job with a design company in London. It's a very attractive situation but his stake in the ground is, "I live and work in Chicago." It's fine with the company that he remains in Chicago. They would prefer it if he relocated to London, but they understand that they want a global business, and it doesn't matter anymore. I'm working at home today because I'm trying to train my staff to do without me more. They're capable of making decisions, and if they make a whole lot of mistakes, they'll be gone, but they haven't made any yet.

SR: Can you talk a little about the concept of work at home and in other locations?

MB: Well, here I am talking to you from a small summer cottage. I have a good view. I look out on a body of water. I have a phone, a fax, a computer, a pad of paper. The refrigerator is another tool, so that when my brain is fried, I have a cup of tea and a piece of fruit and look at the water for a while and suddenly something comes to me. I'll race back in and jot it down. There's nothing beyond the most basic electronic things; there's no magic formula to mobile work at all. But it certainly integrates life and work more fully than the early-twentieth-century nine-to-five work model.

SR: In summary, what brief would you give designers on how to improve work, in the context of the contemporary issues we've talked about?

MB: Well, what's blindingly obvious and unbelievably overlooked is doing the hard work to find out what people in organizations really do and what they need to do. Most designers do a perfunctory analysis so they can get to the "hot" part, which is creating. What that means is they're leaping over the reality of the lives of their clients and focusing on the reality of their own lives, which often involves creating something dazzling to look at. Since they don't have a whole lot of information about the actual situation, they bring a lot of their imagination, which may or may not serve their clients well. For me the breakthrough is paying attention to what people do, what's needed. Developing solutions comes from engaging with what's inside an organization.

Interview with Francis Duffy
Paola Antonelli

PAOLA ANTONELLI: When did you start working in the office design field?

FRANCIS DUFFY: I began in 1964. I have been lucky in having a world perspective, working for American organizations in Europe and seeing their attitude toward the work environment. Americans assumed that Europeans were united in the way they worked; it was a shock for them to see that in Northern Europe an open-plan model had been rejected in Sweden and accepted in Finland. It created a challenge to understand why this was so. I couldn't understand it. During a study for IBM in the late 1970s in Italy, Switzerland, Germany, and elsewhere, we looked at different pressures in each country and compared what was happening because of nonrational considerations (which were surprising because we expect that the office is rationally organized and thus should be the same everywhere). That was a revelation, a cross-cultural study that was not amazing because of culture but because of anthropology.

PA: What has happened in the past twenty-five years in terms of office development in the United States and Europe?

FD: One critical threshold was in 1967, when office landscaping reached the United States. The Schnell Brothers in Hamburg in the late 1950s had championed the idea of a work environment based on communication rather than on a hierarchy of workspace. The basic idea was to study the pattern of action of the workplace as the starting point on which to develop a building. Radical design methods for building were formed as a result of these concerns.

Immediately after this, Northern Europe went through a pattern of rejecting open planning. [Herman] Hertzberger's Centraal Beheer Office Building in Apeldoorn, The Netherlands, was, in effect, the last important open-plan office design of the structuralist tradition. It was a very complicated building based on a honeycomb of open spaces that could be individually decorated. This was the end of the open plan in Europe, or at least the last respectable open-plan building. It dates from 1973.

Workers' councils in Europe then began to have statutory power. It became compulsory to negotiate with employees before changing their working conditions or before any changes in workspaces were made. Since then, buildings have become thinner and thinner. They are all the same. A variant is the Comby Office from the early 1980s, where each employee had his or her own office, with a common space in the center. Northern Europe still follows that pattern today. Britain is a mix of the Northern European patterns and the States.

In 1967 North America, in contrast to Northern Europe, began to adopt the Action Office, a screen-based office. Robert Propst in Ann Arbor, Michigan, developed this office design in conjunction with Herman Miller, reinventing the open plan with a stratagem. It became known as the Action Office 2 (it was preceded by Action Office 1, dating from 1964). Despite this office plan, the States, for the most part, remained extremely conservative, and the plan transmuted into the "Dilbert-like" cubicle that is standard in the United States today. The passive nature of workers in the U.S. contributes to their thinking that they have no choice or control over their environment. They are still working far away from windows.

Europe was more interested in reinventing features, and much more change took place there than in the United States. Key moments came from the explosion of information technology in the early 1980s, when the computer made it possible for one to work outside the office. There was an explosion of change on both sides of the Atlantic, a new fantastic mobility. The rules for location could be rewritten; the city now became an exercise in synchrony. The idea that office workers should all show up at the same time and do work that comes from the mill, as in factory labor, was becoming obsolete. Because information technology is reliable and everywhere, the patterns of location, aggregation, and time will all be rethought. The city will be accessible in a more nineteenth-century kind of way. It will be a much freer timetable.

The workplace is precisely at the cusp of change. The impact on the culture of organization is immense. Corporations have suddenly begun to discover that design, the physical environment, is capable of working in a catalytic sense and can enhance cultural change. Offices are taking advantage of the automating of professional work so that what remains is the intellectual work.

PA: So essentially the office should become like a private club.

FD: Yes, the office becomes like an oasis in a cultural desert.

PA: There also needs to be a brand loyalty.

FD: Well, the boundaries between organizations are beginning to shift. With more work outsourced, there is permeability. There are more career shifts, people as individuals can pick and choose, which creates a different attitude toward the boundaries in organizations and buildings. Mobility is encouraged. It would be better to have more fluidity designed within the architecture.

For architects, it means inventing the iconography of new culture and having an enormous effect on the power of design. Architecture has the ability to express cultural ideas—mobility, transparency, etc. Architecture has been used by companies as a powerful agent for change.

PA: Sometimes that power is almost abused.

FD: Architecture in North America had become technocized; its focus is on the delivery of a cheap product. The idea that it is *for* something is an idea that can, in the next five years, be revived.

PA: What is the most culturally challenging culture design project you have done?

FD: The Orbit Study done at the beginning of the 1980s in the United States. There were also versions done in the United Kingdom and Japan. It addressed the impact of information technology on office design. We realized the office was going to change because of technology; we realized early on that it would be the sociological consequences of technology that were going to matter. Second, it was about land development, regarding the possibilities for building intelligence, the possibility of building architecture that was anticipatory of and responsive to change. This was in 1985. Third, it involved the idea of what a building is. Is it a separate entity or a *utility*? This is a question that has lately developed into a question of what a knowledge-rich environment would be like. Most offices are dull and sterile. But, for example, if we have voice recognition, if you can talk to your machine, this creates a different acoustic environment. Another example: there is an oil company that has a device called HIVE, which is like a small 3-D Imax cinema. It simulates an oil field in 3-D, and sections can be cut through it in different ways. Around this model are placed different groups who debate how best to exploit the model. The effect is inherently interdisciplinary; it is designed like architects gathering around a model. It is independent of space and time. This is a glimpse into what a knowledge-based environment is like. It can invade space.

PA: Do you have much contact with the Japanese?

FD: The Japanese have been very good at that kind of thing; they are fascinated by the concept of intelligent buildings. But they are even more conservative than Americans in office layouts. Their structures are highly hierarchical and inefficient, but they are fascinated by electronically enhanced environments. They have been slow in adopting the personal computer (partially due to character incompatibility). But there is some really good thinking going on, which hasn't found its way into the architectural realm.

PA: Which country do you think comes closest to the ideal workspace?

FD: It's surprising. Silicon Valley has the highest level of technological development and the greatest level of entrepreneurial environment, but it also has the dullest real estate in the world. Sweden is undergoing a renaissance at the moment. It is socially sensitive to political issues (environmental matters, sustainability, health, etc.). Yes, that a building shouldn't kill you should be taken for granted. In certain aspects of personal health, the U.S. is advanced, and with personal computer issues too. Holland is very interesting, especially in terms of all things in architecture. There are some interesting things in the U.K. and Australia, with land lease, for example.

PA: What about relaxation?

FD: Interesting things are happening with mobility and space planning. Because of telephony, offices can be zoned like the city; there can be a place for a meeting, for concentration, for relaxation. You can still be connected when you want to be, but the timetable is more in your control.

As far as anthropology goes, there is microanthropology and macroanthropology. There are the differences between sectors—media, electronics, lawyers, etc.—versus macroanthropology, the differences among cultures. Both are important. In a way, this has been my career. If someone says, "Oh, you can't do that here," it's usually nonsense. They're talking about a value system. The general movement toward a greater autonomy is promising. I'd put my money on diversity.

Testimonials

Working at the Visible Language Laboratory at the MIT Media Lab, Cambridge, Massachusetts
DAVID SMALL, MULTIMEDIA DESIGNER

The MIT Media Lab in Cambridge, Massachusetts, and in particular the Visible Language Workshop, offered a unique approach to the research environment. Professor Muriel Cooper had an abiding interest in the Bauhaus, having designed the ultimate compendium of its work for the MIT Press, and she would often describe our workspace in terms of the spaces for collaborative design that had been explored by the Bauhaus.

Although we occupied a beautiful building designed by I. M. Pei, most of our use of the space was contrary to the original architectural plan. Cooper deliberately eliminated offices from Pei's plan in order to get a large, open, common space that was the heart of the workshop. The space was dark; most of the functional illumination came from the computer screens themselves, creating little pools of activity around the computers. One didn't see much of the environment; one saw the work. The desks were arranged so that students would work side by side and back to back. Two or three people could carry on a quiet conversation around one computer workstation while others would work alone nearby. This was managed either by masking sound with music or by the use of headphones to create closed workspaces.

Most of the "real work" happened in this large, fluid, nonlinear space and not in the offices. Another strange quality of the work environment was created by the full-length glass walls along the corridor. Students were exhibited to sponsors and VIPs, not unlike rare animals in their native, dark habitat. A soft lounge space and a large student office accommodated nonprogramming activities (such as sleeping and writing), which would have otherwise intruded on the more focused intensity of the lab space.

The Visible Language Workshop at the MIT Media Lab, Cambridge, Massachusetts. 1990–95

Working at *The New York Times*
STEVEN HELLER, WRITER AND ART DIRECTOR

Steven Heller's office at *The New York Times*

I work in chaos, at least it's chaos to anyone walking into my rabbit warren of an office. There are envelopes galore, piles of books and papers personified, flat files of unorganized junk and valuables that will not close. My desk is similarly endowed. Most of the space is taken up by a Power Mac 9600/233, a bulky, flatbed scanner, and a twenty-eight-inch monitor. To one side of the hardware are high piles of disks dating back to the days of the smaller Mac Classic, if not before. I just can't bear to dump them. The problem is that I fancy myself as organized, if not regimented. In fact, I can find virtually anything I need, and yet I hate entering my office in the morning only because I feel helpless amid the growing mounds. The more I discard, the less I make an impact on my environment. Nevertheless, work gets accomplished. As long as the keyboard is clear, I can function. I may have stacks of paper atop my scanner, but with a little leverage I can still open the hood. I am resigned.

I also have a so-called home/office in the building where I live. It is an apartment all to myself designated as a library. I originally thought that since this was more than four times the size of my office, it would be my sanctuary from clutter. But, alas, the mounds began a year or two ago and have not abated. Despite the installation of more bookshelves for books and archival boxes, the piles grow and grow. I continually try with all my strength to keep the desktop in a narrow portion of the divided room (under a skylight) relatively clear. Indeed, I put much of my work in folders, which are then filed in drawers after every use. But the force is beyond my control. The books are stuck in wherever there is space; the papers rule the roost.

I'm thinking of getting another working apartment, but what's the use?

Living and Working in Sydney
MICHAEL ALVISSE, FURNITURE DESIGNER

As I write this, here in Oz, we are only a few weeks away from the Olympic Games in Sydney, and I've just booked my flights to escape the crowds and chaos to enjoy a deserted beach in the warm north of western Australia. Yesterday was a magical mid-winter Sydney morning. It was just before sunrise and I was on the cliffs overlooking Bronte Beach when I thought I saw a large, dark dorsal fin of a shark cutting through the waves, a dangerously close thirty meters from the coastline. Given that a six-meter white pointer had been caught off Bronte only a few months before, I was about to run down to warn the dawn surfers who were already catching the morning waves. As I ran, however, I noticed that there was not one but half a dozen dorsal fins skimming the waves, and their relaxed, playful movements told me they were not sharks but probably dolphins or pilot whales. It was amazing to watch them actually bodysurfing with the human surfers! Can you think of many cities of four million people where you can expect to see dolphins frolicking in the surf?

Experiences like this are a powerful anchor for an otherwise hectic urban life. After a frenetic day buffeted by a storm of deadlines and meetings, I rely on the comfort of diving into the still warm (even in the middle of winter) Pacific Ocean to keep me sane. A few bracing laps of the ocean pool are enough to remind me that all is well with the world once more. Being so intimately in touch with the ocean—its power and beauty—is enough to remind me how complicated we've chosen to make our lives, and how much delight there can be in simplying BE-ing.

Working in Maui
ADRIAN OLABUENAGA, DESIGNER AND ENTREPRENEUR

We had been living in a big city, Los Angeles, and had grown tired of the crime, noise, and brown air, but we were concerned about leaving and moving our business, Acme Studios, anywhere that might not provide the services we need. The place we were considering was the island of Maui, where we vaca-

Ettore Sottsass and Johanna Grawunder. Casa Olabuenaga, Maui, Hawaii. 1989–97

tioned every few months. It's not exactly a metropolitan center from which to run a product-design studio that works with the world's leading architects, artists, and designers, but we moved there anyway in 1988.

Had we remained in a big city, business would have been a lot easier. In the first few years, we had to work harder at staying connected. We had a satellite dish, subscribed to tons of design magazines, overdosed on CNN, and spent hours on the telephone with our customers. Even with these efforts, the business probably lost a little momentum back then. However, in the last few years, with the Internet, E-mail, websites, E-commerce, etc., we became better connected in ways that we could not even have considered just a few years ago.

Because of this "reconnection" with the new technology, which is not that new anymore, we have made a serious commitment to being away from the big city. We have built a house, designed by Ettore Sottsass, on the hillside of Haleakala (the world's largest dormant volcano, overlooking the Pacific Ocean). A warehouse and an enlargement and renovation to our office are now under way, again designed by Mr. Sottsass.

We now live in what we consider paradise, in a world-class example of architecture. Our office is on the same property as the house, so our morning commute is just a few steps away. We literally stop and smell the roses every morning on our way to the office. Technology enables us to be totally connected to the world. We travel when it's needed, and visit New York several times a year. Our projects are the best we have ever worked on, and our income is better than ever. We are living proof that you can now do anything from anywhere. All you have to do is want it badly enough.

Working at Word Webzine, New York
DARON, EDITOR

Our webzine, Word, has no office. We had one for almost five years, but we lost our lease and all work is now done at home. The change has been really great, but, ironically, it has made me realize that I don't like the Internet very much.

The myth that the Internet is a freeing medium is a false one. It was meant to liberate us from the earthbound constraints of physical space. The old paradigm of office headquarters, where workers have to toil side by side in padded beige cubicles under the cold glare of industrial fluorescent lighting, can be made obsolete by the web. Working from home, I am able to send and receive electronic files to and from locations all over the world with relative speed and efficiency. I can engage in complex, dynamic human interactions with others electronically, discussing projects and exchanging ideas just as if we were right there in the same room. And, as many television advertisements for the web would have us believe, I am able to do all of this in nothing but my underwear.

Existing away from the inevitable vagaries and politics of office life unquestionably enables one to have a better sense of overall well-being. The feeling of liberation is fantastic. The only drawback is the Internet itself. We need it to make this whole thing possible; however, connecting to it from home, over a standard phone line—as opposed to the ultra-fast T1 connection once rigged into our former corporate office space—is a frustrating experience because of the medium's limitations. It's slow, difficult to navigate, and most of the content is substandard. Every time I browse the web and a message comes on the screen telling me that I don't have the proper plug-in or whatever to access what I want to see, I am reminded that, in a few years, a great deal of the content Word has worked so hard to produce may be lost along with the inevitably obsolete technology that it's bound to.

I'm not complaining. I prefer an office space made of pixels and telephone lines to a real one any day. It's just that, living in virtual reality, I've found it has begun to make me dream of things that are really real. I've been craving tangible substance, solidity, timelessness. I have a recurring vision of Word's huge logo blasted into the side of a gigantic, towering mesa in the Utah desert, lit up at night by powerful, 700-megawatt klieg lights. I dream of a theme park surrounding it, a gambling casino, a golf course, tennis courts, a hotel complex. People could come there to see our work printed indelibly in bright colors onto giant, billboard-sized synthetic banners hung ostentatiously in enormous gallery spaces. They could E-mail their friends pictures of themselves standing in front of it. They could bring laptops and work while luxuriating in opulent Roman-style spa baths. They could eat meals with their families at gargantuan buffet tables, drinking out of jumbo souvenir cups bought at discount prices. And perhaps, in a thousand years, they would still continue to come, like so many tourists swarming over ancient Aztec pyramids. Or maybe not. Maybe the whole place would sit in ruins, forgotten. In either case, it doesn't matter. Word will still be there, carved into solid granite, waiting for glaciers and oceans to swallow it. That, I think, would be enough for me.

Luis Galliussi's studio, Madrid. 2000

Working the Spanish Way
MONICA CEÑO, ART CRITIC

Spain has changed considerably during the last decades, yet some habits prevail when it comes to work. First of all, work hours are not from nine to five, as in most places, but from nine to two and from five to eight-thirty or nine. Dinner is at ten. Why? In Spain we work in order to live; we don't live in order to work. Food is extremely important to us. Almost nobody eats in front of the computer. People either go home for lunch or eat in a nearby restaurant, where they chat and discuss business. The typical Spaniard does not stay during his lunchtime searching the web; he or she will go out to a park or to one of the department stores that are open at lunchtime. Some places like "Masajes a 1000," where you can get a quick massage, have incorporated siesta rooms for those unfortunate enough not to be able to return home for a short nap in the afternoon. The most important meetings take place not at the office headquarters but in restaurants over a bottle of wine and a few cigars.

At the workplace, computers are a must. Open spaces prevail so that everyone sees everyone, except for the boss, who usually reserves for himself a big office where he will not be watched. Smoking is forbidden in workspaces, but nobody seems to care. Everybody smokes in banks, public spaces, airports, and universities, disregarding nonsmokers.

Sometimes the streets of Madrid are suddenly deserted as if World War III had been announced, but the fact is probably that an important soccer match is being broadcast on television. Offices are abandoned in a rush to get home so that one can sit comfortably and watch while eating some Spanish ham and chips. The next day, if the favored team won, you can tell from the faces of your coworkers; if the opposite is true, it may affect important meetings, which are often postponed for a better time.

Another striking thing in Spain is trying to do business around eleven o'clock or one o'clock. At that time, everybody is out for breakfast and tapas, and no work gets done. Some offices are shortening lunchtimes to two hours, from 2:30 to 4:30, but Spanish ways are ingrained, and a change won't be easy, nor will it come soon. It is not such a bad idea, frankly, to have time to eat and relax; most Spaniards like it that way.

Plates

The Official Office

The official office awaits most of us every weekday morning at the appointed time and typically hosts us for about eight hours, with a one-hour lunch break. Yet, it often does not reflect the space we would choose to inhabit for so many hours at a time. Nor does it resemble the ideal place where our best work would get done. Privacy, noise level, conflicts of personality, and visual and physical comfort are some of the obvious concerns.

The impersonality of most office systems is a natural and obvious consequence of the necessity to generalize and standardize resources. With the currently available technology and real estate, it would be unrealistic to expect that each worker could have what he or she wants, that is, a larger, homier, and completely customized space—with openable windows. As far as real estate is concerned, most buildings and facilities in North America that date to the second half of the twentieth century dictate the final plan, which reflects an unmistakable centripetal hierarchy with the perimeter reserved for executives. The industrial manufacturing processes currently available to furniture and partition makers, moreover, albeit enormously improved in the four decades since the introduction of the Action Office, are still very restrictive. Many manufacturing companies have tried to overcome these limitations by widening the range of the elements that compose the system, by implementing assembly options, and by giving more choices of finishing colors and materials. One recent design is an office configuration that relies on a central pole or on a more organic arrangement, as opposed to a perimeter of partitions disposed orthogonally. A selection of recent exemplary office systems of all kinds is the subject of this section.

It will be a long time before we can completely customize our worksphere in the official office. Even given economic realities, however, many details could be improved. Carnegie Mellon University in Pittsburgh, Pennsylvania, hosts a "Living Laboratory" devoted to the intelligent workplace: an office space where scholars work together, study, and test new solutions. The laboratory, whose web address is http://www.arc.cmu.edu/cbpd, researches all scales of workplace design, from architecture to furniture, and addresses the most crucial issues, from the availability of clean air and the efficiency of the energy system to the customization of the individual worksphere and the sensibility of the furniture. The laboratory's goal is to develop "plug and play technologies for individual comfort and productivity; organizational flexibility; technological adaptability; and environmental sustainability."

Like this example, based on the alliance between academia and a selected consortium of companies, many other similar experiments are initiated every month worldwide. Some deal pointedly with how design can influence the socialization dynamics, others with the physical boundaries among individuals. Some are convincing and successful; others remain at the surface and are not able to develop viable solutions. Some take into account the real needs and means of the employers. All aim at recognizing the necessity to make the office a better place, because, according to one writer, "in the immediate future, your workplace will have to provide an excellent sense of balance in order to attract, keep and motivate your employees. A place where they can balance work and family, comfort and energy, new and old technology. A space that offers more communication choices, more freedom, more inspiration, more chances to interact, better methods of collaboration. An environment that sparks ideas, rewards talent and allows for a quick adaptation on a minute-to-minute basis. An office where privacy is available, where large groups can gather formally or informally, where a person who spends seventy percent of the time on the road can feel at home, where opportunities for learning abound."

P. A.

Clive Wilkinson Architects. TBWA Chiat/Day, Los Angeles. 1998. Interior

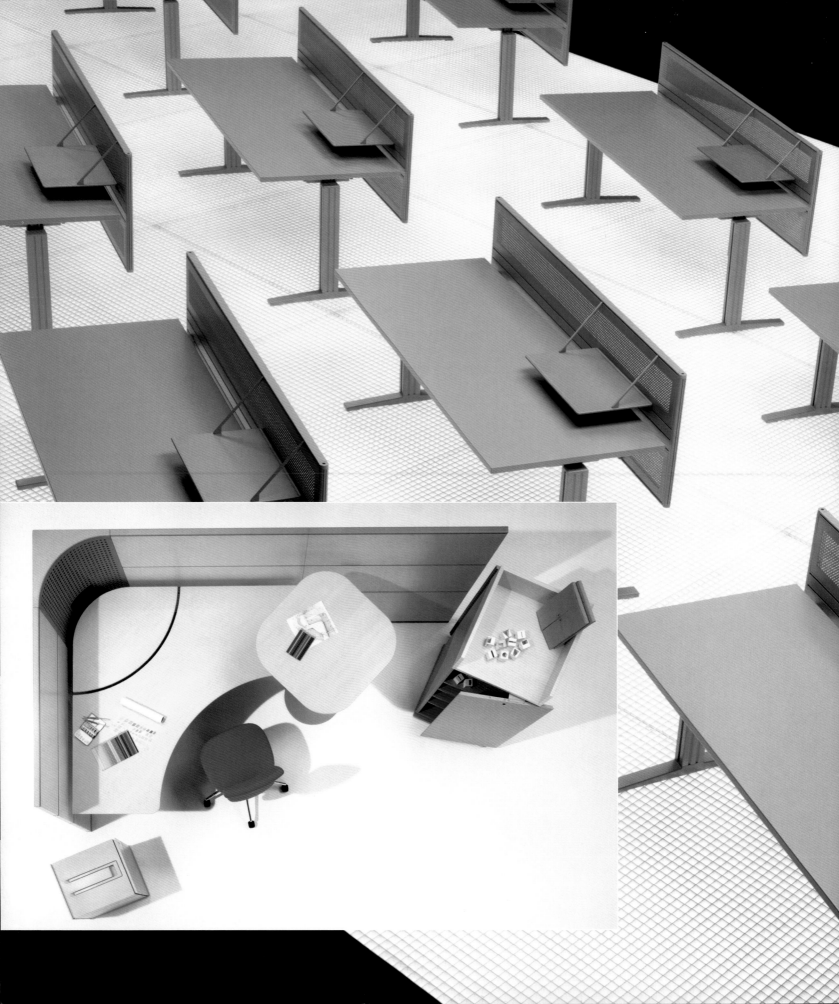

This page:
Robert Reuter (American, b. 1950) and
Charles Rozier (American, b. 1951).
Currents Office System. c. 1997. Materials
and dimensions vary. Mfr.: Knoll, Inc.,
USA, 1998

Opposite:
Luca Meda (Italian, b. 1936). Misura
Office System. 1979. Post-formed lami-
nate, particleboard, and painted metal,
29" x 6'6¾" x 29½" (73.7 x 200 x 74.9 cm).
Mfr.: Unifor SpA, Italy, 1980

Opposite, inset:
F & L Design. I Satelliti S/200 Office
System. 1997. Laminate, particleboard,
glass, and painted metal. Dimensions
vary. Mfr.: Unifor SpA, Italy, 1998

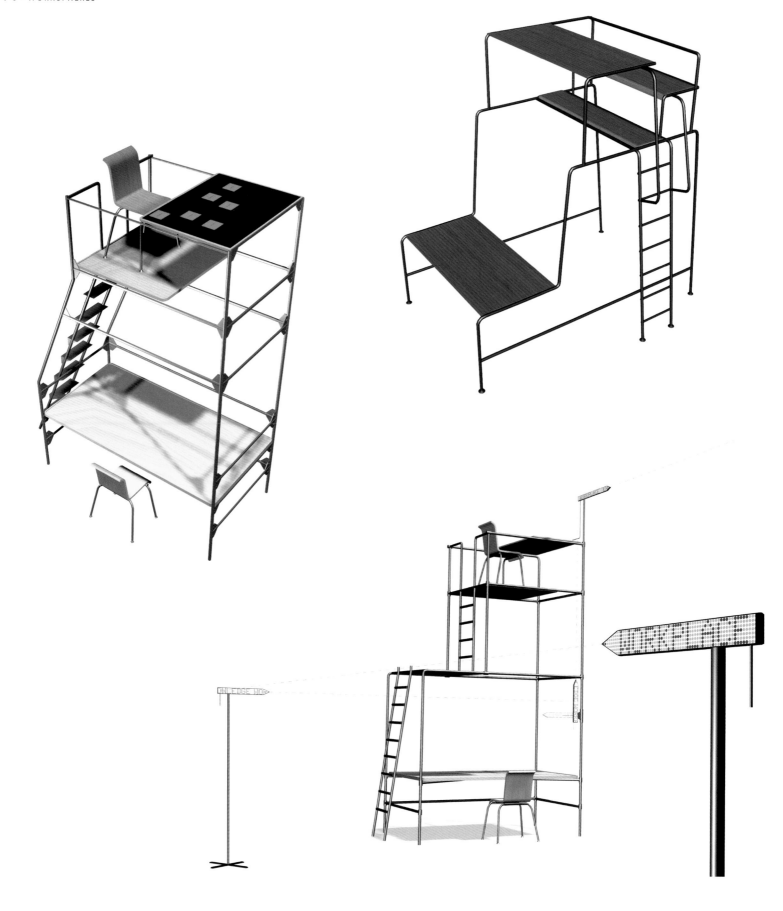

Opposite, left:
William Gaver (American, b. 1959), Heather Martin (British, b. 1970), and Andy Boucher (British, b. 1974). Double Deck Desk 4, version A. Tubular steel space frame and veneered particleboard, 10' 6" x 63" x 37½" (320 x 160 x 95.3 cm). Concept, 2000

Opposite, top right:
Gaver, Martin, and Boucher of The Appliance Design Studio, Royal College of Art, London. Double Deck Desk 2, version A. Tubular steel space frame and veneered particleboard, 8' 2½" x 63" x 7' 10½" (250.2 x 160 x 240 cm). Concept, 2000

Opposite, bottom right:
Gaver, Martin, and Boucher. Double Deck Desk 5, version F, and Digital Display. Tubular steel space frame and veneered particleboard, 11' 6" x 71" x 35½" (350 x 180.3 x 90.2 cm). Concept, 2000

This page:
Gaver, Martin, and Boucher. Double Deck Desk 2, version B. 2000. Tubular steel space frame and veneered particleboard, 9' 10" x 71" x 71" (300 x 180.3 x 180.3 cm). Concept, 2000

This concept, a research project developed in the Royal College of Art's Appliance Design Studio, proposes a new version of the workspace. The Double Deck Desk incorporates a standard-size office desk with a raised platform and table about ten feet above the floor. Like a crow's nest or fire lookout, the built-in ladder to the upper level can be climbed by the user, thus allowing him or her to literally rise above mundane chores, exploiting the psychological effects of elevation to pursue high-level insights and long-range planning. Bespoke hardware and software support the user in extracting key words from everyday documents and communications, finding associated words and images, and organizing the results into high-level "mind-maps" that can be printed for further reflection.

Opposite and this page:
Steelcase Design Team. Pathways®.
1993–98. Materials and dimensions vary.
Mfr.: Steelcase Inc., USA, 1998

Pathways® is a portfolio of products based on a unifying design concept that integrates architecture, furniture, and technology. It is intended to give design professionals the tools to create new kinds of work environments to support the changing and diverse ways people work. The system comprises reconfig-urable floor-to-ceiling walls—ideal for pri-vate offices or enclosed team spaces—assorted work surfaces, mobile tables, and flexible storage. Pathways® offers plug-and-play access to technology via lay-in wiring and cabling zones found throughout the environment. Raised flooring provides a permanent zone for routing wires and cables, and for heating and cooling distribution.

This page:
Sulan Kolatan (Turkish, b. 1958) and
William Mac Donald (American, b. 1956)
of Kolatan/Mac Donald Studio. Slices
Furniture Line: Junior Table. Materials
vary. 10 x 10 x 10" (25.4 x 25.4 x 25.4 cm).
Concept, 2000

Opposite:
Kolatan and Mac Donald. Slices Furni-
ture Line: Executive Table. Composite.
Dimensions vary. Concept, 2000

This project is based on the relationship
between personal and corporate identity, and individual design and mass
production. Traditionally, there has been
very little room in these relationships for
the unique, singular, personalized, and
eccentric. The notion of mass-customi-
zation, however, permits a different
approach. It allows for multiple identities
to be organized as unified systems, and,
in the realm of computer-aided manufacturing with composite materials, it
makes a large range of permutations
possible, as illustrated in the renderings.
By linking these two effects of mass-
customization, the new workspace
model that is being proposed here not
only embeds individual identities and
performances into a larger structure but
also registers change and growth within
the workspace.

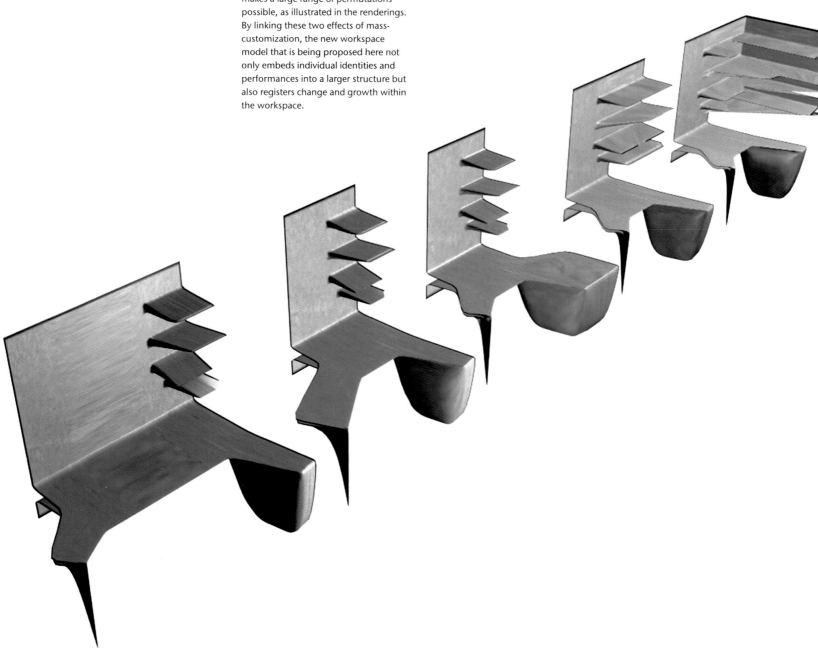

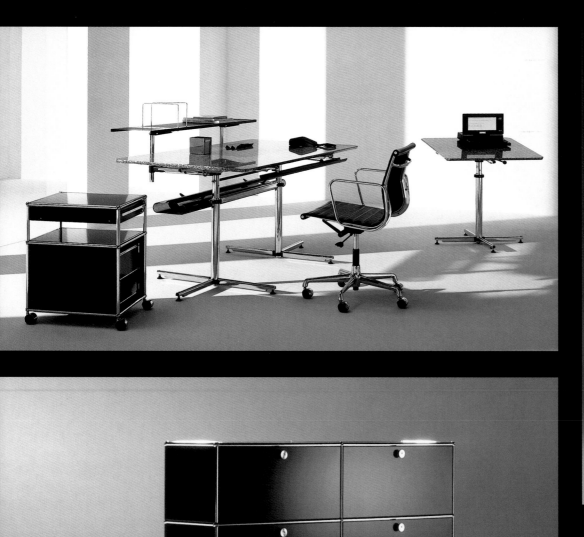

Opposite, top:
Fritz Haller (Swiss, b. 1924). Group of
Office Components. Left: Haller Systems
Rolling Pedestal. 1963. Steel and chrome,
20 x 13 x 16½" (50.8 x 33 x 41.9 cm).
Mfr.: USM U. Schaerer Sons Inc., USA,

This page:
Knoll Design Team. The Calibre Collection. 1990. Materials and dimensions
vary. Mfr.: Knoll, Inc., USA, 1990

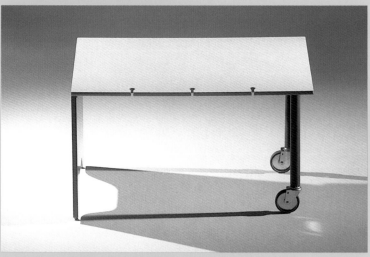

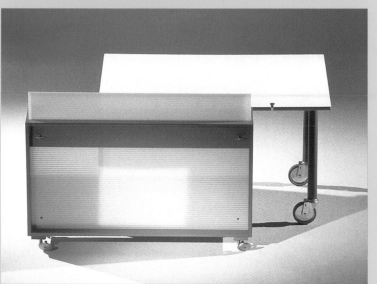

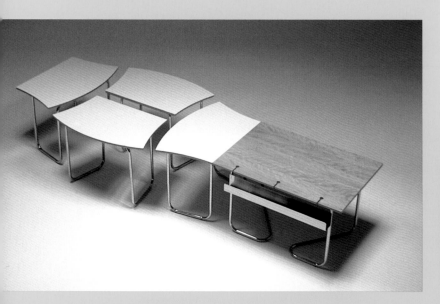

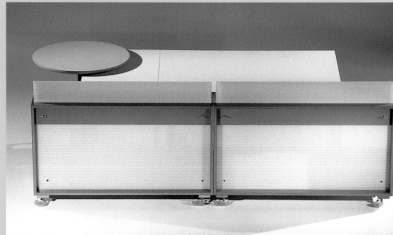

Opposite, left:
Sam Hecht (British, b. 1969) and Bill Moggridge (British, b. 1943) of IDEO. Axis Hotel System. 1994. Stainless steel, cherry veneer on fiberboard substrate, Colorcore, and polypropylene; desk: $27^{15}/_{16}$ x $55^{1}/_{8}$ x 31" (71 x 140 x 78.7 cm); subdesk: $27^{15}/_{16}$ x $23^{5}/_{8}$ x 31" (71 x 60 x 78.7 cm). Mfr.: IDEO UK, 1994

Opposite, right:
Sam Hecht (British, b. 1969) and Ian MacColl (American, b. 1963) of IDEO. San Fran Furniture System. 1995. MDF, Colorcore, powder-coated steel, Lexan, and polycarbonate, desk: $27^{15}/_{16}$ x 63 x 33" (71 x 160 x 83.8 cm); subdesk: $27^{15}/_{16}$ x 33 x $23^{5}/_{8}$" (71 x 83.8 x 60 cm); round monitor desk: $27^{15}/_{16}$ x $23^{5}/_{8}$ x $23^{5}/_{8}$" (71 x 60 x 60 cm); wall cabinet: $27^{15}/_{16}$ x $55^{1}/_{8}$ x $9^{7}/_{8}$" (71 x 140 x 25.1 cm). Mfr.: IDEO, 1996

According to designer Sam Hecht: "Thousands of workers are having to change to a new way of working called hoteling. Like booking a hotel room, the worker can call up a concierge at the office, reserve a workspace, and arrive at the booking time. The objective of this design is to embrace the interior, furniture, and graphics to form a new holistic infrastructure—necessary for such a change in a working pattern. Each hoteler has at a station a wall-mounted hoteling cabinet with privacy panel; a hoteling desk; a team desk that can connect to other hotellers; and a mobile storage trolley. This allows enough flexibility to move from quiet working to team meetings and social interactions. Because hoteling work is temporal, the design reflects the concept that these stations would be reused again and again by different people. Three key elements of design were incorporated: transparency, surface and mobility in order to overcome the territorial issues associated with hoteling, and a deliberate absence of physical connections of furniture, since the workers needed to 'get to work fast,' and not have to learn how to operate it."

Above:
Henner Jahns (German, b. 1968), Zoe Vidali (Greek, b. 1968), and Bernard Brucha (American, b. 1972). Swell Station, options 1 and 3. 2000. Tubular steel, perforated metal, MDF, RTF, cork-linoleum welding, and CNC; main table: 30" x 8' x 52" (76.2 x 243.8 x 132.1 cm); side table: 29 x 48 x 24" (73.7 x 121.9 x 61 cm). Mfr.: Sitag International Inc., USA, 2000

This page and opposite:
Antonio Citterio (Italian, b. 1950) and
Glen Oliver Löw (German, b. 1959).
Ad Hoc System. 1992. Materials and
dimensions vary. Mfr.: Vitra Inter-
national, Switzerland AG, 1994

Ali Tayar (American, b. 1959). Icon 20
Work Wall. 1999. Sheet metal and Baltic
birch plywood, 8½ x 16⅛ x 7⅜" (21.6 x
41 x 18.7 cm). Prototype. Mfr.: Parallel
Design, USA, 1999

Eric Chan (American, b. 1952) and Jeff
Miller (American, b. 1952) of ECCO
Design. Kiva Wing Table and Kiva Pebble
Table. 1999. Powder-coated CNC milled
MDF board, vinyl-wrapped CNC milled
MDF board, powder-coated fabricated
steel, and one-piece gas-assisted injection-
molded ABS. Dimensions vary.
Mfr.: Herman Miller Inc., USA, 1999

Below:
Robin Donaldson (American, b. 1957),
Russell Shubin (American, b. 1960), Henner
Jahns (German, b. 1968), and Zoe Vidali
(Greek, b. 1968) of Shubin and Donaldson
Architects. Alumina. 2000. Aluminum, 29" x
6' 8" x 30" (73.7 x 203.2 x 76.2 cm). Mfr.:
Sitag International Inc., USA, 2000

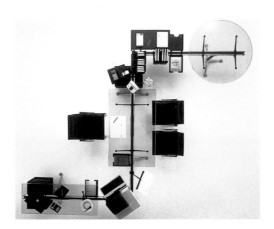

Bruce Burdick (American, b. 1933). Burdick
Group Furniture. 1977–81. Glass and die-
cast aluminum. Dimensions vary. Mfr.:
Herman Miller Inc., USA, 1981

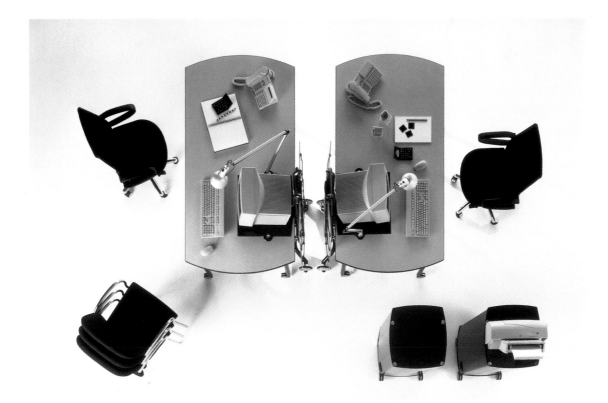

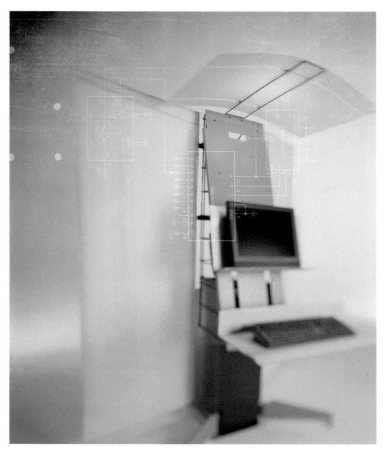

Above:
Arriz Hassam (Canadian, b. 1964), John Tong (Canadian, b. 1959), and Paul Syme (Canadian, b. 1949). Rug. 2000. Flat conductor with protective layer and underlayer of various materials, 1" x 15' x 10' 6" (2.5 x 456.9 x 320 cm). Mfr.: Teknion Inc., USA, 2000

This product is an electronically enhanced area rug that defines and activates a working environment for individuals, teams, and groups in an open plan. It provides a matrix of power and data connections, like a flat-access floor. Flat conductor technology is used to create circuits of power and data point connections. The circuits are laminated with protective layers over cushion.

Top right:
Donald McKay (Canadian, b. 1948). Meadow Call Center. 2000. Painted steel frame with adjustable monitor and keyboard attachments, draped fabric screens, and laminated wood veneer

shade, 5' 2" x 47" x 33" (159 x 120 x 84 cm). Mfr.: Teknion Inc., USA, 2000

The Meadow workstation is designed to offer flexibility. With the easel, an operator can move a flat screen and keyboard to any position without effort or distraction. A curtained partition hides a raceway that brings power and communication to the group of easels.

Bottom right:
Andrew Jones (Canadian, b. 1966). Jack Flexible Workstation. 1998. Painted steel base, acoustic wrap with fabric-covered wired inner frame and foam, and painted MDF tops. Dimensions vary. Mfr: Teknion Inc., USA, 1999

This workstation system was designed to provide a better environment for high-pressure Call Center employees. Individual workstations cluster around and plug into the branching cable beams, which carry power and voice and data cables and allow for flexible organic planning.

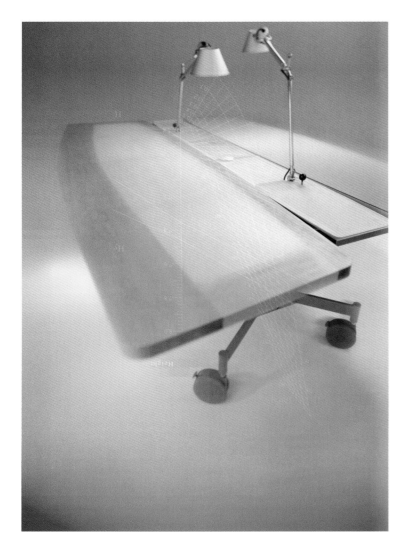

Arriz Hassam (Canadian, b. 1964), John Tong (Canadian, b. 1959), and Paul Syme (Canadian, b. 1949). Work Table. 2000. Steel frame, honeycomb polyurethane core with wood surround tops, and plastic laminate, 36" x 6'4" x 48" (91.4 x 193 x 121.9 cm). Mfr.: Teknion Inc., USA, 2000

The folding table makes an ideal work surface for individual stations and can also easily accommodate team sessions and conference settings. Both table leaves can be folded into a vertical position so the table takes up minimal floor space when not needed. Two task lights are built into the design, thus ensuring the user has enough illumination to work comfortably. A trough runs between the two table surfaces, servicing several functions: power and data cable lay-in, storage for desktop accessories and mounting brackets, and storage of the integrated lighting. Oversized wheels make it easy to move the table over bumpy floors.

Martin Kohn (Canadian, b. 1953) and Rick Galezowski (Canadian, b. 1954). Spandrobe. 2000. Aluminum frame on MDF shell, fabric with spandex, and mirror glass, 6' x 45" x 7" (182.9 x 114.3 x 15 cm). Mfr.: Teknion Inc., USA, 2000

The Spandrobe is a storage product for personal possessions such as a coat, shoes, umbrella, and handbag. It is designed to hang on the wall so it has a minimal footprint. The spandex panel can expand to accommodate bulkier items such as a gym bag. The mirrored panel opens to provide shelves for smaller items such as battery chargers and shirts. The lighting is built in. This concept embraces the idea of having a personal storage space in the office while keeping its size to a minimum.

Opposite and below:
Mark Baloga (American, b. 1957),
Paul Siebert (American, b. 1961),
Steven Eriksson (American, b. 1952),
Greg Draudt (American, b. 1959), and
Michael Tingley (American, b. 1958) of
Robert Luchetti Associates. The Personal
Harbor® Workspace. 1992. Steel, fabric,
and plastic laminate, 7' 6" x 8' x 6'
(229 x 244 x 183 cm). Mfr.: Steelcase
Inc., USA, c. 1994

When closed, the Personal Harbor®'s
sliding, curved door with frosted-glass
windows gives complete visual, acoustic,
and territorial privacy (see model below).
It comes with a partial ceiling and two
work surfaces, one stationary, the other
mobile. A tower of shelves provides additional book and binder storage. To keep
clutter off the work surfaces, the telephone, shelves, drawers, and fingertip-
filing system are vertically stacked in
what is aptly called a totem. A control
panel lets the individual employee adjust
lighting and ventilation. The unit has a
special ledge for accessories such as
pens, paper clips, and coffee cups, and
one part of the wall is a floor-to-ceiling
marker board. The Harbor can also come
equipped with a CD player with a wireless headset.

This page and opposite:
Ayse Birsel (Turkish, b. 1964) of Olive 1:1.
Resolve. 1997. Extruded aluminum,
plastic, coated MDF, and proprietary
display fabrics. Dimensions vary.
Mfr.: Herman Miller Inc., USA, 2000

Resolve redefines the shape of systems
furniture by replacing the right-angled,
paneled cubicle with more versatile
workstations composed of 120-degree
angles. Steel poles provide hang-on
capability and easy access to power and
data delivered from a system of overhead
trusses. This simple, lightweight infrastructure makes installation and reconfiguration faster. Fabric screens and
canopies define space and modulate
privacy without using solid walls, incorporating clear sight lines to help keep
communication flowing.

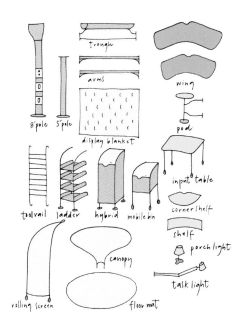

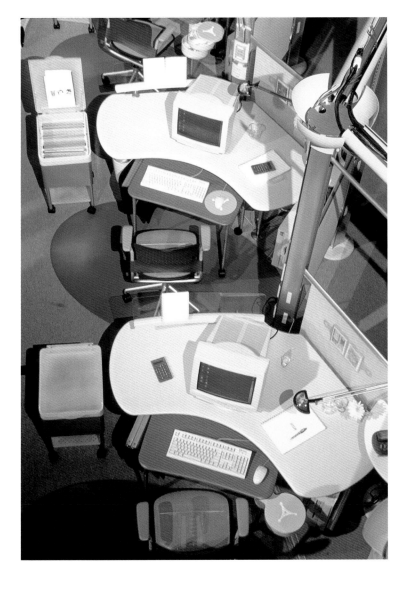

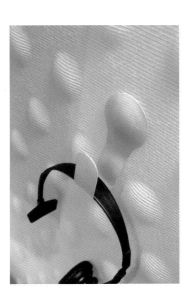

The Individual Workstation

This section addresses the subject of the personal workstation in the official office and its microcosmic nature. Many workers reveal their true selves in the way they arrange their personal worksphere. Hiroaki Kitano, the Tokyo-based scientist whose workshop developed AIBO robot dogs for Sony, says that he needs and craves chaos in order to work and produce good results, and he is not alone. Other workers have the opposite need—a tidy, orderly work environment in which well-built piles of papers, if any are present on the surface, are placed orthogonally and everything has its designated place.

An article by Jack Cox in the July 8, 1998, issue of the *Denver Post* listed the different ways people tend to express their personality and mark their territory, from the harmless family pictures to the much more disruptive habit of blowing bubblegum bubbles when under stress. Just by looking at one desktop—mine—one can notice the Kitano predicament—chaos is the mother of all good ideas. Large manufacturers of office furniture have enlisted the help of cognitive scientists to better arrange the degrees of freedom that come with the workstation. It is nonetheless clear that much emphasis is placed on the need to allow room for personal belongings and statements. These studies, applied to a neighboring field, brought us the bud vase Volkswagen provides with its new Beetle.

Several new workstation designs take into account the relative position of the worker with all of his or her different tools, such as the telephone and the computer; in some cases these designs provide new postural options. One example is the Netsurfer workstation developed by the Finnish company Snowcrash, which offers a reclining chair and sets the computer dangerously cantilevered toward the user. Many desks are highly adjustable, like the Levity Desk developed by Herman Miller: its technology enables one to work sitting on the floor, on a chair, or even standing—all by adjusting the desk height. Many stations are also provided with acoustic barriers.

The right paradigm for personal workstations seems to be the cabin of a truck, a highly personalized worksphere that is insulated both visually and acoustically. The Intelligent Workplace Laboratory at Carnegie Mellon University has developed an individual control unit that regulates the light, airflow, and temperature at a microenvironmental scale, even in an open office. The same control panel also carries a white noise device that makes telephone conversations inaudible just a few feet away. Other university labs, such as the MIT Media Lab, are working on acoustic cones, a new technology that concentrates sound only in a precise area around the worker. Acoustic technology will provide designers with a new tool to extend the boundaries in which we work and will help focus on the individual worksphere.

P. A.

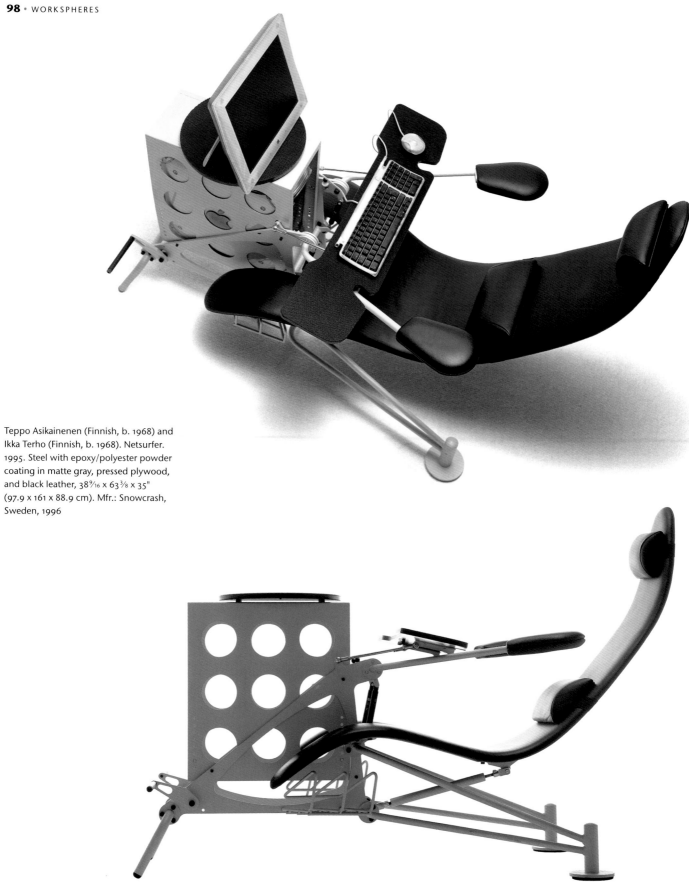

Teppo Asikainenen (Finnish, b. 1968) and
Ikka Terho (Finnish, b. 1968). Netsurfer.
1995. Steel with epoxy/polyester powder
coating in matte gray, pressed plywood,
and black leather, 38⁹⁄₁₆ x 63³⁄₈ x 35"
(97.9 x 161 x 88.9 cm). Mfr.: Snowcrash,
Sweden, 1996

Stefan Brodbeck (German, b. 1962) and
Andreas Struppler (German, b. 1964).
Werndl™ Emerge™ Desk. 1996–97.
Materials and dimensions vary. Mfr.:
Steelcase Inc., USA, 1998

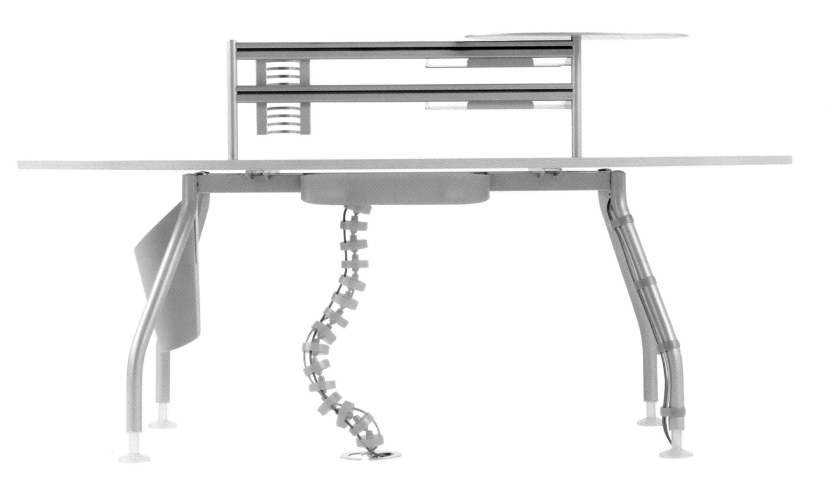

Opposite:
Ayse Birsel (Turkish, b. 1964) of Olive 1:1. Red Rocket Desk. 2000. Steel, plastics, particleboard, and textiles, 41" x 7' x 60" (104.1 x 213.4 x 152.4 cm). Herman Miller Inc., USA, 2000

This page:
Eric Chan (American, b. 1952), Jeff Miller (American, b. 1968), and Rama Chorpach (American, b. 1969) of Ecco Design. Red Spider Neck. 2000. Particleboard with melamine top, steel, and plastic feet, 26½ x 57 x 30" (67.3 x 144.8 x 76.2 cm). Mfr.: Herman Miller Inc., USA, 2000

Fast-growing companies tend to purchase technology before they buy anything else for their offices. They need furniture that they can view and purchase on the web, receive the next day, install in a matter of minutes, and deploy every time a new person or a visiting team walks in. Red Rocket and Red Spider are designed specifically for people for whom time and efficiency play an essential role. Inspired by film and camera equipment, Red Rocket in particular is designed like a tripod for computers. It ships and stores flat, and opens up to a three-legged structure that supports a height-adjustable monitor pod and a peanut-shaped work surface. The canopy and the butterfly-wing screens, on the back pole, provide a sense of individual space. Accessories like a cable bag, phone tray, and tackboard either hang from the legs or are inserted into the surface.

Above:
Brian Alexander (American, b. 1963). Flo
Concept Work Station. 1997. Fiberglass,
aluminum, steel, leather, and ABS, 48" x
6' x 48" (121.9 x 182.9 x 121.9 cm). Prototype. Mfr.: Haworth, Inc., USA, 1997

Flo consists of a surfboardlike work top
with a wire mesh display area, designed
to provide a visual connection to work-
in-progress, thus making it accessible
and easy to recall. Flo adds several flat-
panel monitors to the desktop, but treats
the flat panels simply as tools or big
Post-it®notes that can be shuffled seamlessly in and out of the individual's work
process. It has a carryall that allows work
and the context in which it was created
to travel with the user. In addition, Flo's
storage structure breaks from the tradition of repetitive, camouflaged, paper
management units (files, in boxes) by
providing open cells that help make the
contents— and their location— easier to
remember.

Opposite, bottom:
Clarkson Thorp (American, b. 1968) and Steve Beukema (American, b. 1966). Eddy. 1997. Polished fiberglass, plexiglass, upholstered leather and fabric, die-cut silicone, latex rubber, laser-cut steel, and water-based matte-finish paint, 54 x 60 x 60" (137.2 x 152.4 x 152.4 cm). Prototype. Mfr.: Haworth, Inc., USA, 1997

Eddy is a tiered workspace that allows users to display reference materials that would normally end up in stacks on the fringes of a work surface. This arenalike arrangement provides greater visibility of work that is often concealed in piles. Eddy's curvilinear, writable, fiberglass tiers and gooseneck fittings accommodate smaller materials and act as mental scratch pads. The folding organizers allow work to be put into packets of related information while their key ingredients are on view.

Below:
Brian Alexander (American, b. 1963). Drift. 1996. Hand-laid fiberglass, aluminum tubing, butted steel tubing frame, and resin-coated top surface, 50" x 6' x 6' (127 x 182.9 x 182.9 cm). Prototype. Mfr.: Haworth, Inc., USA, 1996

Drift is an organizing element for office and paper work. It attempts to be a natural extension of the need to keep certain projects or topics visible. This need manifests itself in Post-it®note clouds and paper piles turned geographical in nature. Drift makes pending projects accessible and visible, creating a theoretical possibility of increasing short-term memory capability. The reason that people "pile" in the first place is that if they put the work away, it disappears from their mind's eye as well. Drift is a planar form that can be pieced together to form a "cocoon" or opened to act as a backdrop for computers and tables or to subdivide an open area. The scooter desk brings together the chair and work surface in the context of hands-free mobility.

Opposite, top left:
Steve Beukema (American, b. 1966), Rogue Corpuz (American, b. 1970), Ralph Reddig (American, b. 1967), and Clarkson Thorp (American, b. 1968). Idea Factory Installation, version C. 1998. Plywood, aluminum tubing, metal mesh, and silicone rubber; low table: 15 x 63 x 63" (38.1 x 160 x 160 cm); stools: 15 x 24 x 15" (38.1 x 61 x 38.1 cm); foldable display boards of various sizes. Prototype. Mfr.: Haworth, Inc., USA, 1998

Opposite, top right:
Beukema, Corpuz, Reddig, and Thorp. Idea Factory Installation, version E. 1998. Plywood, aluminum, metal mesh, silicone rubber, steel, tackable foam, aluminum, polypropylene, nylon, fabric-backed marker sheets, rubber, and nylon wheels; low table: 17 x 63 x 63" (43.2 x 160 x 160 cm); stool: 15 x 24 x 15" (38.1 x 61 x 38.1 cm); postings spool: 29 x 6'6 x 29" (73.7 x 198.1 x 73.7 cm); expanding wall of various dimensions. Prototype. Mfr.: Haworth, Inc., USA, 1998

Above:
Clarkson Thorp (American, b. 1968) and Steve Beukema (American, b. 1966). Chunk Houses. 1997. Polished fiberglass, die-cut silicone, laser-cut steel, and water-based matte-finish paint. Dimensions vary. Prototype. Mfr.: Haworth, Inc., USA, 1997

Right:
Jeff Reuschel (American, b. 1959). Sit-Stand Chair. 1996. Vacuum-formed ABS over a welded steel frame, injection-molded polypropylene shells, suedelike nylon upholstery, cast-aluminum arms coated with a low-durometer and air-dry polyurethane, 25 x 25 x 20" (63.5 x 63.5 x 50.8 cm). Prototype. Mfr.: Haworth, Inc., USA, 1996

The prototype chair focuses on movement—that of the user in the chair and the movement of the chair and user together within the environment. The seat hinges across (left to right), allowing the front edge of the seat to drop away as the height increases. It thus serves two functions. First, it decreases the pressure points on the back of the thighs as the seat is raised. Second, it allows the user's feet to move back and under the body, a much more active posture. The seat is also much smaller than a typical task chair to encourage movement in the chair and make it easier to move through a furniture jungle.

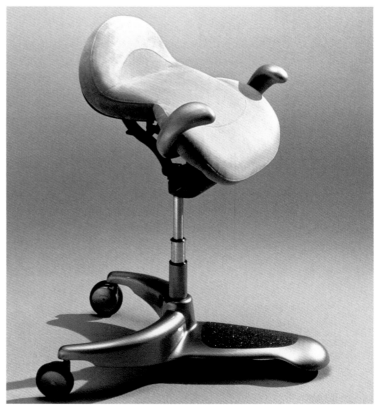

Bottom right:
Beukema, Corpuz, Reddig, and Thorp.
Idea Factory Installation, version F. 1998.
Fluted polypropylene, polyester foam, aluminum tubing and sheets, marker board
laminate, fiberboard, tackable foam, aircraft cable, sound-absorption foam, plywood, metal mesh, and silicone rubber;
acoustic dome: diameter 10' (304.8 cm);
foam wall: 65 x 60 x 12" (165.1 x 152.4 x
30.5 cm); postings spool: 29 x 29 x 6'6"
(73.7 x 73.7 x 198.1 cm); low table: 63 x 63 x
17" (160 x 160 x 43.2 cm); stools: 15 x 15 x
24" (38.1 x 38.1 x 61 cm). Prototype. Mfr.:
Haworth, Inc., USA, 1998

The partnership between Haworth's
Ideation Group and John Kao's Idea Factory
in San Francisco aims to learn how an environment can better support the capture of
ideas generated in a co-active space. The
resulting experiments seek to create an
environment that makes it easy for a group
to interact, store and display ideas and
information, and revive what was created.
The 180-degree Learning Curve combines
marker and tack surfaces to give the
group a tool to focus and organize information in a nonhierarchical manner. It is
height-adjustable and can be raised above
standing height to create additional vertical space for information to cascade down
and around the group. It can also be
hoisted to the ceiling in order to clear the
space for other purposes. The Acoustic
Dome reflects the verbal exchanges of
members within the group space while
absorbing the ambient noise outside the
collaborative area and is translucent to dif-
fused light. The low table and stools provide an "everyone-is-equal" place to sit
and share ideas and information.

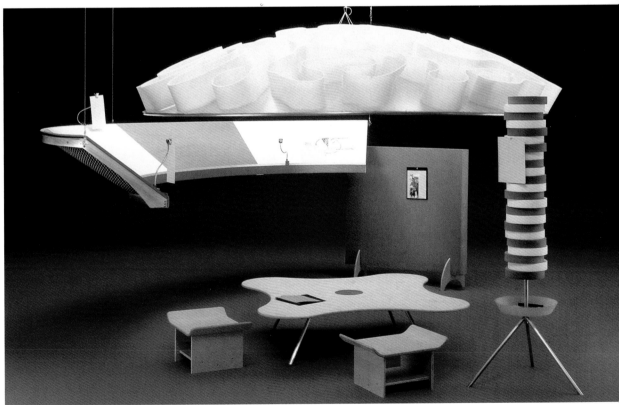

Top:
Clive Wilkinson (British, b. 1954).
Nest. 1998. Cast-aluminum
frame, vinyl-wrapped wood-core
top, perforated steel screen, and
steel binder box; work surface:
1¼ x 7'3 x 41½" (3.2 x 221 x 105.4
cm); mobile storage unit: 24¾ x
43½ x 23" (62.9 x 110.5 x 58.4
cm). Mfr.: Turnstone, USA, 1999

Bottom:
Jouni Leino. Link X Chair. 1999.
Form-pressed plywood shell,
cross-coated aluminum, and
steel tube. Dimensions vary.
Mfr.: Avarte Oy, Finland, 2000

Jouni Leino. Web Table. 1998.
Birch plywood, keyboard tray
with linoleum surface cover, and
jalousie of birch, high: 45⁵⁄₁₆ x
47¼ x 36¼" (115.1 x 120 x 92.1
cm); low: 28³⁄₈ x 47¼ x 36¼"
(72.1 x 120 x 92.1 cm). Mfr.:
Avarte Oy, Finland, 1998

Richard Holbrook (American, b. 1959). Levity Interaction Tower. 1997. Materials and dimensions vary. Mfr.: Herman Miller Inc., USA, 1998

The Levity Collection is a suite of tools, including the interactive tower, equipment carts, and height-adjustable tables, that allows users to spontaneously change their position and their environment throughout the workday. The interactive tower can switch to any working position—from sitting on the floor to sitting in a chair to standing. The 13- to 50- inch height-adjustment range accommodates users of any size, from the first percentile female to the ninety-ninth percentile male, in all positions. The tower height-adjustment mechanism is a simple gravity-driven counterbalance system allowing "touch of the finger" adjustments. It works like a weight machine. The tower rests on six casters to allow easy movement within the office. It can be folded to roll through a doorway as narrow as 30 inches wide and can easily fit into a 48-inch corner.

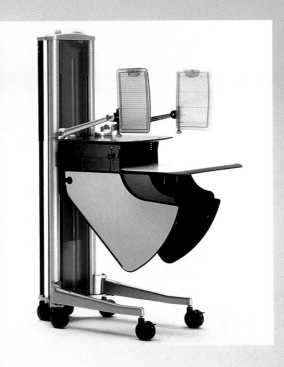

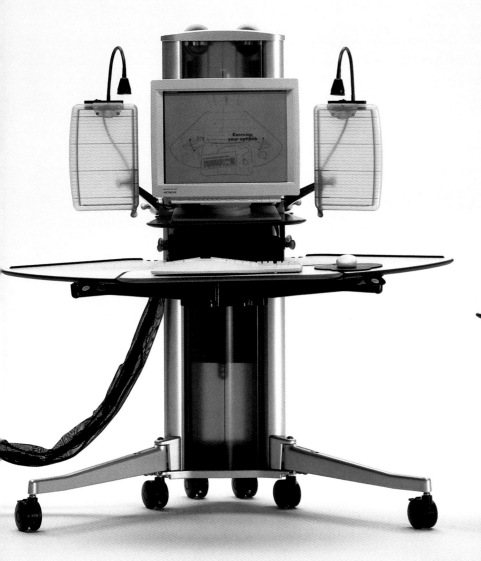

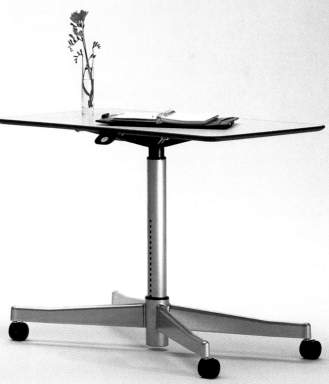

Chairs, Tables, and Other Furniture

Some offices are not designed as systems, but rather are furnished in a manner similar to what would be used in a home. This section examines stand-alone elements, primarily chairs and tables, but also screens and foldable cots that are designed especially for the office.

Chairs are a staple of our lives and of designers' lives. Anyone asked to come up with an example of good design is likely to choose either a car or a chair, because they are objects that seem to most embody everybody's conscious experience of design. For designers, moreover, chairs are a ritual of initiation. They tend to teach designers about imperfect control. In chairs, more than in any other designed object, human beings are clearly the unit of measure to which everything has to defer. Office chairs, on the other hand, are where designers seek "perfect" control.

Decades of in-depth studies have been devoted to designing the best chair. The 1960s and 1970s were the years of the ergonomic breakthroughs, when designers like Henry Dreyfuss and Niels Diffrient set the scientific parameters of comfort with their groundbreaking studies. According to an article in *Design World* in June 1983, "When seated and virtually immobile for long periods, the effect can be manifold. The sitting posture causes the abdominal muscles to slacken, curves the spine and impairs the function of some internal organs, especially those concerned with digestion and respiration. It is not just the sitting posture but the lack of corrective movement which leads to chronic ailments. A well designed chair does not confine the seated person to any one posture."

The past thirty years have seen tremendous progress in the design of chairs, resulting in exceptional comfort, accessories such as footrests, handrests, and lumbar supports, new and better fabrics, and enhanced adaptability. The novel appearance of the most recent ergonomic chairs, however, took adjusting to. The introduction of Chadwick and Stumpf's Aeron Chair in 1992 startled the world. Not only was a hefty instruction card included with the chair that explained the operation of several levers and pulleys, but the chair also looked like a giant black mechanical insect from a science-fiction movie. Its transparent seat and back looked like wings, while the mechanical box under the seat resembled its digestive organs. Together with some of Frank Gehry's buildings and Pedro Almodóvar movies, it contributed to a re-examination of our centuries-old idea of classical beauty—and of our decades-old idea of modernist beauty as well. The Ypsilon Chair, designed by Mario and Claudio Bellini and recently introduced by Vitra, carries the similitude even further by featuring a visually and functionally enhanced exoskeleton of sorts.

Several office managers counteract the high-tech feeling of comfortable chairs with wood and steel tables purchased from stores that sell old-fashioned kitchen appliances. The kitchen, being one of the most technical rooms in a house, is the closest metaphor and resource available to those who want their offices to feel more domestic—and also who have less money to spend on startup costs. Office lighting, not included in this exhibition because of display limitations, is an area that is as deep and varied as chair design, and its recent progress is part of the studies that are transforming the workplace into a much more comfortable and healthier place to be.

P. A.

Konstantin Grcic (German, b. 1965). 1 + 1 = 1. 1994. Polystyrene, 6' 2 13/16" x 9' 10 1/8" x 17 11/16" (190 x 300 x 45 cm). Model. Mfr.: Association J. Vodoz & B. Danese, Milan, 1994

Left and above:
Maarten van Severen (Belgian, b. 1956). Schraag Table on Foldable Trestles. 1999. Cast-aluminum box with natural rubber, anodized aluminum legs, and red stained plywood top, 29" x 6'7" x 35" (73.7 x 200.7 x 88.9 cm). Mfr.: Bülo Office Furniture, Belgium, 1999

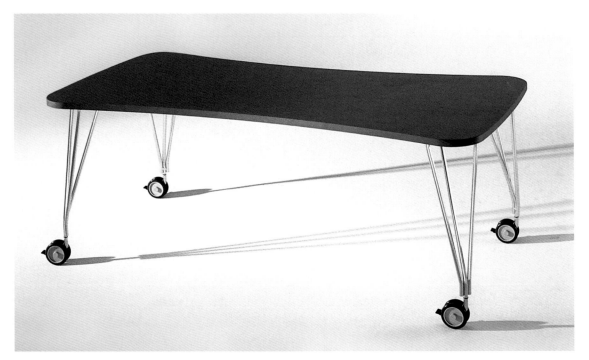

Right:
 Ferruccio Laviani (Italian, b. 1960). Max Table. 1998. Polished steel and laminate, 31½ x 63 x 27⁹⁄₁₆" (80 x 160 x 70 cm). Mfr.: Kartell SpA, Italy, 1998

Donald Chadwick (American, b. 1936) and William Stumpf (American, b. 1936). Aeron Office Chair. 1992. Die-cast glass-reinforced polyester, aluminum, Hytrel® polymer, polyester, and Lycra®, 43½ x 27 x 19" (110.5 x 68.6 x 48.3 cm). Mfr.: Herman Miller Inc., USA, 1994

In this innovative chair, the body rests on little more than a fiber net supported by a skeletal frame. The Pellicle™ mesh fabric relieves sitter strain by changing its shape and responding only in localized areas. Once the user stands, the fiber's almost perfect elastic memory cancels the deformation. The chair features seat-height adjustment, reclinability, and armrest manipulation.

Left and below:
Tom Eich (American, b. 1961), Thomas Overthun (German, b. 1959), George Simons (American, b. 1955), and Steelcase Design and Engineering. Leap Chair. 1998. Injection-molded glass-reinforced nylon, gel-encapsulating injection-molded plastic arms, ABS, and progressive die-formed robotically welded steel frame, 40 x 30 x 26" (101.6 x 76.2 x 66 cm). Mfr.: Steelcase Inc., USA, 1999

Ann Demeulemeester (Belgian, b. 1959).
Table Blanche. 1995. Wood and canvas,
31" x 9'2" x 30" (78.7 x 257 x 76.2 cm).
Mfr.: Bülo Office Furniture, Belgium, 1996

Opposite:
Luigi Baroli (Italian, b. 1951). Cartoons Screens. 1992. Corrugated paperboard and die-cast aluminum, $66\,^{15}/_{16}$ x $39\,^{7}/_{16}$ x $1\,^{3}/_{16}$" (170 x 100.2 x 3 cm). Mfr.: Baleri Italia, 1992

This page:
Niels Diffrient (American, b. 1928). Freedom Chair. 1999. Materials and dimensions vary. Mfr.: Humanscale, USA, 2000

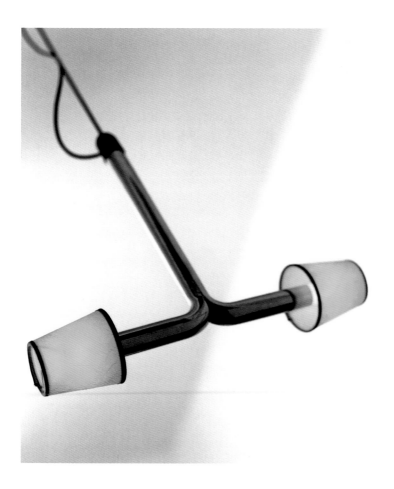

Opposite:
Thomas Bernstrand (Swedish, b. 1965).
Sugar Ray. 1999. Stainless steel, fiber
optics, and silicone rubber, 16⁹⁄₁₆ x
16⁹⁄₁₆ x 7⁷⁄₈" (42.1 x 42.1 x 20 cm). Mfr.:
Bernstrand & Co., Sweden, 1999

"Sugar Ray" is a hall lamp that can turn
into a frustration and tension reliever. It
is made of silicone rubber, and the light
comes from a fiber-optic cord. It will
withstand a Tyson punch.

Above and right:
Thomas Bernstrand (Swedish, b. 1965).
Do Swing Ceiling Lamp. 1999. Stainless
steel and second-hand lampshades,
18⅛ x 19¹¹⁄₁₆ x 3¹⁵⁄₁₆" (46 x 50 x 10 cm).
Mfr.: Bernstrand & Co., Sweden, 2000

"Do Swing" is designed to do what its
name says—swing. Normal chandeliers
are difficult to grasp, are seldom strong
enough to hold a person, and often have
sharp edges. "Do Swing" has smooth,
stainless-steel handles for grasping so
that the user will feel safe swinging on it.
This lamp is convenient for a stretching
pause during a hard day at work.

Left:
Antonio Citterio (Italian, b. 1950) and Glen Oliver Löw (German, b. 1959). Axess. 1995. CFC-free polyurethane foam on polypropylene shell. 35½ x 22 x 17½" (90.2 x 55.9 x 45 cm). Mfr.: Vitra International AG, Switzerland, 1996

Above:
Antonio Citterio (Italian, b. 1950) and Glen Oliver Löw (German, b. 1959). T-Chair. 1992–93. Fiberfill-wrapped CFC-free polyurethane foam over polypropylene foam, plastic, fiberglass-reinforced polyamide, and fabrics, 35½ x 22 x 16" (90.2 x 55.9 x 40.6 cm). Mfr.: Vitra International AG, Switzerland, 1994

Mario Bellini (Italian) and Dieter Thiel
(German). Figura 2000. 1993. Fiberfill-
wrapped CFC-free polyurethane foam
over polypropylene foam, 35 1/2 x 22 x 19"
(90.2 x 55.9 x 48.3 cm). Mfr.: Vitra
International AG, Switzerland, 1994

Below left:
Antonio Citterio (Italian, b. 1950) and
Glen Oliver Löw (German, b. 1959).
AC2 Chair. 1995. CFC-free polyurethane
foam on polypropylene shell, steel, and
wicker, 34¾ x 19 x 19" (88.3 x 48.3 x
48.3 cm). Mfr.: Vitra International AG,
Switzerland, 1996

This page:
Alberto Meda (Italian, b. 1945). Meda 2
Chair. 1998. Polyamide (30% glass filled)
and other materials, 37 13/16 x 26 3/8 x 26 3/8"
(96 x 67 x 67 cm). Mfr.: Vitra International AG, Switzerland, 2000

Robert Scheper (American, b. 1961). Please
Chair. 1998. Aluminum, leather, and other
materials; seat height: 16–21" (40.6–53.3
cm); seat depth: 15½–17½" (39.4–44.5 cm);
seat width: 19" (48.3 cm). Mfr.: Steelcase
Inc., USA, 1998

Peter Opsvik (Norwegian, b. 1939).
Capisco Chair. 1988. Leather, steel, and
other materials, 34½ x 22½ x 19" (87 x 56 x
48.3 cm). Mfr: Håg, Norway, 1988

Hans Roericht (German, b. 1932). Stitz 2 Stools. 1991. Polypropylene, steel, rubber, cork, and quartz sand, heights 25–35" (64.8–90.2 cm); diameter 12$^{15}/_{16}$" (31.3 cm). Mfr.: Wilkhahn, Germany, and Vecta Inc., USA, 1992

Sari Anttonen (Finnish, b. 1966). Kiss Chair. 1998. Polyurethane seat and back and tubular steel frame, 32 $^{11}\!/_{16}$ x 18 $^{15}\!/_{16}$ x 20 $^{7}\!/_{8}$" (83 x 48.1 x 53 cm). Mfr.: Püroinen Inc., Finland, 1998

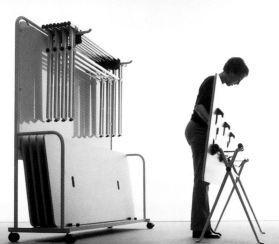
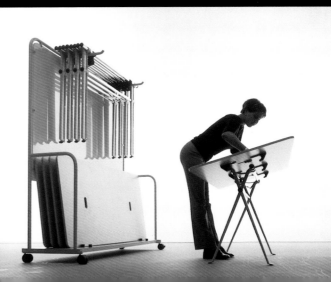

Below:
Burkhard Vogtherr (German, b. 1942).
Spin Chairs. 1994. Materials vary. 36⅝ x
8⅝–10⅝ x 16⁹⁄₁₆" (93 x 22–27 x 42 cm).
Mfr.: Fritz Hansen A/S, Denmark, 1996

Opposite:
Jasper Morrison (British, b. 1959). Tate
Chairs. 1999. Plywood and stainless steel,
29½ x 18⅛ x 20½" (74.9 x 46 x 52 cm).
Mfr.: Cappellini SpA, Italy, 1999

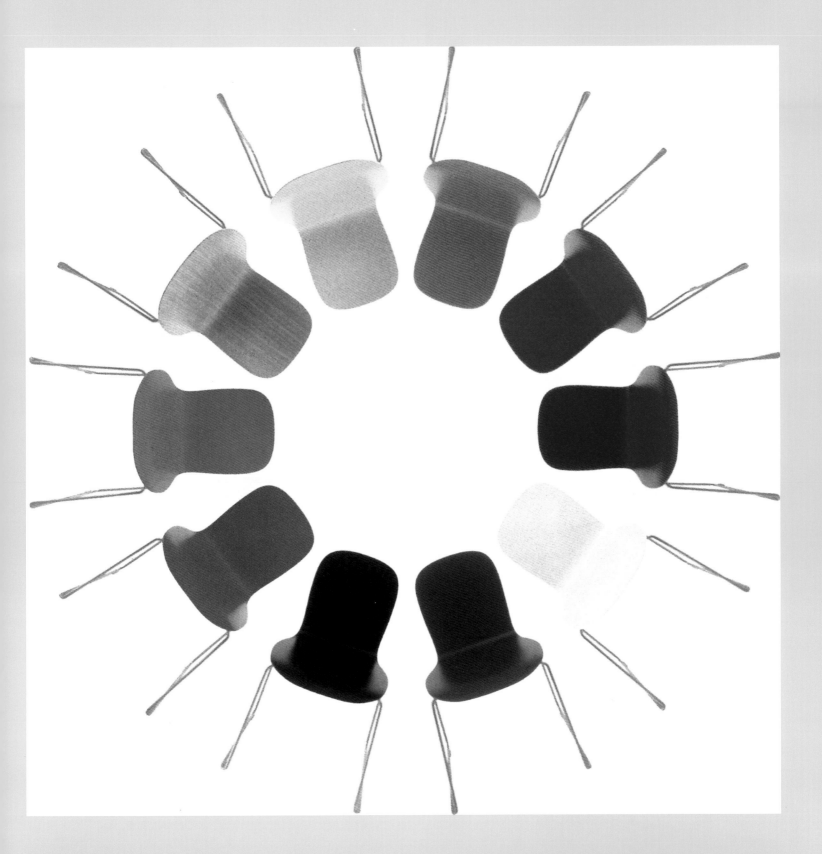

Thomas Bernstrand (Swedish, b. 1965).
Newspaper Recycle Carrier. 1995. Plywood and wood, 21½ x 13¾ x 7" (55 x
35 x 18 cm). Prototype. Mfr.: Bernstrand
& Co., Sweden, 1995

Matali Crasset (French, b. 1965). Téo de 2 à 3 Folding Mattress. 1998. Fabric, foam, and wood, closed: 20 x 15 x 15" (52 x 40 x 40 cm); open: 3$^{15}/_{16}$ x 70$^{7}/_{8}$ x 20" (10 x 180 x 52 cm). Mfr.: Domeau & Pérès Inc., France, 1999

Taking an afternoon nap is frowned on in our culture, but it is a sure way to regenerate oneself and therefore be much more efficient during the rest of the afternoon. Téo de 2 à 3, a stool that unrolls into a mattress, enables one to take a siesta at work. It also contains a "do not disturb" sign.

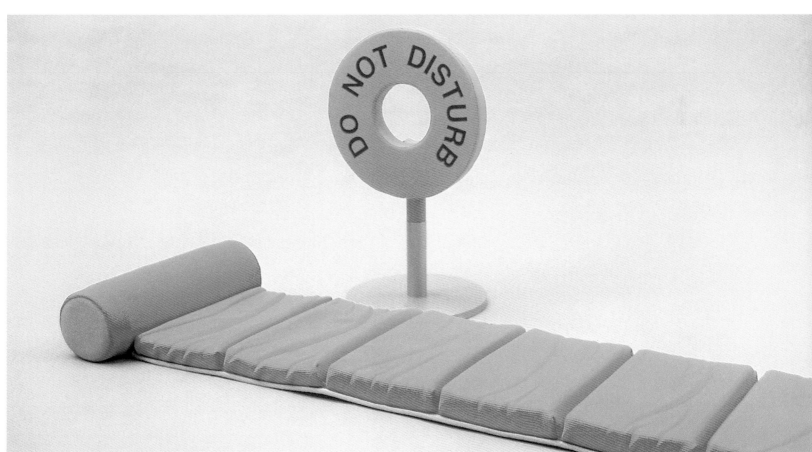

The Nomadic Office

For many individuals, work no longer necessarily entails a routine contained in a dedicated box called "the office," but may comprise a new system adapted to everyday life within the larger structure of a working community. The advantages of an unmitigated nomadic worklife can be many: "You get to see how the world really turns. And the benefits of having an eclectic soap collection shouldn't be underestimated," explains the professional nomad, John Gruetzner. But even among those of us who still occupy a desk in an official office, the experience of nomadic work is familiar.

Nomadic workers range from traveling salesmen and consultants to couriers and executives of multinational companies. They conduct their work in many different places— cars and vans, hotel rooms, poolside tables, seats in business or coach class on airplanes and trains, airport lounges, business or press lounges at trade fairs and conventions, or strangers' offices. They tend to use similar equipment—laptops, cell phones, organizers—and are always looking for the right plug to recharge their batteries, make their presentations available locally, and connect via Internet to the mothership and to other like-minded satellites. "Road warriors," Jeremy Myerson calls them.

Steve Mann was a pioneer of nomadic work in the Internet age. He was the first person to put his life on the Internet, in 1994, while a student at MIT in Cambridge. Via his portable apparatus, which involves a helmet with camera, a private-eye lens that displays all information directly into his right eye, a few cables, wires, and backpacks, and a glove with keys aptly called "Keyer" as an input device, Mann designed the first online bicycle, which he currently calls his office. "Actually, my office is my right eye. In the morning, I put on my office." Year after year, his equipment has become less bulky and more refined. When asked how he can be reached, he hands out an E-mail address and says: "Just put a message into my right eye." His example is the epitome of a nomadic worksphere, as immaterial and integrated with the human body as possible, a fluid and continuous connection with the big Internet global workspace.

Among workspheres, the nomadic one is the most dependent on technology and the most vulnerable to its idiosyncrasies and limitations. The different standards for electricity, cellular telephones, modem connectivity, and television systems in different countries, for instance, are still responsible for panic and frustration. Design cannot do much for these global issues except, perhaps, provide more compact and reliable travelers' kits. Yet, at its many scales of intervention, it can offer more conducive and better-organized environments and intermediate stations than we have now.

A trend analysis carried out by the British Design Council effectively delineates what design can do for nomadic workers: "Developing work equipment that is portable and usable; developing and placing Internet kiosks in public places; addressing the car interior and onboard information systems to support people working from the road; rethinking transport nodes, such as airports, train stations, motorway service stations to allow nomadic workers to log on and carry out work; redesigning high street, roadside and transport terminal leisure facilities to create opportunities for work; developing software and communication systems to support virtual teams." Much has been achieved recently, especially in airports, many of which now provide business facilities for travelers' without business-class seats or VIP lounge privileges, as well as gyms, massage parlors, and short-term hotel rooms. A well-functioning nomadic worksphere needs to count on a healthy mind in a healthy body, and not only on healthy technology.

P. A.

Robert Mangurian (American, b. 1941), Mary-Ann Ray (American, b. 1958), and Jeffrey Hannigan (American, b. 1949) of Studio Works. Portable Person. Ink and pencil on paper, 7' 1" x 55" (215.9 x 139.7 cm). Concept, 1976 (revised 1999)

People wear things that serve as environmental protection (clothing, foul-weather gear), that correct or enhance the senses (glasses, portable speakers), that extend the physical and mental self (tools, portable calculators), or that project the psychological self (clothing, jewelry). The Portable Person comprises a headset with brain implants and space-enhancing virtual settings, wristbands, and a bodysuit with electronic implants.

Headset
TV/camera skull cap containing universal lens and back-up clip-on systems for TV/cameras. (Sony xxxx)

Antenna for sending and receiving signals. (Garth Brooks)
Brain sensor for keeping track of brain functions.

Vision and sun correcting glass with built in digital readout chip and micro/macro capability. (The Private Eye)
Microphone linked for audio input into tape, TV, phone, and sound amplification systems.
Headphone for sound input and environmental dampening.

Coaxial cable for connecting headset to waistbrain.

Whole system life pac
Health pac containing body chemistry pills, health aids for dealing with physical breakdowns, microfilm medical history. (including Smart Dust)

Food pac containing vitamin pills, food wafers, and taste sensations.

Weather pac containing rain/wind wear.

Information pac containing information storage cards (computer inputs),cassettes, and microfilm. (Visor)

Tools pac for repairing portable person and dealing with the outside mechanical world.
Protection pac with a built-in aggression bomb.

Transporters pac with collapsible containers.

Wrist bands
Information indicator band for time, date, weather, and health (endo system for body and ecto system for mechanical and electrical systems).

Control input band for phone, computer, TV, radio, tape, and other systems. (Twiddler, Visor, Wristwatch Cell Phone)

Waist brain
Fuel cell for operating electronic systems and heating/cooling systems (rechargeable cassettes for exchange at 'City terminals').

Plug-in jack for using local power source.
Coaxial cable connection to body suit connecting all systems to waist brain.

Internal circuitry with jacks for connecting all hardware.

Minicomputer with both built-in programs and slot for program card inputs (interfacing mechanism for external communication with larger computer). (Visor)

Medical monitoring storage and analysis unit connected through belt to medical sensors.
Card input for medical history (up to date).
Transmitter/receiver for phone, TV, and radio linked to headset antenna and
Amplifier/preamplifier/converter for phone, TV, radio, and tape systems.

Mini-cassette tape dock.
TV monitor for head, hand or table use. Camera storage.

Body suit
Heating system with grid of heating elements.
Cooling system with insulating/heat dissipating material.
Clothing projecting desired image, including customizing updating
Body health sensors.
Internal coaxial cables connecting head set, wrist bands, and waist brain.

Additive
Back pack/carry-all bag containing professional, recreational, comfort, shelter items.

Motorized collapsible feet.

Service terminals for exchanging fuel cells, input, output, power terminals and acquiring expendables.

Smart Dust

Portable Person
1999

Robert Mangurian (American, b. 1941) and Mary-Ann Ray (American, b. 1958) of Studio Works. Cabinet Vest. 1997. Recycled wool felt, 36 x 24 x 1" (91.4 x 61 x 2.5 cm). Prototype. Mfr.: Studio Works, USA, 1997

The Cabinet Vest builds a body clad with storage, with many drawers scattered across the chest. Made of scrap wool felt, it is constructed as a lamination of three layers with the body occupying the space between the front and middle layers; storage facilities are located between the middle and back; and there are display options on the outward-facing surface of the front layer. The over-the-heart "drawer" opens only to the inside for more precious possessions, and the dead-center drawer has a leak for a hand to reach out.

Takashi Sogabe (Japanese, b. 1960).
Digital Blocks. 1996. ABS and steel, cellular video phone: 5⁵⁄₁₆ x 2 x 1" (13.5 x 5.8 x
2 cm); PDA set: 4⁵⁄₁₆ x 2 x 1" (11 x 5.8 x 2
cm); cellular phone set: 3 x 2 x 1" (9.5 x
5.8 x 2 cm); digital camera set: 2¹⁵⁄₁₆ x 2 x
1" (7.5 x 5.8 x 2 cm); pager set: 2⅛ x 1 x
2" (5.4 x 5.8 x 2 cm); voice memo unit:

1¹⁄₁₆ x 2 x 1" (2.7 x 5.8 x 2 cm); battery
unit: 1¹⁄₁₆ x 2 x 1" (2.7 x 5.8 x 2 cm).
Prototype. Mfr.: Sony Technoworks
Corporation, 1996

Above:
Motorola. Mobile Telephone System.
c. 1967. Mfr.: Motorola, Inc., USA, 1967

Right:
Albert Nagele (American, b. 1935). Dyna
Tac, first cellular handset by Motorola.
1978. Injection-molded polycarbonate,
7⅛ x 2⅛ x 1¹¹⁄₁₆" (18.1 x 5.4 x 4.3 cm).
Prototype. Mfr.: Motorola, Inc., USA, 1978

Albert Nagele (American, b. 1935) and
Leon Soren (American, b. 1945). Star Tac
Cellular Telephone. 1993. Injection-
molded polycarbonate blend, 3^{11}/$_{16}$ x 2^{1}/$_{16}$
x ^{3}/$_{4}$" (9.4 x 5.2 x 2.1 cm). Mfr.: Motorola,
Inc., USA, 1995

Albert Nagele. V 3620 Cellular Telephone.
1995. Injection-molded polycarbonate
blend, 3^{1}/$_{4}$ x 1^{5}/$_{8}$ x 1" (8.3 x 4.1 x 2.5 cm).
Mfr: Motorola, Inc., USA, 1997

Above:
Rudolph W. Krolopp (American, b. 1930).
Pageboy Pagers. 1965. Mfr.: Motorola,
Inc., USA, starting in 1965

Right:
Wagon Wang (Chinese, b. 1972) of
Motorola PCS Beijing Design Center.
Accompli A6188 GSM Phone. 1999. Plastic, $3^{15}/_{16}$ x $2^3/_8$ x $1^1/_8$" (10 x 6 x 2.9 cm). Mfr:
Motorola Electronics Ltd., China, 2000

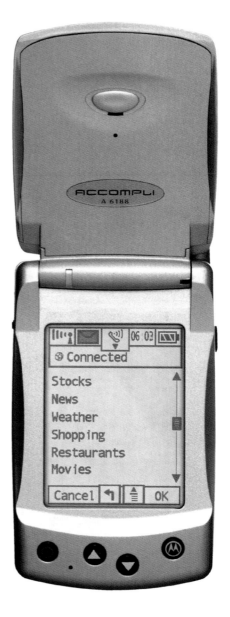

Eliron Koronyo (Israeli, b. 1973). Ground Zero: Privacy in Public Space. 1999–2000. Painted bent plywood, lumisty MFX-1515 film, polycarbonate, bent aluminum, polyurethane, Engelhard iridescent pigment, and vinyl, 60 x 41 x 50" (152.4 x 104.1 x 127 cm). Prototype. Mfr.: Eliron Koronyo, 2000

Ground Zero is a response to a growing need for individual privacy in public space. Airport terminals are filled with business travelers managing hectic schedules. Many would like to have the option of privacy in the midst of a crowded public lounge. This thesis project by a student in the furniture department at the Parsons School of Design in New York was designed as an individual seating unit to provide privacy and comfort without compromising the need for security surveillance. This is achieved by using side panels to modulate the user's peripheral vision. The result gives the individual traveler a brief sanctuary to rest, relax, and gather his or her thoughts before continuing on.

Teiyu Goto (Japanese). Vaio / PCG-Z50C
Laptop Computer. c. 1998. Mfr.: Sony
Corporation, 1998

Swatch Design. Net Invader (left). 1999.
Webmaster (right). 1998. Mfr.: Swatch
Ltd., Switzerland, 2000

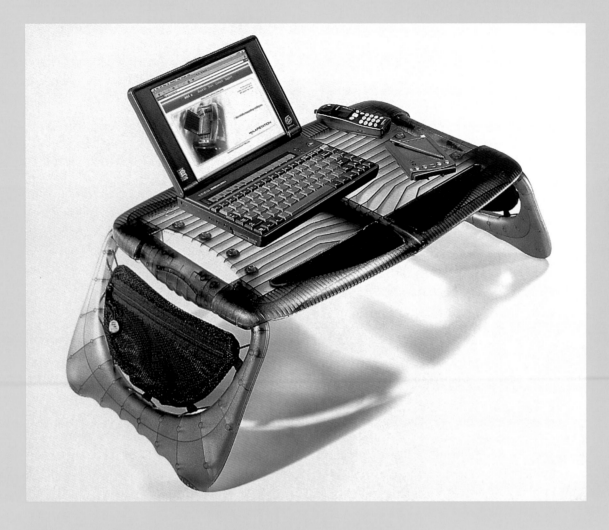

Opposite:
Noel Zeller (American, b. 1936). Long
Reach Flexible Flashlight. 1993–94. ABS
plastic, polycarbonate, and crayton poly-
elastomer tube, 3 x 1½ x ⅝–9" (7.6 x
3.8 x 1.2–22.9 cm). Mfr.: Zelco Industries
Inc., USA, 1994

Above:
Ravi Sawhney (American, b. 1956).
Lapstation. 1999. Injection-molded polycarbonate; folded: 3¹³⁄₁₆ x 16 x 12⅝" (9.7 x
40.6 x 32.1 cm). Mfr.: Intrigo, USA, 2000

Right:
Noel Zeller (American, b. 1936). Itty Bitty
Booklight. 1999–2000. ABS, plastic, and
steel, 7 x 1½ x 3" (19.1 x 3.2 x 7.6 cm).
Mfr.: Zelco Industries, Inc., USA, 2000

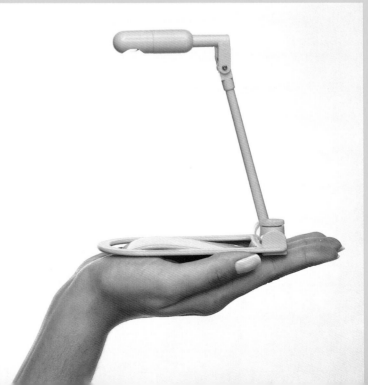

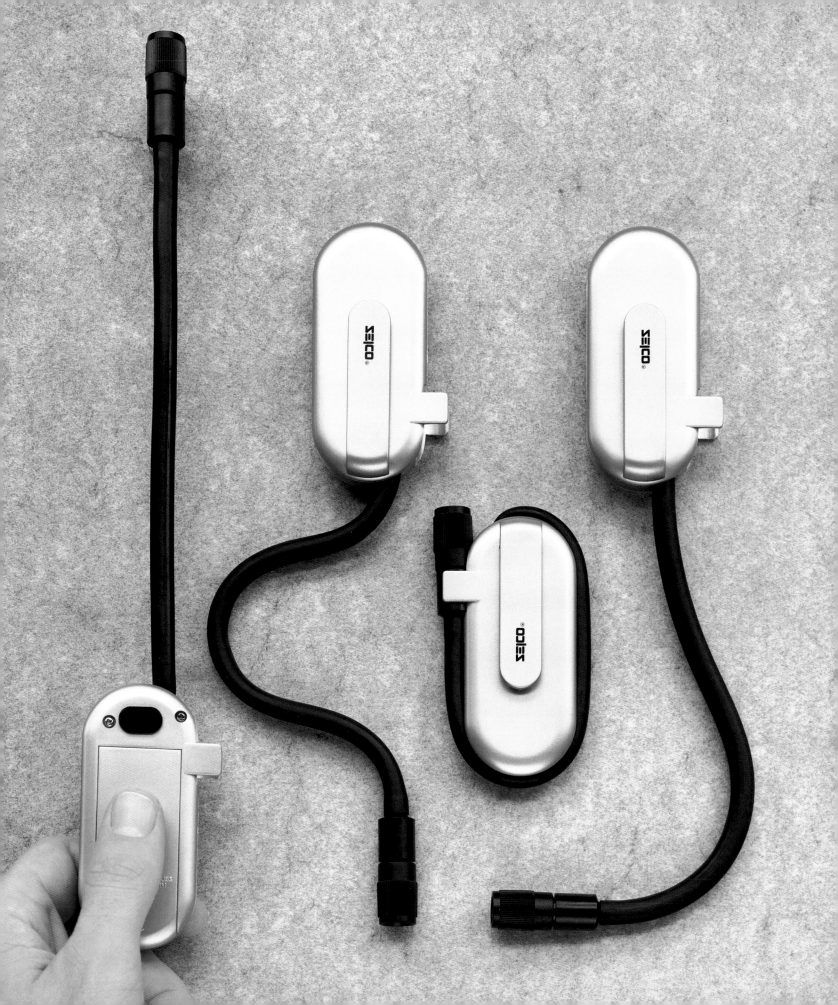

Ericsson Bluetooth™ Headset and T28
World Cell Phone. 2000

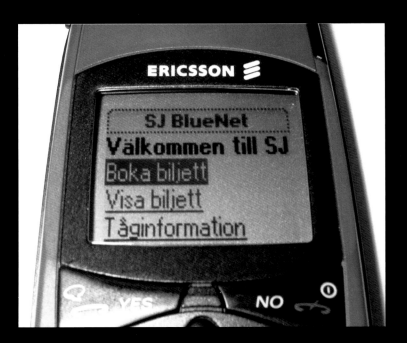

This page:
An example of Bluetooth™ Access System.
2000

Bluetooth™ is a new technology currently being tested in Europe. By means of fixed stations and fixed or portable receivers, it can connect and synchronize wirelessly different devices—i.e., a computer, a PDA, and a cell phone—that may be in close range at any time, without needing a physical docking information-sharing system. A cell phone being carried around by a user thus potentially enters many wireless local networks and can take advantage of them. The operation simulated on this screen—the purchase of a train ticket in Sweden—could in theory happen at home, in connection with the home Bluetooth™station's Internet connection, or even at the railway station, connecting to the station's Bluetooth™ area.

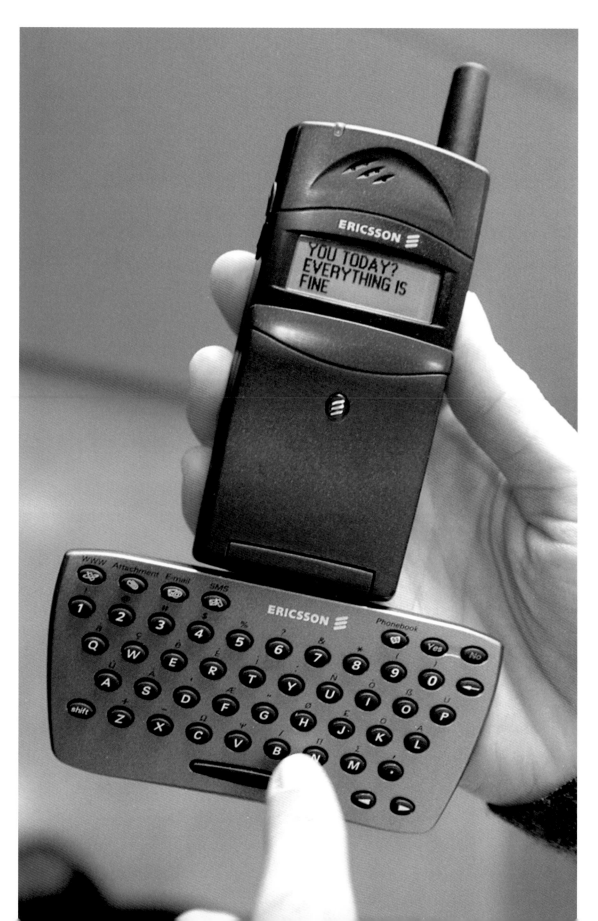

Left:
Ericsson T18 with Chatboard™. 2000

Instant messaging has become a world-wide habit. The albeit small Chatboard™ keyboard bypasses the complex writing system based on the phone keys' assigned letters and renders the operation more expeditious.

Opposite, top:
Ericsson Communicator Platform. Concept, 2000

The concept represents a literal hybrid between a cell phone and a personal organizer, maintaining the screen size close to those already in use by most PDA carriers.

Opposite, bottom:
Ericsson R380s Cellular Phone with Personal Organizer. 2000

The R380s is an example of a PDA/cell phone hybrid already on the market. Besides storing a complete address book and scheduling program, it facilitates the Internet connection and other WAP services.

This page and opposite:
Prada Sport Design Team. Prada Sport, assorted examples from fall/winter 1999–fall/winter 2000 collection. Nylon and other materials. Mfr.: Prada USA Corporation, 1999

Taking their inspiration from sports gear and their impulse from the several small devices people are constantly carrying on their person, Prada and Prada Sport launched a new trend in the past four years. They have designed garments and accessories that, albeit elegant and at times formal, have many evident or hidden storage pockets in obvious and less-obvious places, from the back and chest to the knees and elbows.

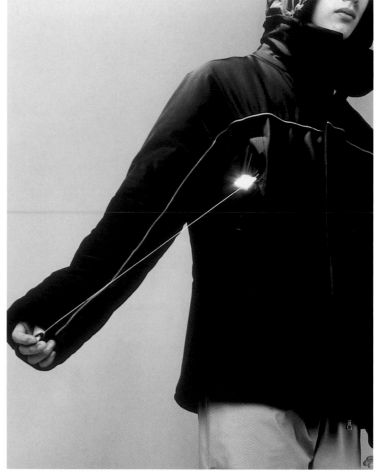

Right:
Nokia Design International. 3G Terminal
Concept III. 1998. Aluminum, 4⁵⁄₁₆ x
2¹⁄₁₆ x ⅝" (11 x 5.2 x 1.4 cm). Concept.
Mfr.: Nokia Mobile Phones Inc., USA, 1998

Below:
Nokia Design International. 3G Terminal
Concept I. 1998. Aluminum, 6⁹⁄₁₆ x 2⅜ x
⅜" (16.7 x 6 x 1.5 cm). Concept. Mfr.:
Nokia Mobile Phones Inc., USA, 1998

Above:
Nokia Design International. Nokia 9110 multifunction digital phone with integrated organizer. 1998. Polycarbonate and ABS plastic, 6 3/16 x 2 1/4 x 1 1/16" (15.8 x 5.6 x 2.7 cm). Mfr.: Nokia Mobile Phones Inc., USA, 1999

Right:
Nokia Design International. Nokia 8850/8890 GSM digital phone. 1998. Polycarbonate and ABS plastic, and aluminum covers, 3 15/16 x 2 x 5/8" (10 x 4.4 x 1.4 cm). Mfr.: Nokia Mobile Phones Inc., USA, 1999

This page and opposite:
Sofia Anna Varanka Hudson (American, b. 1977). Field Office. 1999. Nylon backpack with steel telescoping legs, 20 x 19 x 10" (50.8 x 48.3 x 25.4 cm). Prototype, 1999

The Field Office is a diverse, collapsible workstation contained within a backpack designed by Varanka while a student in the furniture department at the Parsons School of Design in New York. When the center zip closure is released, the pack expands to become a module office area with a detachable briefcase. The telescoping legs can be adjusted or released to full length, allowing the office module to be leaned against any solid, vertical surface for use anywhere.

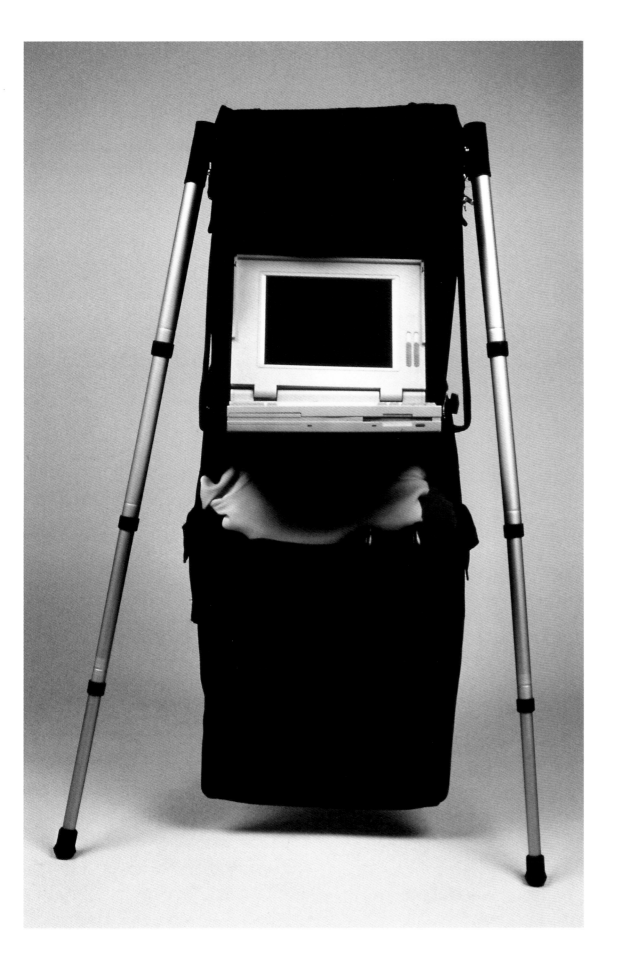

Palm Company Design. Palm m100
Handheld (below) and Cradle (right).
2000. 4½ x 3⅛ x ½" (10 x 7 x 1 cm).
Mfr: Palm, Inc., 2000

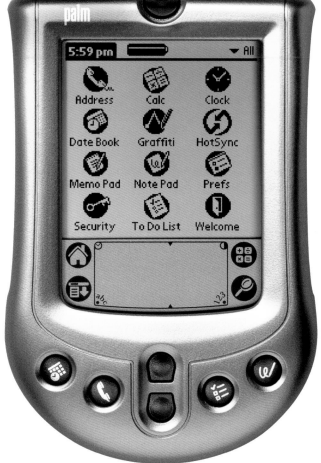

Robert Brunner and Benjamin Chia of Pentagram Design. Stowaway Portable Keyboard. 1999. Injection-molded ABS and stamped and formed aluminum; folded: 5⅛ x 3⅝ x 1" (13 x 9.2 x 2 cm); unfolded: 5⅛ x 13⅞ x ½" (13 x 35.2 x 1 cm). Mfr: Think Outside, Inc., USA, 1999

This page and opposite:
Naziha Mestaoui (Belgian, b. 1975),
Yacine Aït Kaci (French, b. 1973), and
Christophe Beaujays (Belgian, b.1972).
Écharpe Communicante (communicat-
ing scarf). 2000. Wool/fabric scarf with
computer screen, keyboard, and tele-
phone, length 39⅜" (100 cm). Proto-
type. Mfr.: N. Mestaoui, Y. Aït Kaci, C.
Beaujays, and France Telecom, 2000.

Conceived as a second skin for communication, this extra- long, detachable
scarf is equipped with built-in communicating interfaces, including a hands-free
telephone, screen, keyboard, and camera, allowing the wearer to be at once
here and potentially everywhere but still
within a private sphere of communication. By wrapping the scarf around the
neck, the wearer is isolated, both physi-

cally and acoustically, from the outside
world. Inserting the arm into one length
of the scarf, as if through a large
bracelet, allows access to the computer.

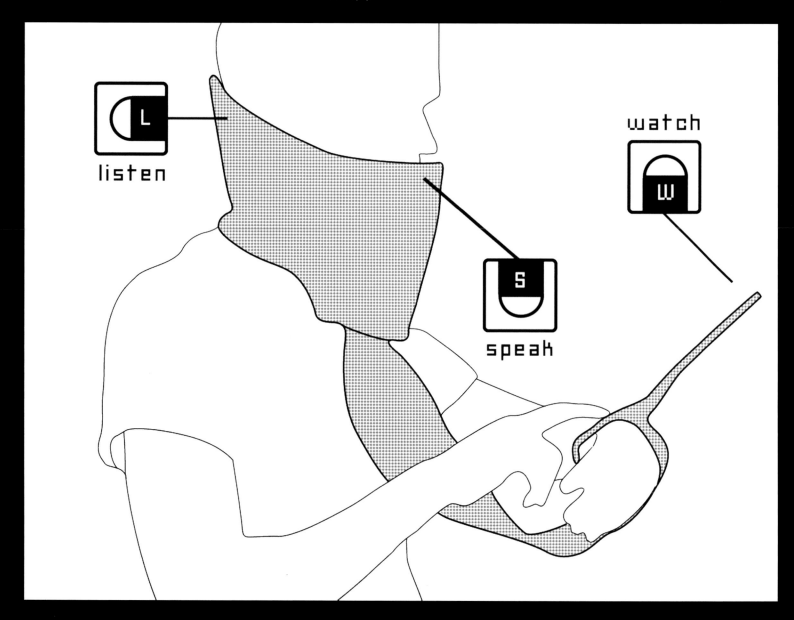

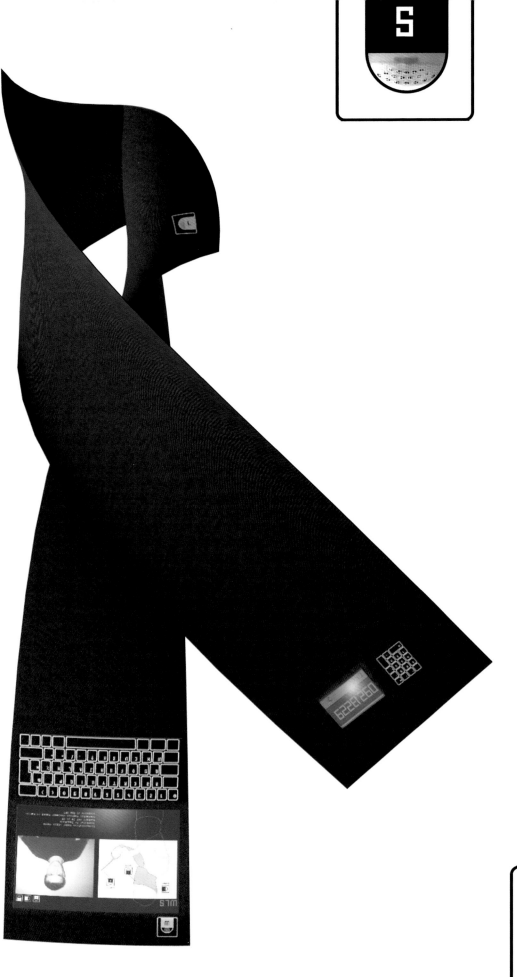

Below:
iGo Design Team. Road Warrior International Access Pack AC and RJ 11 Bundle. 1997. Modem saver international (a polarity tester), dual modeler adapter, alligator clips, in-line coupler, modem cord, and "high tech tips" book. Mfr.: iGo Inc., USA, 1997

The ultimate, essential traveling companion and an emblem of the need to rationalize telecommunications and electrical standards in the world, Road Warrior contains all the adapters and plugs necessary to achieve a connection in different countries.

Opposite:
Ann Lindberg. Promotional photograph of Letosh Working Snob laptop computer. See page 160

Dan Grettve (Swedish, b. 1967) and Anna Lenskog (Swedish, b. 1964). Letosh Working Snob (right). 1998. Silicon and soft-feel lacquer, 1 x 11$\frac{11}{16}$ x 9$\frac{1}{16}$" (2.5 x 29.7 x 23 cm). Tank (bottom). 1998. Silicon and soft-feel lacquer, 1$\frac{3}{4}$ x 12$\frac{1}{4}$ x 9$\frac{1}{16}$" (4.8 x 31.2 x 23 cm). Mfr.: AB Pro Lack, Sweden, 1999

Apple Industrial Design Group. I-Book
Portable Computer. 1998. Materials and
dimensions vary. Mfr.: Apple Computers,
Inc., USA, 1998

This page:
Jennie Pineus (Swedish, b. 1972). Head-cocoons. 2000. Polyamide fabric, 13¾"
(35 cm) high; 10½" (27 cm) diameter.
Prototype. Mfr.: Jennie Pineus, Sweden,
2000

Opposite:
Pineus. Cocoonchair. 2000. Steel,
polyamide fabric, and plastic, 55⅛ x
35⅜ x 39⅜" (140 x 90 x 100 cm). Prototype. Mfr.: Jennie Pineus, Sweden, 2000

These cocoons are intended to provide a
simple and accessible solution to shelter
us from a stressful, intense environment.
They may be used in public spaces,
where pressure is high and it is difficult
to escape and take a break. The cocoonchair provides a space in which you can
relax, read, prepare a lecture, or even fall
asleep. The shape of the chair clearly
communicates that you are not to be dis-
turbed and provides privacy. It can be
used at the airport, office, library, or in
any public space. The headcocoon
instead is a portable version that can be
taken anywhere. It folds up and comes
with its own bag: an individual personal
relaxation sheath.

Claus-Christian Eckhardt (German,
b. 1965). Siemens S42 Cellular Phone.
1998. Galvanized plastic and stainless-steel
wire mesh, 4¾ x 2 x 1" (11.5 x 4.4 x 2.3 cm).
Mfr.: Siemens, Germany, 2000

Trium Company Design. Mondo Digital
Mobile Phone. 2000. Mfr.: Mitsubishi
Electric Telecom Europe, 2000

Centre de Recherche et Développement,
Rennes, France. Cosmo Digital Mobile
Phone. 2000. Mfr.: Mitsubishi Electric
Telecom Europe, 2000

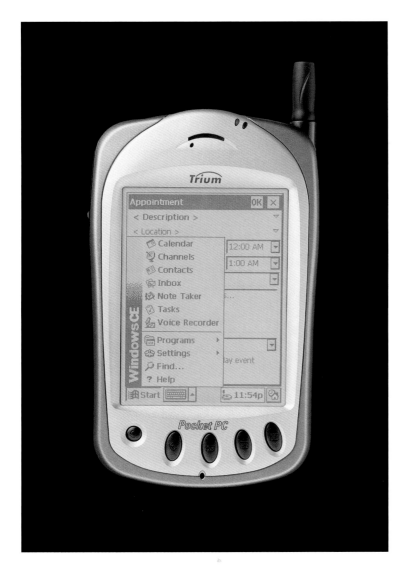

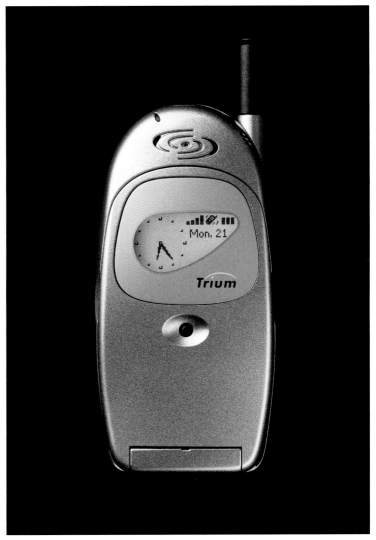

Data Mining
The New Goldrush

Martin Bone (British, b. 1968), Tom Eich (American, b. 1961), Thomas Elders (German, b. 1967), Danny Stillion (American, b. 1967), and Andre Yousefi (British, b. 1970) of IDEO. IDEO 2010 Concepts. Manufactured by IDEO, USA 2000

Opposite, inset:
Agent (Personal Digital Assistant).

Opposite:
Tube (Tomorrow's Laptop).

Top right:
E-Quill (Connected Pen).

Bottom right:
Agent (Personal Digital Assistant), open

IDEO 2010 represents the designers' belief that active objects will become smaller, and smaller objects will become more active in the future. Advances in low-power circuit design and chip-fabrication technologies will lead to a proliferation of extremely fast, widely affordable computer and communication devices that will use very little power and process speeds at least one hundred times faster than today's PCs. Intelligent objects will have to do a much better job of selecting and organizing the information they provide via rudimentary artificial intelligence. Devices will hold simple applications locally (voice and handwriting recognition, for instance), but will rely on a link to central databases for access to project data, or to coordinate appointments with coworkers. This will increase flexibility, as an immense array of services and applications will be available at a moment's notice via wireless access.

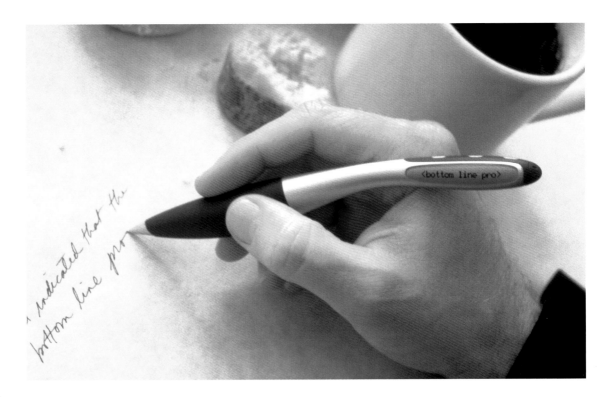

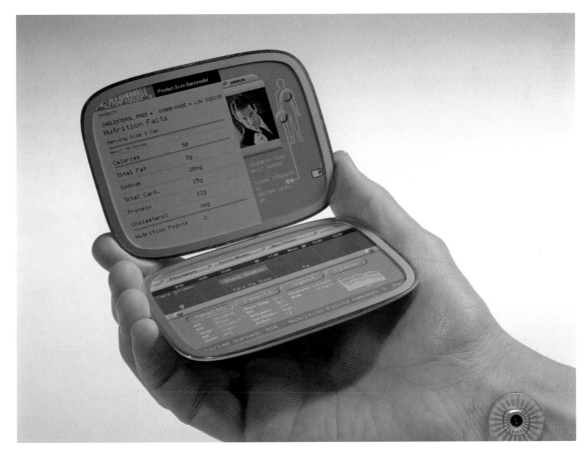

This page and opposite:
Bran Ferren (American, b. 1953) and
Thomas Ritter (German, b. 1958). Maxi-
Mog Global Expedition Vehicle System.
1998–2000. Various materials. 10'6" x 6'
8" x 19'10" (320 x 203 x 604.5 cm). Mfr.:
Unicat Fahrzuegbau GmbH, Germany,
1998–2000

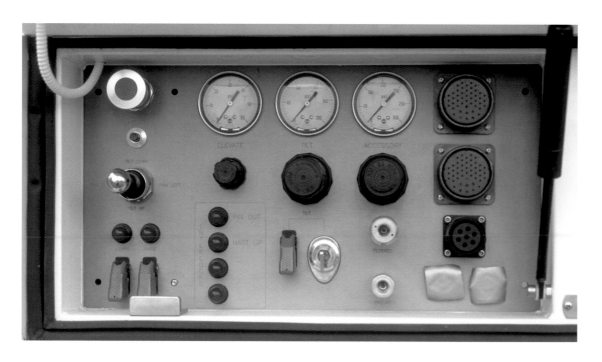

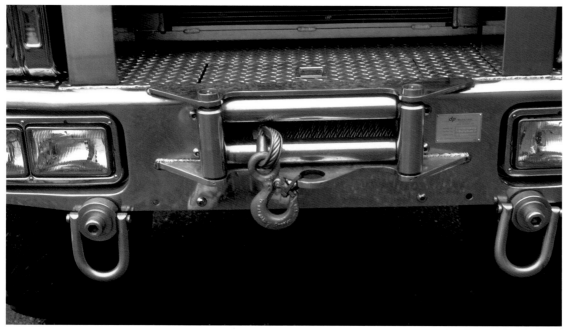

This custom-built high-mobility vehicle is based on a Mercedes Benz Unimog chassis and was designed as a high-performance environment from which one can work in any part of the world. It features a modular engine system, automatic transmission with on-and off-road modes, and computer-controlled air suspensions. It is capable of climbing a forty-five degree gradient, fording six feet of water, and cruising at ninety miles per hour on improved roads. The vehicle is road legal worldwide and includes a complete secure global communications system supporting voice, data, video, fax, E-mail, and full Internet access with both terrestrial and satellite communication paths, and a dual computer-based information-management system which provides worldwide digital moving maps, imaging, and systems-management capabilities. The highlights of the powered trailer include a sleeping deck, kitchen pod, bathroom pod, and BMW off-road motorcycle for scouting, and for routine and emergency travel.

Desktop Objects

Despite the expansion of our work practice into the meta-physical and meta-spherical dimensions available today—thanks to laptop computers and cell phones—the desktop, to everybody's relief, remains a reliable horizontal surface. Used as a metaphor in the design of computer interfaces, the top of the desk is the last resource for personalization. Even in the most suffocating cubicle, it is the place where one can create a familiar landscape to return to every morning. Some offices, such as those of Chiat/Day, designed by Gaetano Pesce, asked their employees to give up this one last inalienable right and pick a different surface almost every morning. The results were discordant: managers and executives, who were usually responsible for implementing the innovation, expressed their satisfaction; normal employees, from their perspective, felt depressed and displaced.

The top of the desk is where flowers, family pictures, and memorabilia—ranging from Pokémon to beaded boxes—can vivify the austere presence of the desktop computer and the telephone. Personal computers made a relatively recent appearance and became ubiquitous in the second half of the 1980s. They do, of course, perform faster and are more capacious, but they are not always more efficient. Paradoxically, while every other appliance has shrunk in size, they have not. For a short while in the mid-1980s, the cozy smiling box called Macintosh—in its SE and Classic models—represented an attempt at reduction, but it was mainly marketed for the home. Moreover, workers crave monitor space, which the small Mac could not provide; workers also want space for "the other desktop." Nor have desktop computers evolved much from a formal or an aesthetic point of view. With the exception of Apple's recent forays, the iMac and the Cube, and IBM's choice of total black, and despite other companies' discrete attempts with alternative colors, desktop computers remain in a safe zone of grays, enhanced vents, and boredom.

Our desk is filled with surprises that come from its connection to other desks and people, from its electrification and animation. Yet, some of the most persistent and eternal masterpieces of design that still command their spot on the desktop have no plugs. Bic pens, Post-It® notes, paper and binder clips, file folders—these beautiful objects continue to populate our work lives. Not only do we need them, we really want them. It will take time before we will truly be able to do without paper, if ever. This brings us to the most important feature in desktop design: the various degrees of order and chaos. One could call it "personal landscaping," but the way we distribute our desktop, our piles of paper, our reminders, is always organized, even when it looks most chaotic.

P. A.

Tibor Kalman (American, 1949–1999), Douglas Riccardi (American, b. 1962), and Alexander Brebner (American, b. 1960) of M&Co. Mystery Book. 1989. Pencils, metal ruler, paper, eraser, rubber bands, metal pencil sharpener, licorice candies in metal tin, and cardboard, 10 x 8 x 1" (25.4 x 20.3 x 2.5 cm) Mfr.: M&Co., 1989

Below:
Apple Industrial Design Group. iMac
desktop computers. 1998. Materials vary,
15 x 15 x 17$\frac{1}{16}$" (38.1 x 38.1 x 43.3 cm).
Mfr.: Apple Computers Inc., USA, 2000

Right:
Apple Industrial Design Group. Apple
Pro Mouse. 2000. Materials vary, 1$\frac{5}{16}$ x
2$\frac{7}{16}$ x 4$\frac{3}{8}$" (3.3 x 6.2 x 11.1 cm). Mfr.:
Apple Computers Inc., USA, 2000

Left:
Apple Industrial Design Group. Cinema Display, 22" Flat Panel. 1999. Materials vary. Mfr.: Apple Computers Inc., USA, 1999

Above:
Apple Industrial Design Group. G4 Cube with 15" Studio Display, Pro Mouse, keyboard, and speakers. 2000. Materials vary. G4 cube: 10⅛ x 7¹¹⁄₁₆ x 7¹¹⁄₁₆" (24.8 x 19.5 x 19.5 cm); studio display: 15¹³⁄₁₆ x 16¹⁄₁₆ x 6¹¹⁄₁₆" (40.2 x 40.8 x 17 cm). Mfr.: Apple Computers Inc., USA, 2000

Below:
Apple Industrial Design Group. Apple Studio Display (17") CRT. 2000. Materials vary. 8½ x 17 x 17 1/16" (21.6 x 43.2 x 43.3 cm). Mfr.: Apple Computers Inc., USA, 2000

Below, right:
Harman Kardon iSub Subwoofer for Apple iMac. 2000. Various materials. Mfr.: Harman Kardon, USA, 2000

Opposite, bottom:
Tibor Kalman (American, 1949–1999). Paperweight. 1984. Vinyl and lead paperweight inside, 3½ x 4 x 4" (8.9 x 10.2 x 10.2 cm). Mfr.: M&Co., 1984

Left:
Décolletage Plastique Design Team. Bic®
Cristal®. 1950. Polystyrene, polypropy-
lene, and tungsten carbide**.** Mfr.: Société
Bic, France, 1950

Below:
Tipp-Ex GmbH Design Team. Tipp-Ex®
Rapid Correction Fluid. 1965. Barex and
high-density polyethylene. Mfr.: Société
Bic Corp., USA.

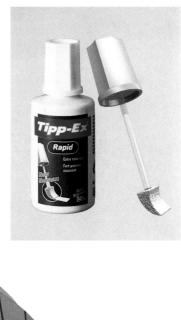

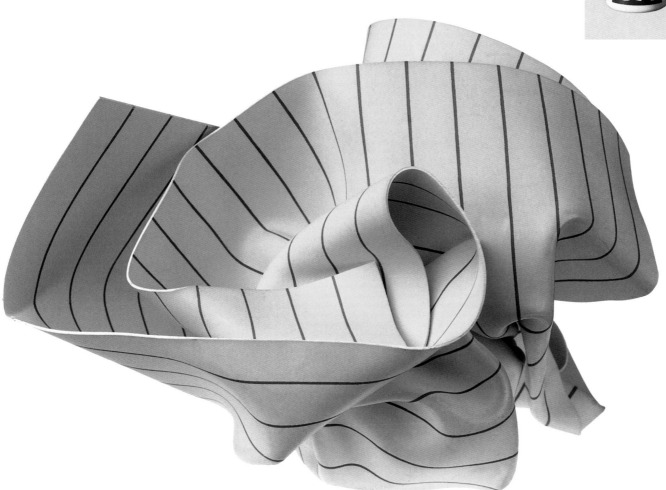

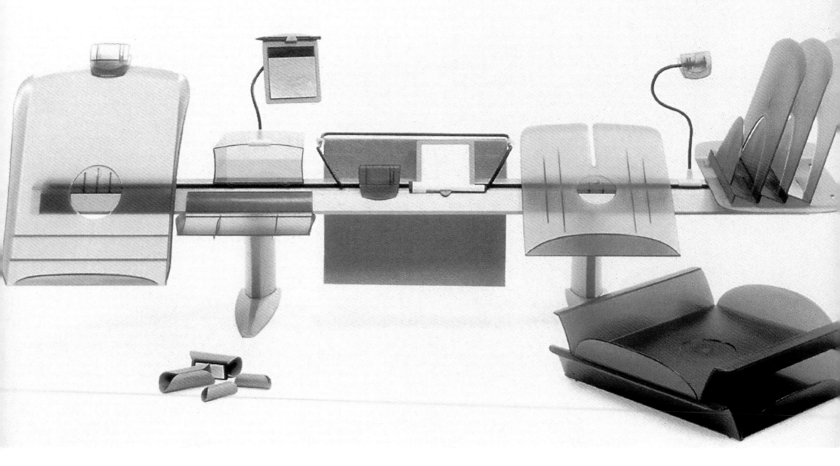

Chuck Taylor (American, b. 1949) and
Gary Fitzgerald (American, b. 1958).
Jump Stuff Desktop Accessories. 1999.
Injection-molded ABS and aluminum.
Various dimensions. Mfr.: Haworth, Inc.,
USA, 1999

Below:
Raul Barbieri (Italian, b. 1946) and Giorgio Marianelli (Italian, b. 1939). Babele Letter Tray. 1981. ABS, $2\frac{1}{2}$ x $9\frac{7}{8}$ x $13\frac{1}{2}$ " (7 x 25.1 x 34.9 cm). Mfr.: Rexite SpA, 1981

Right:
Philippe Starck (French, b. 1949). Liberté (freedom) and Pensées (thoughts) all-purpose boxes. 1997. Melamine, $2\frac{1}{3}$ x 9 x 7" (6 x 23 x 18 cm). Mfr.: Alessi SpA, Italy, 1998

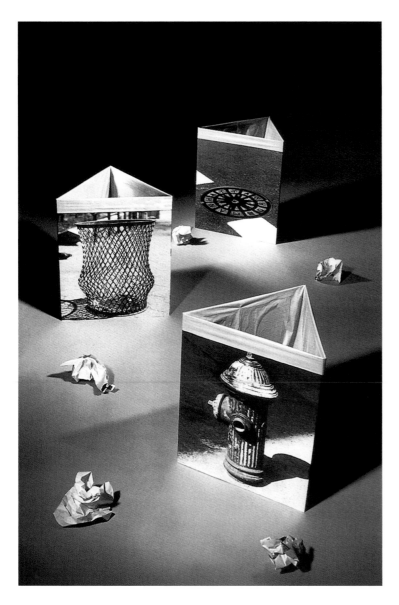

Left:
Giovanni Pellone (Italian, b. 1964) and
Bridget Means (American, b. 1965) of
Benza. Zago Folding Trash Cans. 1992.
Recycled cardboard and polyethylene
liner, 17½ x 15 x 15" (44.5 x 38.1 x 38.1
cm). Mfr.: Benza Inc., USA, 1996

Below:
Matali Crasset (French, b. 1965). Artican
(wastepaper basket). 1999. Plastic and
metal, 23⅝ x 16⁹⁄₁₆ x 16⁹⁄₁₆" (60 x 42 x 42
cm). Mfr.: Sas/OO, France, 2000

Enzo Mari (Italian, b. 1932). In Attesa
(Waiting) Wastepaper Baskets. 1970.
Polypropylene, 16⅛ x 11 x 11" (41 x 26 x
26 cm). Mfr.: Danese Milano, Italy, 1971

Carl Ledbetter (American, b. 1963),
Steve Fischer (Canadian, b. 1966), Hugh
McLoone (American, b. 1961), and Ken
Fry (American, b. 1968). Intellimouse
Optical Mouse. 1999. Injection-molded
ABS, paint, polycarbonate, Kraton brand
polymer, injection-molded nylon, PVS
sheaths, injection-molded overmolds,
and Teflon-coated polyethylene, 1$\frac{9}{16}$ x
2$\frac{11}{16}$ x 4$\frac{15}{16}$" (4 x 6.8 x 12.5 cm). Mfr.:
Microsoft Corp., USA, 1999

Asprey and Garrard Design. Sterling Silver Internet Mouse. 1999–2000. Sterling
silver, 1 x 2$\frac{3}{4}$ x 4$\frac{3}{4}$" (2.5 x 6.4 x 11.4 cm).
Mfr.: Asprey and Garrard Inc., USA,
1999–2000

Giovanni Pellone (Italian, b. 1964) and
Bridget Means (American, b. 1965) of
Benza. Squiggle Mouse Pad. 1997. Poly-
carbonate and foam rubber, ⅜ x 9½ x
9½" (.37 x 24.1 x 24.1 cm). Mfr.: Benza
Inc., USA, 1997

This page:
Michele de Lucchi (Italian, b. 1951). Artjet
10 Bubble Ink-Jet Printer. 1997. Materials
vary. 6⁵⁄₁₆ x 13³⁄₁₆ x 8¾" (16 x 33.5 x 21 cm).
Mfr.: Olivetti Lexikon, Italy, 1999

Opposite:
Michele de Lucchi (Italian, b. 1951). Artjet
20 Bubble Ink-Jet Printer, 1997. Materials
vary. 7⅞ x 18⅛ x 7⅞" (20 x 46 x 20 cm).
Mfr.: Olivetti Lexikon, Italy, 1998

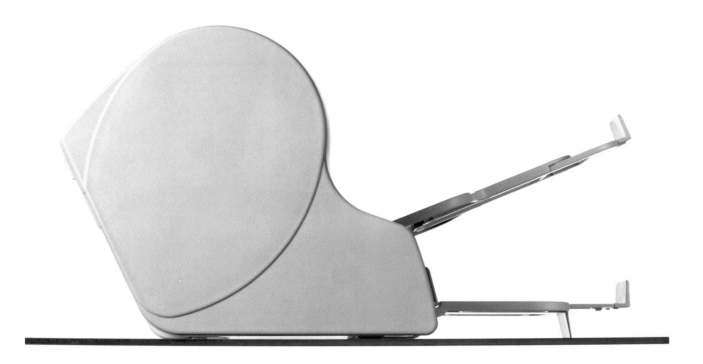

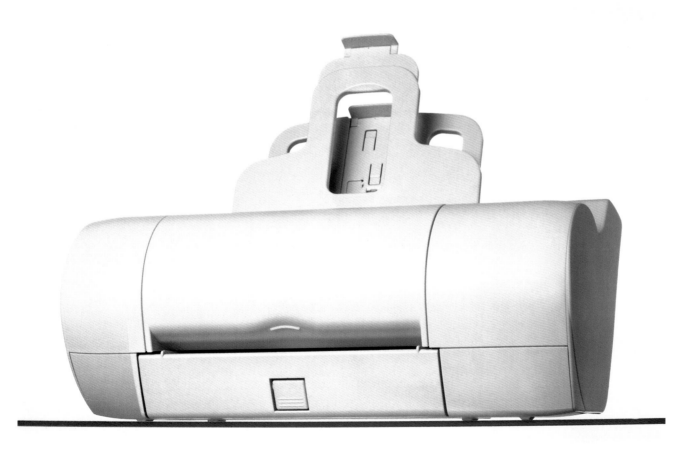

Laurence Sarrazin (Canadian, b. 1977).
The Banana Bag. 2000. Ethylene-vinyl-
acetate, 3 x 10 x 18" (7.6 x 25.4 x 45.7 cm).
Banana Wrist Pad. 2000. Foamed poly-
urethane, 2 x 2 x 8" (5.1 x 5.1 x 20.3 cm).
Prototypes. Mfr.: Laurence Sarrazin, 2000

Work environments are resistant to
humor, yet it is an essential ingredient for
creativity. This product, designed while
Sarrazin was a student at Parsons School
of Design in New York, introduces play
into the workplace, presenting a set of
hand-held and desktop containers for
work tools. By forcing this organic form
of a seemingly purposeless and highly
connotative fruit out of its usual context
and placing it in a new one, these containers inject humorous tension into the
office.

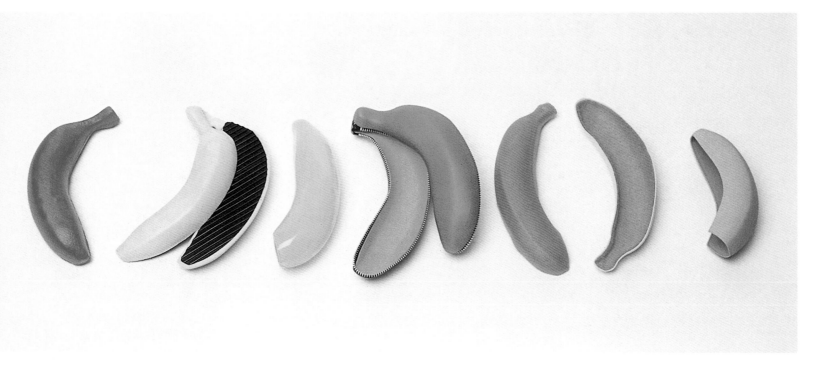

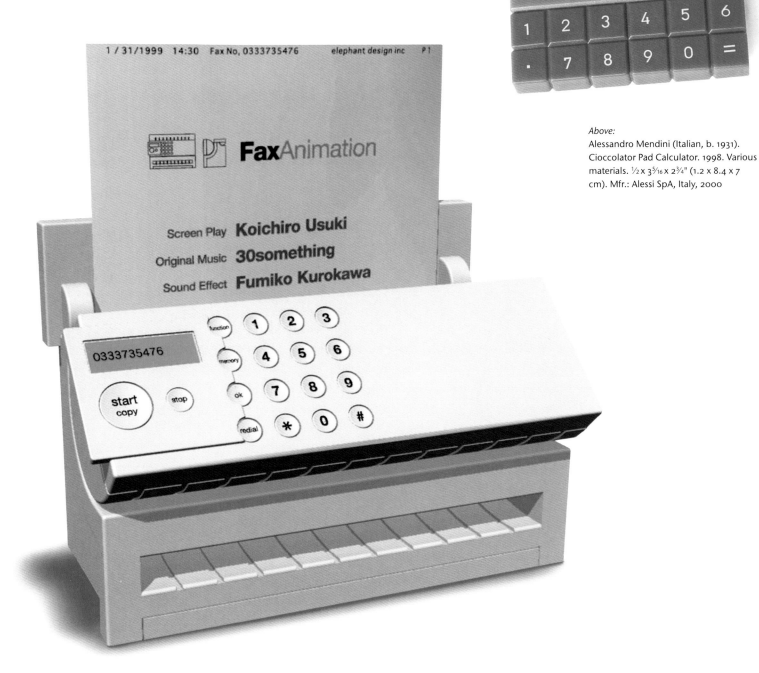

Below:
Elephant Design, Tokyo. TPF Fax
Machine. 2000. Materials vary. 11¾ x
15½ x 7" (29.9 x 39.4 x 17.8 cm). Concept, 2000

Above:
Alessandro Mendini (Italian, b. 1931).
Cioccolator Pad Calculator. 1998. Various
materials. ½ x 3⁵⁄₁₆ x 2¾" (1.2 x 8.4 x 7
cm). Mfr.: Alessi SpA, Italy, 2000

Richard Sapper (German, b. 1932), John
Swansey (American, b. 1960), David Hill
(American, b. 1957), and Brian Leonard
(American, b. 1967) of IBM Corporate
Design. IBM NetVista X40. 1999. Ther-
moplastic resin, steel, printed circuit
cardboard, and thin film transistor display, 18 15/16 x 18 1/2 x 23 5/8" (48 x 47 x
60 cm). Mfr.: IBM Corp., USA, 2000

Richard Sapper (German, b. 1932),
Tomoyuki Takahashi (Japanese, b. 1958),
Kazuhiko Yamazaki (Japanese, b. 1955),
and David Hill (American, b. 1957) of IBM
Corporate Design. IBM ThinkPad 570.
1998. Carbon fiber, reinforced plastic, and
ABS, $1\frac{1}{8}$ x $11\frac{13}{16}$ x $9\frac{7}{16}$" (2.8 x 30 x 24 cm).
Mfr.: IBM Corp., USA, 1999

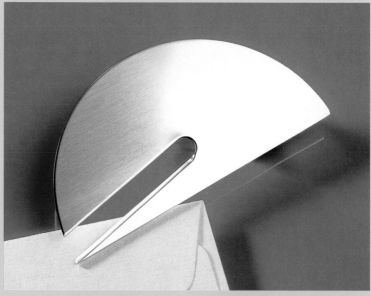

Top:
Folmer Christensen (Danish, b. 1911).
Classic Folle Stapler. 1946. Satin polished
stainless steel, $3\frac{1}{4}$ x $1\frac{11}{16}$ x 5" (9.5 x 4.3 x
12.8 cm). Mfr.: Folle, Denmark, 2000

Bottom:
Folmer Christensen (Danish, b. 1911).
Tape Dispenser. 1995. Satin polished
stainless steel, 5 x 4 x $\frac{1}{2}$" (13 x 10 x
1 cm). Mfr.: Folle, Denmark, 2000

Top:
Folmer Christensen (Danish, b. 1911).
Paper Knife. 1991. Satin polished stainless
steel, $3\frac{5}{16}$ x 4 x 2" (10 x 10.2 x 5.1 cm).
Mfr.: Folle, Denmark, 2000

Bottom:
Folmer Christensen (Danish, b. 1911).
Document Holders. 1999. Satin polished
stainless steel, 2 x 2 x 2" (5.1 x 5.1 x 5.1
cm). Mfr.: Folle, Denmark, 2000

Left:
Takahiro Tsuge (Japanese, b. 1966).
Stereo Headphone SRF-H5. 1997. ABS, 2 x
25 ⅝ x 5 ¹⁵⁄₁₆" (5 x 65 x 15 cm). Mfr.: Sony
Corp., USA, 1997

Right:
Yasufumi Yamaji (Japanese, b. 1968).
Caller ID Display TLID-10. 1997. ABS,
19 ¹¹⁄₁₆ x 3 ¹⁵⁄₁₆ x 6 ¹³⁄₁₆" (50 x 10 x 17.3 cm).
Mfr.: Sony Corp., USA, 1997

Below:
Enzo Mari (Italian, b.1932). Suva Letter
Tray. 1976. Technopolymer. Mfr.: Danese
Srl, Italy, 1987

This page and opposite (detail):
Shunji Yamanaka (Japanese, b. 1957).
Tagtype Keyboard. 2000. ABS and ther-
moplastic elastomer, 2⅛ x 5⁹⁄₁₆ x 5⅛"
(5.4 x 14.1 x 13 cm). Working prototype.
Mfr.: Leading Edge Design Corp., Japan,
2000

Tagtype is a new system for entering
Japanese text into a computer. It replaces
the traditional keyboard with a handheld controller, making input easier to
learn and ergonomically better. The
broad aim is to diminish the barrier
between the technologically illiterate or
less physically able and the information
society. The keyboard generates Japanese
HIRA letters, each of which consists of a
consonant and a vowel drawn from a
matrix of ten consonants and five vowels. The controller has ten main buttons,
each assigned one of ten consonants.
Then the vowel is entered. The two rows
of buttons are both assigned with the
five vowels. Most Japanese speakers
know the matrix of HIRA letters and will
therefore be able to quickly form a mental map relating to the Tagtype system,
thus facilitating the learning process. The
characteristic button layout of this system makes the product very compact so
it can be held comfortably in the hands
like a video game controller.

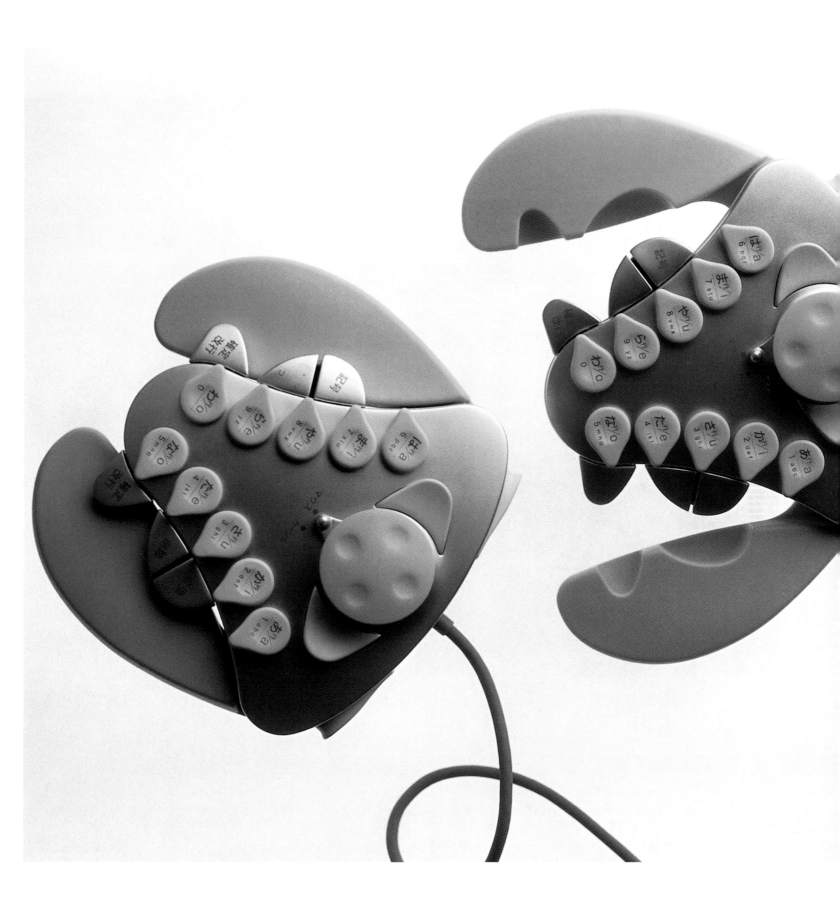

Noel Zeller (American, b. 1926). Mouse
Minder. 1995–96. ABS plastic, 5¾ x 3 x 7"
(13.3 x 7.6 x 17.8 cm). Mfr.: Zelco Industries Inc., USA, 1996

Eric Bertes (French, b. 1970). Stone Voice
Recorder. 1999. ABS plastic and quartz
LCD movement, 4¹¹⁄₁₆ x 3⅜ x 1" (11.9 x
9.2 x 2.2 cm). Mfr.: Lexon Design Concept, USA, 2000

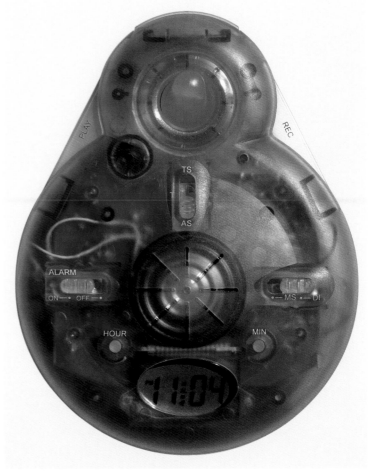

Jean-Marie Massaud (French, b. 1964). Prima Calculator (LC 30). 1994. ABS plastic and LCD screen, 3 $^{13}/_{16}$ x 1 $^{7}/_{8}$ x $^{3}/_{16}$" (9.7 x 4.8 x .1 cm). Mfr.: Lexon Design Concept, USA, 2000

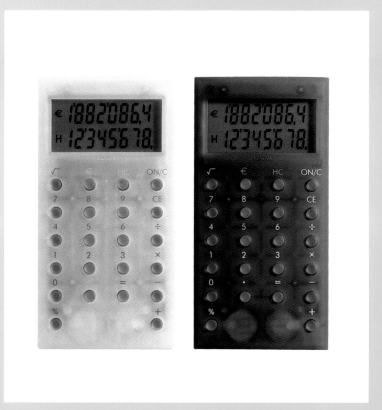

Marc Berthier (French, b. 1935) and Frédéric Linz (French, b. 1971). Euroquation Calculator (LC 34). 1997. ABS plastic and LCD screen, 4 $^{15}/_{16}$ x 2 x $^{3}/_{8}$" (12.5 x 5 x 1.4 cm). Mfr.: Lexon Design Concept, USA, 1998

Enzo Mari (Italian, b. 1932). Manhattan
Letter Trays. 1991. ABS, 2 x 9⅞ x 13" (5 x
25 x 33 cm). Mfr.: Danese Milano, Italy,
1992

Enzo Mari (Italian, b. 1932). Set Salina Blu desktop accessories. 1984. Glass. Pencil holder: 1$^9/_{16}$ x 11$^7/_{16}$ x 7$^1/_4$" (4 x 29 x 18.5 cm); paper holder: 1$^9/_{16}$ x 5$^3/_4$ x 7$^1/_4$" (4 x 14 x 18.5 cm); table calendar: 1$^9/_{16}$ x 8$^5/_8$ x 7$^1/_4$" (4 x 22 x 18.5 cm); letter tray: 2$^1/_4$ x 11$^3/_8$ x 15" (7 x 29 x 38 cm). Mfr.: Danese Milano, Italy, 1985

Sony Multiscan® N50PS liquid crystal display. 1999. Various materials. 9 x 12 x ¾" (23 x 30.5 x 2.3 cm). Mfr: Sony Electronics, USA, 2000

Masamichi Udagawa (Japanese, b. 1964), Sigi Moeslinger (Austrian, b. 1968), and Mitch Stein (American, b. 1955) of Antenna Design New York. IBM LifeNetwork InfoPortal. 1999. Injection-molded plastic and cast-aluminum structure, 17$\frac{1}{2}$ x 11$\frac{3}{16}$ x 17$\frac{5}{16}$" (44.5 x 28.4 x 44 cm). Prototype. Mfr.: IBM T. J. Research Center, USA, 2000

InfoPortal is a mobile information tablet that can stand on a flat surface or be docked and operated in a wall or counter-mounted configuration, with or without the use of an articulating arm. The mounting pillar also provides an easel-like support for use alone and folds away in the tablet configuration. In addition to an integrated video camera, which folds away when not in use, it features a fingerprint reader for biometric authentication, a hard button for deploying the on-screen soft keyboard, and an ingenious two-part articulated fold-away physical keyboard. All told, there are more than ten possible configurations of the basic system. Designed to take advantage of the latest advances in Human Computer Interaction technologies being developed by IBM Research, it contains a fully integrated "sensory bezel," a combination of sensing technologies that enable the InfoPortal to automatically adjust its user interface by sensing and reacting to the user's presence and position. The InfoPortal also introduces "touchless pointing," which allows the user to navigate the interface without physically touching the device or using any sort of stylus.

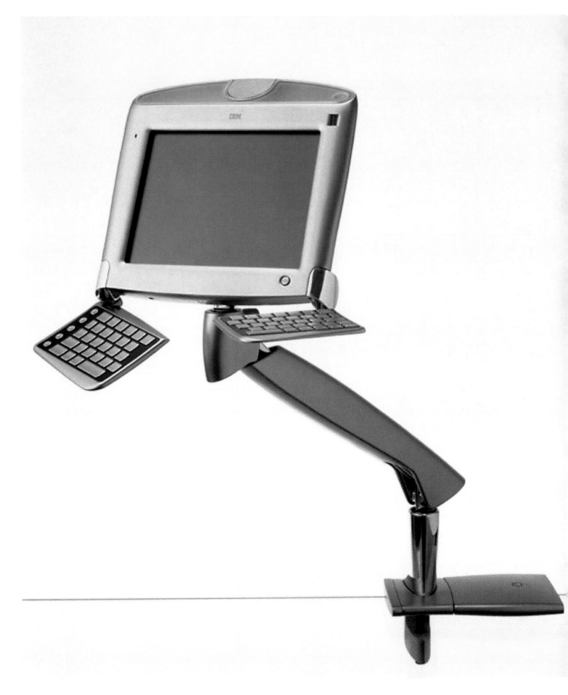

The Domestic Office

The home office requires fortitude and the ability to set boundaries and impose limits. Professional life and private life are invariably mutually exclusive, and their proximity can be dangerous. The conventional commute to work, which many scorn, provides a natural buffer between professional and private time. When that physical distance is obliterated, a psychological one needs to replace it to avoid malfunction. There are new words to describe this malaise, too. "Blending," for instance, is a term coined to define "a new mind-body problem," says Arlie Russell Hochschild of the University of California at Berkeley. "For some people, like your neighbors and sometimes your children, your body is there but your mind is not." Different home workers use different stratagems. Some clearly separate the work space with walls and doors, when available, or partitions, plants, screens, and colors. Others observe a very strict schedule, sometimes setting their work equipment on timers. Some even change clothes to go to the next room and perhaps take a walk around the block to simulate a commute.

As complex as the problem is at the individual level, working at home, if kept under control, can have several advantages and lead to overall satisfaction. In a family setting, for instance, "we see a kind of neo-medieval life with its close spatial integration of work and life, with kids seeing work done first-hand, demystifying both work and that portion of their parents' lives that they don't normally see," explains Michael Brill. More progress, Brill continues, can be seen "for community life, as the nature of the bedroom community alters due to the presence of more working adults, who need and use more local support services and amenities. Through this increased presence, people become more active and interested in local affairs, exert more control over the local economy and governance, and the community itself changes." The domestic office is a fascinating concept that engages design at all levels, from the urban and suburban scale, as new nodes need to be designed to provide workers with decentralized functions—from having meetings to accessing color copiers—to the architectural one, as homes have to be rethought to accommodate the new requirements.

Design can also become an important consideration in domestic office furniture. People who work at home and who need one or two workstations are less likely to buy their furniture from a large office systems manufacturer. The retail features are rarely available to individuals, the choices are more complicated, and the style appears at first glance too "official." They would rather go to a home furniture retailer and purchase the few solutions that are marketed under the "Home Office" label. So, while they will still have the warm feeling of furnishing a home, they will not take advantage of the research and development efforts that large companies have devoted for decades to ergonomy and rationality. Many such companies have recently started home-office divisions. Some, like Herman Miller, Knoll, and Vitra, have the advantage of having had a home division since their founding, and find it easier to merge lines and arrange for distribution. This section contains several suggestions of work-furniture designs that keep in mind the dual nature of the domestic office.

P. A.

Piercy Conner Architects. Concept for Shuflehouse. 2000. Computer rendering

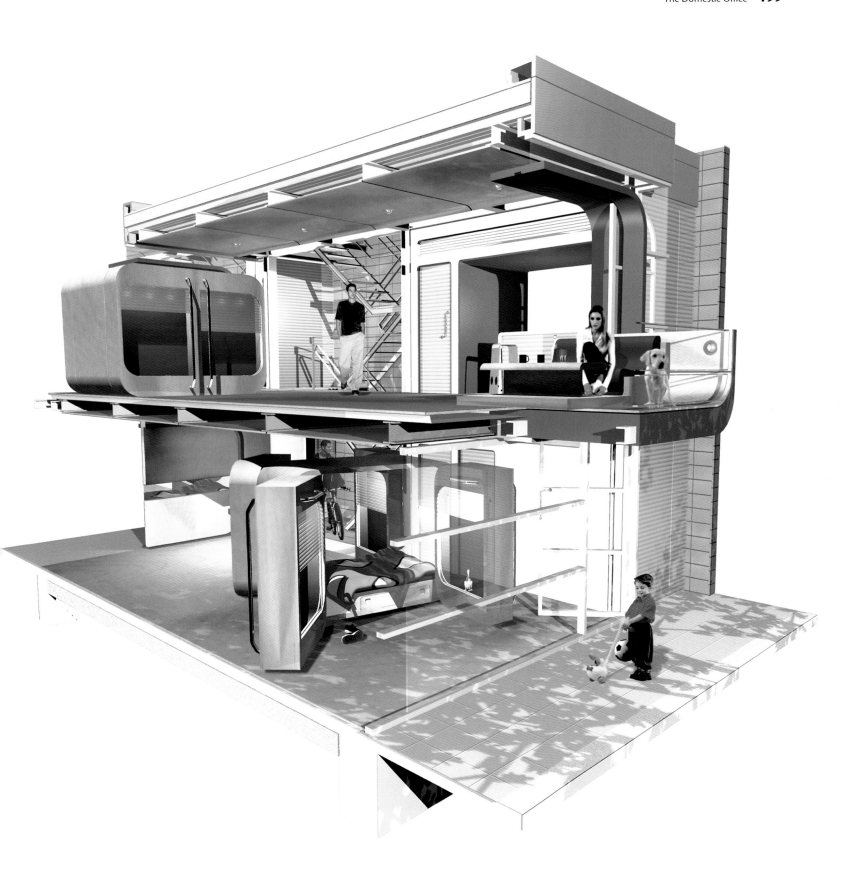

Opposite:
Konstantin Grcic (German, b. 1965). Scolaro. 2000. Beech and lamination, 29¾ x 29¾ x 63" (75 x 75 x 160 cm). Mfr.: Montina International, Italy, 2000

Right:
Edward Barber (British, b. 1969) and Jay Osgerby (British, b. 1969). Loop Desk. 1999. Plywood, veneer, and steel, 33¹⁄₁₆ x 53⅛ x 26⁹⁄₁₆" (84 x 135 x 67.5 cm). Mfr.: Cappellini SpA, Italy, 1999

Below:
Jörg Boner (Swiss, b. 1968) and Christian Deuber (Swiss, b. 1965). Ajax Writing Desk. c. 1998. Formed Multiplex with elm or birch veneer, 32¼ x 43¼ x 36¼" (81.9 x 109.9 x 92 cm). Mfr.: Classicon, Germany, c. 2000

Eunmee Hwang (South Korean, b. 1978).
Sprezuwing Jewel Maker Cabinet. 2000.
Maple, stainless steel, acrylic, MDF, and
maple veneer, 41 x 30 x 21" (104.1 x 76.2 x
53.3 cm). Prototype. Mfr.: Gratz Industries Inc., USA, 2000

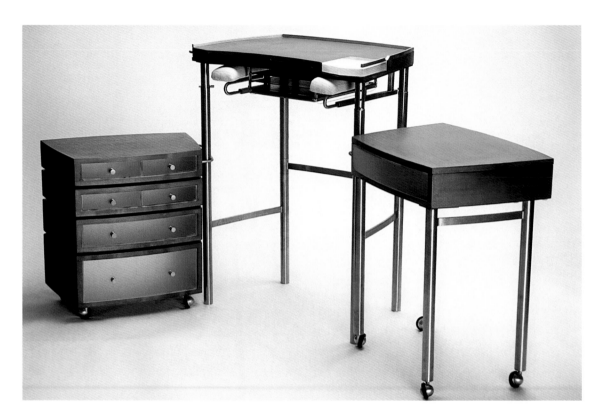

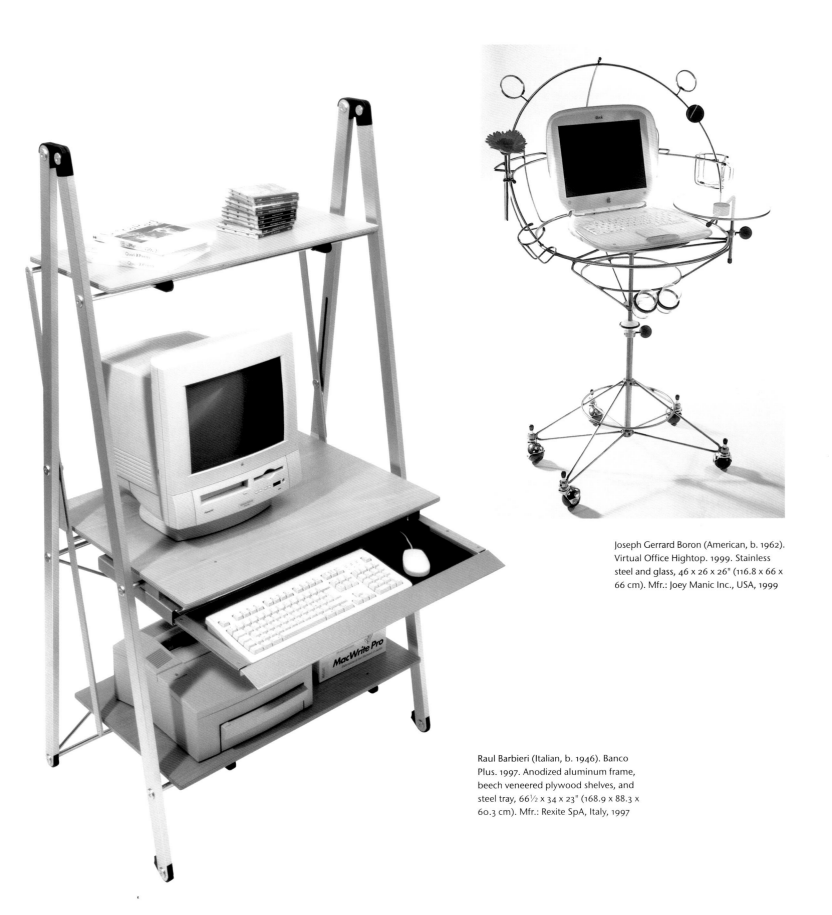

Joseph Gerrard Boron (American, b. 1962). Virtual Office Hightop. 1999. Stainless steel and glass, 46 x 26 x 26" (116.8 x 66 x 66 cm). Mfr.: Joey Manic Inc., USA, 1999

Raul Barbieri (Italian, b. 1946). Banco Plus. 1997. Anodized aluminum frame, beech veneered plywood shelves, and steel tray, 66½ x 34 x 23" (168.9 x 88.3 x 60.3 cm). Mfr.: Rexite SpA, Italy, 1997

Below:
Maurice Blanks (American, b. 1965), John Christakos (American, b. 1964), and Charles Lazor (American, b. 1964) of Blu Dot. 2D: 3D Wall Mount Magazine Rack. 1998. Powder-coated steel, 51 x 12 x 5½" (129.5 x 30.5 x 14 cm). Mfr.: Blu Dot, USA, 1998

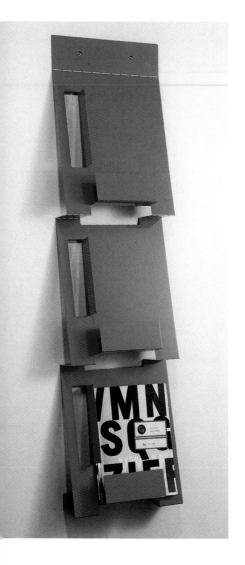

Above:
Blanks, Christakos, and Lazor. 2D: 3D Desk Top CD Holder. 1998. Powder-coated steel, 4 x 6 x 9" (10.2 x 15.2 x 22.9 cm). Mfr.: Blu Dot, USA, 1998

Center right:
Blanks, Christakos, and Lazor. 2D: 3D Catch-All Tray. 1998. Powder-coated steel, 1 x 8½ x 11½" (2.5 x 21.6 x 29.2 cm). Mfr.: Blu Dot, USA, 1998

Bottom right:
Blanks, Christakos, and Lazor. Stackable Files. 1997. Baltic birch plywood and powder-coated steel, 26 x 12½ x 22" (66 x 31.8 x 55.9 cm). Mfr.: Blu Dot, USA, 1998

Konstantin Grcic (German, b. 1965).
Mono A, B, C, D Ledgers. 1994. Powder-
coated steel, 25 ⅝ x 11 ¹³⁄₁₆ x 17 ¹¹⁄₁₆" (65 x
30 x 45 cm). Mfr.: SCP Ltd., UK, 1995

Right:
Ross Menuez (American, b. 1965). CEF Table. 1998. Pressed cloth solid core top, routed profile, and bent welded flat bar, 30 x 45 x 41" (76.2 x 114.3 x 104.1 cm). Prototype. Mfr.: Ross Menuez, USA, 1998

Below:
Konstantin Grcic (German, b. 1965). Prado Desk. 1995. Oak, 29 x 63 x 29" (75 x 160 x 75 cm). Mfr.: SCP Ltd., UK, 1996

Matali Crasset (French, b. 1965). Work at Hôm. 1996. Various materials. Chair: 32^{11}/$_{16}$ x 19 x 21" (83 x 48 x 55 cm); desk: 47 x 70^{7}/$_{8}$ x 23^{5}/$_{8}$" (120 x 180 x 60 cm). Prototype, 1996

Work at Hôm, a project for a domestic office, proposes a fusion between furniture and electronics. It focuses on the thinking process and it uses technology to simplify all administrative functions. It provides an instinctive and flexible configuration of the electronic equipment by taking advantage of wireless connections, applied to the interactive chair and the writing tablet.

Tom Lloyd (British, b. 1966) and Luke
Pearson (British, b. 1967). Homer. 1997.
Steel, aluminum, plastic, and wood, 25⅝
x 13 x 27³⁄₁₆" (65 x 35 x 69 cm). Mfr.: Knoll
International Inc., UK, 1998

Left:
Pascal Tarabay (Lebanese, b. 1970) and
Catalina Tobon (Colombian, b. 1975).
Riding Desk. 2000. Metal, wood, and
rubber, 10½ x 16 x 12" (27 x 41 x 31 cm).
Mfr.: Radice Snc, Italy, 2000

Below:
Jae Kyu Lee (Korea, b. 1964). Piano
Seduto (Seated Plan). 2000. Wood,
pillow, and polystyrene balls, 6 x 19½ x
13½" (16 x 50 x 35 cm). Mfr.: Radice Snc,
Italy, 2000

Workspheres: Six Commissioned Projects

Sarah Robins

In the spirit of The Museum of Modern Art's past design exhibitions and competitions, six design teams were invited to propose realistic solutions that address contemporary issues balancing work and life for the *Workspheres* exhibition. Projects at the Museum, such as the Low-Cost Furniture competition (1948), the Good Design series (1950–55), and the *Taxi Project* (1976), not only presented examples of outstanding design, highlighting the discipline as an art form in its own right, but also played a key role in shaping the design landscape in the United States. This tradition of groundbreaking exhibitions is responsible for such products as Charles Eames's and Eero Saarinen's early wood furniture for Herman Miller, as well as for Charles and Ray Eameses' later fiberglass series for the same manufacturer.

The commissioned projects for *Workspheres* originated with design briefs based on a broad body of research, comprising industry publications, architectural volumes, psychological and analytical studies and theses, newspaper and magazine articles, market research, convention and trade-fair catalogues, lecture transcripts, roundtable discussions, and brainstorming sessions. Each brief was intended to address contemporary frustrations with the workplace and facilitate our navigation and interaction with the numerous factors that influence contemporary life. Design teams were selected for specific briefs according to their previous experience and aptitude for the assigned task; collaborations with manufacturers and technology providers were fostered under the auspices of the Museum. The resulting environments, concepts, and objects are thus the product of multiple contributions, which each design team has incorporated into its proposed solution.

At the time of publication, each commission is still decidedly a work in progress, conceptually defined and currently in production. We hope these projects will provide a valid and thoughtful contribution to the current debate on the integration of knowledge work and contemporary life and draw attention to the integral role of design within the fray.

My Soft Office

Hella Jongerius of Jongeriuslab. Bed in Business. 2000

Hella Jongerius (Dutch, b. 1963), Jongeriuslab, Rotterdam

BRIEF: DOMESTIC OFFICE—A BETTER PARADIGM FOR WORKING AT HOME

More and more people are working at home, either self-employed or as part of a corporate program, but home offices are rarely "designed" and more frequently comprise spare rooms with office furniture and equipment added to them. A worksphere environment needs to be designed so that it can be re-created within an established structure. It should be able to manage physical smallness, minimal infrastructure, and variable conditions and demands, such as the presence of children, pets, elderly family members, the eating and rest functions of the home, etc.

THE PROJECT

Hella Jongerius's work is characterized by an innate sensitivity to materials, history, and juxtapositions: high and low technology; new and old materials; functional and aesthetic qualities. Her products often hold an element of surprise, provoking reconsideration of an object, its function, and the method by which it is to be used. Jongerius's design temperament is manifest in her Soft Office project for *Workspheres*, a series of domestic objects that incorporate technology into their very fabric, thereby facilitating a wide range of activities from within the home, rather than simply ascribing a traditional office environment to one room.

Bed in Business is a high-tech, extra-long bed that brings the tools of the workplace into the bedroom, the heart of domesticity, in an elaborate play on the concept of the home office. The bed, manufactured by the Dutch firm Auping, has corners that can be adjusted to upright and reclining positions in addition to horizontal orientation. Two of the four extremities are equipped with computer screens provided by IBM that may be lowered and raised in accordance with the user's preference, functioning as the foot of the bed. A keyboard and mouse are embedded in "smart pillows" that utilize touch sensor technology, the inherently tactile quality of textiles adapted to a functional use. "The ultimate symbol of rest and relaxation, of dreaming, doing nothing, sleeping, and making love has been fused with work, the symbol of rapid modernity, and with the hectic life of the world beyond the bed," says Jongerius. The introduction of technology into the bedroom not only provides the ability to work while in the comforting embrace of the bed, but also exploits the frequent phenomenon of creative thought while at rest and furnishes the means with which to immediately execute ideas.

Complementing the bed, Jongerius has also conceived Power Patches, cushions that encourage one to lounge comfortably on the floor while working at a computer. A compact version of the bed and pillows, the patches are portable and can thus be used in a bedroom, lounge, dining area, or porch/deck. Cushioned by a soft gel that molds to fit the contours of the body, produced by Royal Medica, Italy, the patches transform the traditionally rigid method of sitting upright to work at a computer into a more relaxed position that is integrated with domestic life. Moreover, the use of color and textile helps to discard the negative associations one may have of bringing work into the home. My Soft Office makes working at home both convenient and congenial to the multiple demands of contemporary life.

Jongerius. Power Patch. 2000

Inspiro-Tainers

Giuseppe Lignano and Ada Tolla of LOT/EK Architecture. A view of cargo containers in an airport. 2000

Giuseppe Lignano (Italian, b. 1963) and **Ada Tolla** (Italian, b. 1964) of LOT/EK Architecture, New York

BRIEF: A SPACE FOR CREATIVITY, ISOLATION, AND RELAXATION

Many businesses, whether technologically sophisticated start-ups or small cottage industries, originate in environments that were initially designed for another purpose: for instance, a spare bedroom in New York City; a garden shed in England; a garage in California; or a basement in Paris. Despite the lack of equipment or infrastructure of an official "office," these are often spaces that induce creativity and inspiration, perhaps precisely because they are not conventional office environments.

Is it possible to design such a space, one that facilitates both serious work and serious relaxation, to be inserted and used within an existing office? It should be a place where one can be isolated or in communication with others, be productive and have good ideas, nap, take a break, and be stimulated through web-browsing, listening to music, or reading. This unit should be modular and of relatively low cost, a realistic suggestion that foresees the potential growth and expansion of the business.

THE PROJECT

LOT/EK Architecture is a New York–based architecture studio that uses preexisting objects and materials as a foundation for its work in conscious reference to the contemporary urban landscape. Among many other projects, in 1998 they exhibited TV-Tank at Deitch Projects, namely, a gasoline tanker sliced into eight elliptical sections, each padded and equipped with

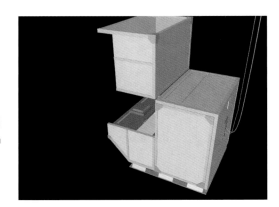

Lignano and Tolla. A view of the exterior of Inspiro-Tainer. 2000

seating and television monitors to provide a comfortable play station akin to a spaceship control deck in which the user would be in an almost reclining position.

Lignano and Tolla are noted for their attention to comfort and playfulness and for their skills and talents with existing containers within structured environments and were thus highly qualified for the brief. They proposed the transformation of an industrial container, used to air freight cargo, into a self-contained environment for work and relaxation. Set on castors, the Inspiro-Tainer is easily mobile and can thus be readily configured within a warehouse or similar space. Moreover, a preexisting panel can facilitate electric cabling, and ventilation and other climatic concerns can be accommodated.

Currently under construction, the container will be padded with soundproof foam. A right-angle cut into one corner will effectively give the pod a hinged lid, allowing the occupant options of privacy and isolation or open interaction with other containers with which it may be configured. Set against the angled end of the container is a reclining three-part chaise longue, also made of soft foam, that facilitates a range of positions between lounging and task, maneuvered both manually and by electric motor. In addition, the desk is embedded with a slim-line computer, keyboard, and mouse that can extend toward the reclining worker, or slide away and fold down against the opposite wall. The space is equipped with a DVD system, stereo, telephone, rear projector, large projection screen, and plexiglass panel that can become opaque or transparent so the screen may be viewed from within the pod or outside, acting as a communication device. Incredibly comfortable and, at the same time, fully equipped with the necessary tools for work and play, Inspiro-Tainer is, indeed, a decompression chamber for today's knowledge worker.

H!Bye

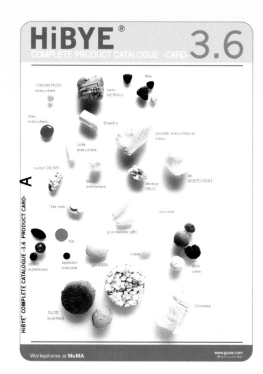

Martí Guixé. H!Bye
instruction card. 2000

Martí Guixé (Spanish, b. 1964), Barcelona and Berlin

BRIEF: NOMADIC OFFICE—COMMON SENSE TIPS FOR THE TRAVELING WORKER

A tool—perhaps a wearable computer—could help us cope with business travel, when we do not have everything at hand. Perhaps this object could offer new ways to relax or even reinterpret the memo pad, a way to retain thoughts and ideas and organize our lives. It should take into account the incompatibility between different countries, different methods of working—such as the effect of siesta on working hours—and the problems associated with taking many objects with you in order to work efficiently.

THE PROJECT

In many ways, Martí Guixé is the ideal candidate to be assigned the concept of nomadic work. Living and working between Barcelona and Berlin, Guixé is representative of the contemporary condition of work. Self-employed, contracted to work on multiple projects at any one time, he has an "office," which is, in fact, a room in his Barcelona apartment.

Guixé's preparation for the project involved both primary and secondary research. The former comprised travel within Europe, moving to a different city every two days over a period of three weeks. The latter involved library and Internet research and consultations. The resulting project, H!Bye, is a system of oral units designed to support nomadic work, providing the necessary elements to exploit the potential for interaction with new people and places, to accommodate the desire for familiar surroundings, and to work well in any environment. Guixé has designed these units in the form of pills, ensuring their portability and ease of use while commenting on the role this commodity plays in our

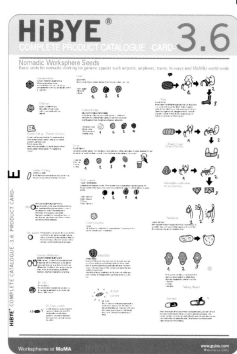

lives: the accepted habitual consumption of vitamins for good health, and of pharmaceuticals in times of sickness. Guixé offers us pills, ostensibly intended to help us work, but with the underlying implication that work, now conducted almost everywhere, is perhaps the drug with which we should most concern ourselves.

The fictitious system of twenty-one units is conceived for dispersion in generic environments such as airports, train stations, and hotels. Each unit pertains to either a psychological, physical, or personal concept and is based on real-time performance. Thus, the pill for concentration is nonedible, hard, and irregularly shaped, intended to be rolled around in the mouth during contemplative moments, much as one might chew the end of a pen or finger. The relaxation pill is instead soft and contains an herbal relaxant, operating as would a cigarette or chewing gum. The "go crazy" unit reacts with dental fillings. The pills are thus conceptual objects, and once explained their need is invalidated.

Model versions of each pill will be produced for the exhibition, based on consultations with a dietician and an anthropologist. An illustrated instruction card/menu of the pills with diagrams and explanations will be made available for the public to take away. Although H!Bye may not represent a literal product for consumption on your next business trip, it may prompt consideration of the mental and physical adjustments necessary to work away from home, the everyday tools of the nomadic worker.

Guixé. H!Bye. 2000

Mind'Space

Brian Alexander. Cell Storage. Filing cabinet from Flo Concept Work Station. 1997. Fiberglass, aluminum, steel, leather, and ABS, 48" x 6' x 48" (121.9 x 182.9 x 121.9 cm). Prototype. Mfr.: Haworth, Inc., USA, 1997

Jeff Reuschel (American, b. 1959) and **Ronna Alexander** (American, b. 1970) of Haworth, Inc.; **Brian Alexander** (American, b. 1963) of Optika Studios; **Christopher Budd** (American, b. 1958) and **Kevin Estrada** (Spanish, b. 1965) of Studios Architecture; and **W. Bradford Paley** (American, b. 1958) and **Hai Ng** (Singaporean, b. 1958) of Digital Image Design, New York

BRIEF: A NEW WORKSTATION FOR THE OFFICIAL OFFICE

In the final stages of commissioning projects for *Workspheres,* the three principals collaborating on this project—Jeff Reuschel, Christopher Budd, and Brad Paley—individually made proposals to the curatorial team for potential inclusion in the exhibition. Each had the common thread of using cognitive processes as the basis upon which to found their proposals, tools for use in the work environment that would exploit the way the brain functions. We suggested that the three parties collaborate on the project as each is associated with a company with a diverse focus—Haworth, Inc., Studios Architecture, and Digital Image Design, respectively—and thus able to contribute complementary resources and skills to the design and production of the workstation.

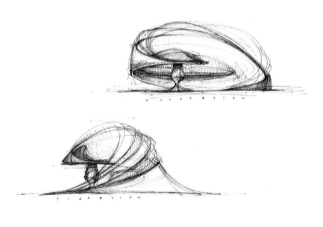

Jeff Reuschel and Ronna Alexander of Haworth, Inc.; Brian Alexander of Optika Studios; Christopher Budd and Kevin Estrada of Studios Architecture, with Brad Paley and Hai Ng of Digital Image Design. Mind'Space. 2000

THE PROJECT

Cognition is basically our ability to think and reason, our active or passive capability to solve problems, make judgments, think about past and future events, and provide the impetus for most of our actions. The state of cognition is how we perceive our environment, how we organize, retrieve, store, and analyze information to make meaning of the world. The Mind'Space project focuses on two of these cognitive processes: attention and memory.

Attention allows us to consciously focus on and filter information, selectively choosing some events and not others. The built model of the workspace will incorporate visual and auditory "input buffers," enabling the user to control the impact of his or her environmental surroundings. The workspace will also separate relevant from irrelevant or lower priority information and either subtly or obviously direct the user to it when most appropriate.

The cognitive process of memory, our ability to record, store, and retrieve information, is applied to Mind'Space by providing an environment that stores information-rich articles (artifacts). These artifacts can be thought of as a portal to a web of associated memory cues organized to bring before the user all information relevant to the particular artifact. An example of how memory theories can be applied to the work environment is a prototype designed by Haworth's Ideation Group in 1997. Cell Storage provides document storage, but rather than using a horizontal/vertical grid format, the system presents the user with irregularly shaped and positioned spaces, which make their contents easier to remember because each cell is unique. Thus, in much the same way as a Post-It® note suggests that attention must be paid to the information written on it, Mind'Space connects a web of associations and sensory cues—visual, auditory, olfactory, and tactile—that signal the user to recall and retrieve that information.

personal skies

Naoto Fukasawa (Japanese, b. 1956) and IDEO, Tokyo

BRIEF: INDIVIDUALITY WITHIN A STRONG CORPORATE IDENTITY

The issue of managing personalization, customization, and privacy within the corporate world is one of much debate. How does one manage to retain his or her own sphere within the boundaries of the organization? This project involves the design of a network of collaborators and considers human behavior and social relationships.

Fukasawa's consciousness of the impact of design on social and work behaviors clearly suggested his aptitude for the task. In initial discussions, for instance, he noted the effect of technology on people's movements, such as the use of mobile phones to access the Internet while waiting on train station platforms, leaning against a wall, or walking along Braille tiles, unconsciously aware of their surroundings. Concepts for the project included further reflections about territoriality, such as a small robot whose function is to set personal boundaries, a flexible bench that would mark dedicated space, a chair that would follow its owner, and a desk whose surface would immediately change to accommodate new objects, such as a computer or a coffee cup.

THE PROJECT

Fukasawa's project comprises two tools that can enhance individuality and privacy: a chair that changes color; and a personalized environment. The chair and environment are poetic gestures that bring a sense of humor and whimsy to the workplace. The chair adapts to the clothing of the user like a chameleon. The final component of the project extends this concept further by projecting the ceiling of choice above one's desk. Thus, one can use images of the sky in various seasons and weather conditions or a particular location, one's home, or a favorite vacation spot. Like the screen saver on one's computer desktop, the projected image not only delineates the user's space, but also sends a visible personal message to the rest of the office.

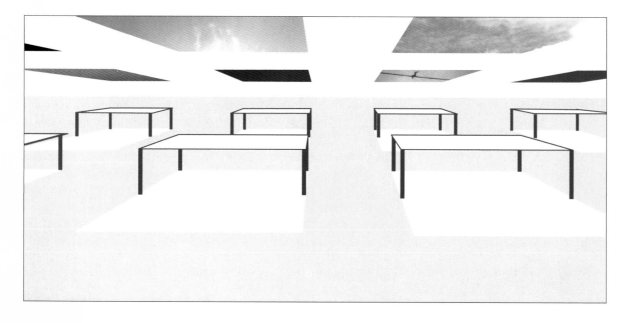

Naoto Fukasawa and IDEO.
personal skies. 2000

MIT Media
Laboratory.
Atmosphere.
2000

John Maeda (American, b. 1966) and **Joe Paradiso** (American, b. 1955) of MIT Media Laboratory, Cambridge, Massachusetts, with **Ari Benbasat** (American, b. 1975), **Elise Co** (American, b. 1976), **Mark Feldmeier** (American, b. 1974), and **Ben Fry** (American, b. 1975)

BRIEF: REDESIGNING TIME
One of the most apparent and widespread problems today is a sense of loss of control over time and information. Regardless of the industry in which one works, it is necessary to have a schedule and routines, whether one chooses to abide by them or break the rules. But as communication tools have slimmed down and become easier to use, the amount of information one receives daily has greatly increased, often so much as to seem unmanageable. Just as the Filofax revolutionized how people consider time and communication, this brief calls for a new, innovative interface product or software to assist people in the organization of their lives.

THE PROJECT
John Maeda's work at the MIT Media Laboratory is consistently innovative, has a highly practical application, and often causes one to marvel at its ingenuity. For *Workspheres*, Maeda has assembled a team of young and experienced designers and engineers, adapting preexisting technology to create a new information interface to manage scheduling and store data such as address books, documents, and spreadsheets.

Atmosphere presents a large cloud of information on a wide presentation screen that can be manipulated by three handheld devices mounted on plinths within the gallery space. The visitor takes one of the devices and physically moves it within a designated area, thereby manipulating the information presented both on the screen and the larger projection. All three devices are able to navigate the same information, but each at a different level of detail—macro, medium, and micro. Thus one might project all the research for a project onto the larger screen and use the macro device to show how the work was initially divided into smaller components, the second to illustrate more detail, and the final tool to show specific points or conclusions, for example, individual documents, correspondence, and notes. The interface presents not only the discrete information but also an organic ensemble view of the intensity of each project and the workload impact distributed across time. The interface has significant potential as a tool for group presentations, organizing the data in a more immediate visual format rather than as the folders and windows to which we have quickly become accustomed through computer usage.

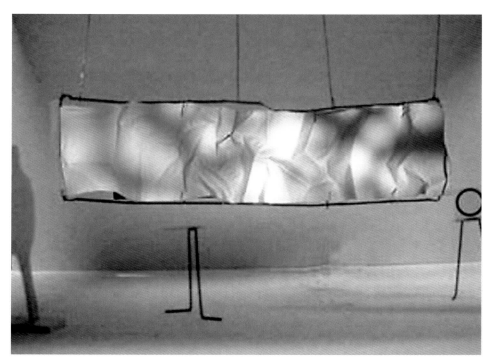

John Maeda and Joe Paradiso of MIT Media Laboratory,
with Ari Benbasat, Elise Co, Mark Feldmeier, and Ben Fry.
Atmosphere. 2000

Acknowledgments

The planning of *Workspheres* began in 1999, and both the exhibition and publication, of necessity, kept to a fast-paced schedule. A complicated undertaking such as this owes its success to the crucial support of numerous colleagues and friends. Many have gone out of their way to help bring this exhibition to fruition, and I owe them an enormous debt of gratitude for their magnanimity of time and effort.

On behalf of The Museum of Modern Art, I wish to thank the designers and manufacturers featured in the exhibition, catalogue, and website for their cooperation, enthusiasm, and generosity. I also want to thank the sponsors for making this endeavor possible; the lenders for agreeing to part, temporarily, with their possessions; and, in particular, the companies and individuals who made generous commitments to various parts of the exhibition and catalogue. Among them are Lee Green, David Hill, and Richard Bartell of IBM, who provided the technology that powers Hella Jongerius's My Soft Office, and Auping Beds, the Dutch company that provided Bed in Business; Manfred Gollent at Nordisk Aviation Products, who lent the two containers for LOT/EK's Inspiro-Tainers; Christine Belich and Jacqueline Krueger of Sony Style for their generous loan of Sony products and their assistance; Crestron for the technology to control the Inspiro-Tainer, Bosch Domestic Appliances in Germany, and Tulp Kitchens and the Mondriaan Foundation in The Netherlands for their support of Henk Stallinga's kitchen model; Takayuki Harada at Inter.office in Tokyo, as well as the Mori Corporation and Maxray Company for their support of Hiroaki Kitano's project; Ralph Pucci at Pucci International for providing the mannequins in the exhibition; Steelcase and Haworth, who, in addition to sponsoring the exhibition, also became deeply involved in two commissions, Atmosphere and Mind'Space, respectively; and finally Massimo Losio and Francesca Bigolin at Royal Medica in Italy for their invaluable help with several projects, including Hella Jongerius's My Soft Office and Takahashi Mirei's Wave Chair. Particular thanks go to IDEO, especially to Whitney Mortimer and David Kelley, for providing so many choices and so much support, and to Bran Ferren and Thomas Ritter for getting the MaxiMog here in the first place, in time and in two pieces.

In the research phase, I was assisted first and foremost by my Advisory Board, and my gratitude goes to Larry Keeley, Bruce Mau, Aura Oslapas, and John Thackara for giving me endless inspiration and advice. Über experts Michael Brill, Jay Chiat, Francis Duffy, Rolf Fehlbaum, Volker Hartkopf, Despina Katsikakis, Andrew Laing, and Robert Luchetti were our authoritative and imaginative interlocutors throughout the process, allowing us to interview them and giving us useful information and insights.

Many friends and colleagues sent ideas and objects for consideration from all over the world and gave precious advice and assistance. I would like to thank them all, but space limitations make this impossible. However, I must single out the following: Jan Abrams, George Beylerian, Fernando and Humberto Campana, Martha Davis, the Danish Design Center, Beth Dickstein, Peter and Stephen Doyle, Margaret Durkan, Georgia Everse, Michele Foyer, Bruce Hannah, Sam Hecht, Arlene Hirst, Marcelo Jünemann, Lisa Krohn, Victoria Milne, Susan Morris, Jane Nisselson, Patrick Norguet, Bruce Nussbaum, Satyendra Pakhale, Allen Prusis, John and Mitchell Rasor, Julie Saul, Turkey Stremmel, Hiroko Sueyoshi, Julie Taylor, and Tony Whitfield. One person who deserves special recognition is Larry Carty.

For their contributions of enlightening and entertaining video interviews about work habits in different parts of the world, I wish to thank Ahn Sang-Soo (Korea), Claudio Arango (Colombia), Georg Bertsch (Germany), Dimitri Bodiansky (France), Mei Mei Ding and Szu-i Wang (Taiwan), Lia Ferrari (Italy), Martí Guixé (Spain), Serge Khripoun (Russia), Lisa Krohn (Los Angeles), Wu Liang (China), Suzanne Linders (The Netherlands), Jane Nisselson (New York), Kayoko Ota (Japan), Trine Fogh Petersen (Denmark), Fernanda Sarmento Barata (Brazil), Anne Sim (New Zealand), Rachel Strickland and Susan Faulkner (San Francisco), Ali Tayar (Turkey), and Ezri Terazi (Israel).

The staff at The Museum of Modern Art deserves special acknowledgment for their enthusiastic support of this endeavor. In particular, I thank Agnes Gund, President, and Ronald Lauder, Chairman of the Board, knowledgeable and enthusiastic fans of design; Glenn D. Lowry, Director, whose early and unwavering support was crucial to the realization of the exhibition; Jennifer Russell, Deputy Director for Exhibitions and Collections Support, for successfully bringing this huge ship to port; and Kirk Varnedoe, Chief Curator, Department of Painting and Sculpture, who graciously permitted the special installation of the MaxiMog in the Garden Hall. I also thank the Contemporary Arts Council for their solid support; Maria de Marco, Coordinator of Exhibitions, for patiently working out the complicated administrative details attached to such a short-term project; Jennifer Wolfe, Senior Assistant Registrar, and John Alexander, Assistant Registrar, for keeping track of so many diverse loan items scattered in dimensions, location, and time; Mary Lou Strahlendorff, Director of Communications, Kim Mitchell, Assistant Director of Communications, and especially Kena Frank, Press Representative, for taking such good care of the press and creating an extraordinary buzz; Michael Margitich, Deputy Director, External Affairs, Monika Dillon, Director, and Jennifer Grausman, Manager, Exhibition Funding, Rebecca Stokes, Director, Campaign Services, and Robert I. Smith, Jr., Manager, Corporate Relations, for their efforts in securing funding for the show. I also wish to thank Stephen Clark, Associate General Counsel, and Nancy Adelson, Assistant General Counsel, for their invaluable advice; Josiana Bianchi in the Department of Education; and my colleague Barbara London for her input and for lending the video that is featured in the Jongerius installation.

A special acknowledgment and my eternal gratitude go to the Department of Publications, headed by Michael Maegraith. Despite this unusually hurried and complex project, he was nonetheless open to all ideas. I want to particularly thank Joanne Greenspun, Editor, for her guidance and for her supervision of the editorial process, and Christina Grillo, Senior Production Assistant, who solved all problems and kept everyone on schedule. The two of them, under exceptional time constraints, are to be commended for this book's appearance in time for the exhibition. Many thanks also to Antony Drobinski, who designed the catalogue beautifully and also quickly. Ed Pusz, Director of Graphics, assisted by Claire Corey, Production Manager, is responsible for the unique *Workspheres* identity featured on the cover, as well as for the graphics throughout the exhibition and its installation.

The installation was indeed a momentous challenge even for our heroic Department of Exhibition Production and Design, directed by Jerome Neuner. Jerry designed the installations, and his incomparable crew, which includes among others Andrew Davies,

Production Manager, actually made it happen. My gratitude goes to them and to K Mita, Manager of Public Technology, assisted by Tanya Beeharrilall and Marianne Goguillon, who performed miracles in order to ensure that the complex technology in the commissioned projects and website kiosks worked smoothly and effectively. For the *Workspheres* website, which has been designed by Method, my thanks go to Astrida Valigorsky, Director of New Media, George Hunka, outstanding Producer, and Bennett Simpson, who not only edited the website with me and contributed a striking photo essay, but also was an inexhaustible source of new ideas and a precious interlocutor. Maggie Lederer, Producer, set up the public survey preliminary to the exhibition.

In the Department of Architecture and Design, I am grateful to Terence Riley, Chief Curator, who believed strongly in this exhibition and offered his support throughout the project. The entire department was supportive and helpful, and I thank each of its members, especially Nobi Nakanishi, our Executive Assistant. Several interns worked on the exhibition and the catalogue and for their efforts I thank Claudia Atencia, Lianor da Cunha, Elyse Deeb, Kristina Kaufman, Emily Kinnemann, Jade Niklai, and Trine Petersen. Thank also to Ulrike Andres for her translations from German.

Lastly, I would like to thank the person with whom I shared all the adventure, Sarah Robins. She was a tireless and indispensable interlocutor in this project, an inventive problem-solver, and an extraordinary improviser, a highly valuable trait in an exhibition of this kind.

This book is dedicated to Jay Chiat and Francis Duffy, two great innovators who, in their own peculiar, personal, imperfect, yet groundbreaking way, are always seeking to bring more humanity and creativity to the workplace.

Paola Antonelli
Curator, Department of Architecture and Design

Photograph Credits

Action Office (Herman Miller), 15, 28, 61
Action Office 2 (Herman Miller), 29, 30
Alexander, Brian: Drift, 103; Flo Concept Work Station, 102; Mind'Space, 215
Alexander, Ronna: Mind'Space, 215
Allen, Davis, 27, 30
Anttonen, Sari: Kiss Chair, 125
Apple Industrial Design Group: Apple Pro Mouse, 172; Apple Studio Display, 174; Cinema Display, 173; G4 Cube with Studio Display, 173; iBook Portable Computer, 161; iMac Desktop Computers, 172
Askainenen, Teppo: Netsurfer, 98
Asprey and Garrard Design: Sterling Silver Internet Mouse, 180

Ball, Douglas, 30
Baloga, Mark: The Personal Harbor® Workspace, 92, 93
Barber, Edward: Loop Desk, 201
Barbera, Joe, 18
Barbieri, Raul: Babele Letter Tray, 177; Banco Plus, 203
Baroli, Luigi: Cartoons Screens, 114, 115
Beaujays, Christophe: Écharpe Communicante (communicating scarf), 156, 157
Becker, Franklin, 33
Bellini, Claudio: Ypsilon Chair, 108
Bellini, Mario: Figura 2000, 119; Ypsilon Chair, 108
Benbasat, Ari: Atmosphere, 217
Bentham, Jan: Netherlands Design Institute, Amsterdam, 36, 37, 41, 42
Bergne, Sebastian: IXIX—Universal Table, 126, 127
Bergson, Henry, 38
Bernstrand, Thomas: Do Swing Ceiling Lamp, 116; Newspaper Recycle Carrier, 130; Sugar Ray, 116, 117
Bertes, Eric: Stone Voice Recorder, 192
Berthier, Marc: Euroquation Calculator, 193
Beukema, Steve: Chunk Houses, 104; Eddy, 102, 103; Idea Factory Installation, version C, 104, 105; Idea Factory Installation, version E, 104, 105; Idea Factory Installation, version F, 105
Birsel, Ayse: Red Rocket Desk, 100, 101; Resolve, 94, 95

Blanks, Maurice: Stackable Files, 204; 2D: 3D Catch-All Tray, 204; 2D: 3D Desk Top CD Holder, 204; 2D: 3D Wall Mount Magazine Rack, 204
Bone, Martin: IDEO 2010 Concepts, 166, 167
Boner, Jörg: Ajax Writing Desk, 201
Boron, Joseph Gerrard: Virtual Office Hightop, 203
Boucher, Andy: Double Deck Desk 2, version A, 74; Double Deck Desk 2, version B, 75; Double Deck Desk 4, version A, 74; Double Deck Desk 5, version F and Digital Display, 74
Brebner, Alexander: Mystery Book, 170, 171
Bretford Design Studios: Free Multi Plus Workstation, 96, 97
Brill, Michael, 14, 33
Brodbeck, Stefan: Werndl™ Emerge™ Desk, 99
Brown, John Seely, 41, 43
Brucha, Bernard: Swell Station, options 1 and 3, 83
Brunner, Robert: Stowaway Portable Keyboard, 155
Budd, Christopher: Mind'Space, 215
Bunshaft, Gordon, 26, 27; Union Carbide Building (later Manufacturers Hanover), NYC, 26, 27
Burdick, Bruce: Burdick Group Furniture, 89
Bürolandschaft, 28, 30

Campana, Fernando and Humberto: Images from "Street Business, Street Leisure," 9
Carnegie Mellon University, Pittsburgh, 70, 96
Cassirer, Ernst, 38
Castells, Manuel, 36
Centre de Recherche et Développement, Rennes, France: Cosmo Digital Mobile Phone, 165
Chadwick, Donald: Aeron Office Chair, 108, 111
Chan, Eric: Kiva Pebble Table, 87; Kiva Wing Table, 87; Red Spider Neck, 100, 101
Chia, Benjamin: Stowaway Portable Keyboard, 155
Chiat/Day offices (Pesce; Wilkinson), 14–15, 24, 34, 35, 71, 170
Chiat, Jay, 10, 14, 15
Chorpach, Rama: Red Spider Neck, 100, 101
Christakos, John: Stackable Files, 204; 2D: 3D Catch-All Tray, 204; 2D: 3D Desk Top CD Holder, 204; 2D: 3D Wall Mount Magazine Rack, 204
Christensen, Folmer: Classic Folle Stapler, 188;

Document Holders, 188; Paper Knife, 188; Tape Dispenser, 188
Citterio, Antonio: AC2 Chair, 120; Ad Hoc System, 84, 85; Axess, 118; T-Chair, 118
Co, Elise: Atmosphere, 217
Conner, Piercy: Concept for Shuflehouse, 198, 199; Full Pod, 21
Corpuz, Rogue: Idea Factory Installation, version C, 104, 105; Idea Factory Installation, version E, 104, 105; Idea Factory Installation, version F, 105
Cox, Jack, 96
Crasset, Matali: Artican (baskets), 178; Téo de 2 à 3 Folding Mattress, 131; Work at Hôm, 207
Crouwel, Mels: Netherlands Design Institute, Amsterdam, 36, 37, 41, 42

Décolletage Plastique Design Team: Bic Cristal, 175
Delacroix, Eugène, 43
Demeulemeester, Ann: Table Blanche, 113
Deuber, Christian: Ajax Writing Desk, 201
Diaz, Orlando, 30
Diffrient, Niels, 16, 108; Freedom Chair, 115
Donaldson, Robin: Alumina, 88
Draudt, Greg: The Personal Harbor® Workspace, 92, 93
Dreyfuss, Henry, 16, 108
Drucker, Peter, 18
Duffy, Francis, 14, 33
Duguid, Paul, 41

Eames, Charles, 8, 211
Eames, Ray, 41
Eckhardt, Claus-Christian: Siemens S42 Cellular Phone, 164
Eich, Tom: IDEO 2010 Concepts, 166, 167; Leap Chair, 112
Einstein, Albert, 25
Elders, Thomas: IDEO 2010 Concepts, 166, 167
Elephant Design: TPF Fax Machine, 185
Ericsson: Bluetooth™ Access System, 145; Communicator Platform, 146, 147; Ericsson T18 with Chatboard™, 146; Headset and T28 World Cell Phone, 144; R3805 Cellular Phone, 146, 147

Eriksson, Steven: The Personal Harbor® Workspace, 92, 93
Estrada, Kevin: Mind'Space, 215
Ethospace (Herman Miller), 32, 33, 61

Fayol, Henri, 28
Felderman and Keatinge Design: Fabergé Corporate Headquarters, NYC, 19; Interface Americas Corporate Headquarters, Cartersville, Georgia, 17; MTV Network West Coast Headquarters, Santa Monica, California, 23
Feldmeier, Mark: Atmosphere, 217
Ferren, Bran: MaxiMog Global Expedition Vehicle System, 168, 169
Financial Times (London), 12, 16
Fischer, Steve: Intellimouse Optical Mouse, 180
Fitzgerald, Gary: Jump Stuff Desktop Accessories, 176
F&L Design: I Satelliti S/200 Office System, 72, 73
Ford, Henry, 20
Formway Design Studios: Free Maxi Workstation—Double Level, 96, 97; Free Mini Workstation—Double Level, 96, 97
Fry, Ben: Atmosphere, 217
Fry, Ken: Intellimouse Optical Mouse, 180
Fukasawa, Naoto: personal skies, 216

Galezowski, Rick: Spandrobe, 91
Gaver, William: Double Deck Desk 2, version A, 74; Double Deck Desk 2, version B, 75; Double Deck Desk 4, version A, 74; Double Deck Desk 5, version F and Digital Display, 74
Gehry, Frank, 15, 56, 108
Gell Mann, Murray, 39–40
Goto, Teiyu: Vaio/PCG-250C Laptop Computer, 140
Grant, Margo, 30
Grcic, Konstantin: Mono A, B,C, D Ledgers, 205; 1 + 1=1, 108, 109; Prado Desk, 206; Scolaro, 200, 201
Grettve, Dan: Le Tosh Working Snob, 159, 160
Gruetzer, John, 132
Guarnaccia, Steven, 18
Guixé, Martí: H!Bye, 214
Guru.com advertisement, 10

Haller, Fritz: Group of Office Components, 80, 81
Hampden-Turner, Charles, 39
Hannigan, Jeffrey: Portable Person, 132, 133
Harman Kardon iSub Subwoofer for Apple iMac, 174
Hassam, Arriz: Rug, 90; Work Table, 91
Hecht, Sam, 83; Axis Hotel System, 82, 83; San Fran Furniture System, 82, 83
Hendriks, Bart, "Frederique," 8
Hertzberger, Herman: Centraal Beheer Office Building, Apeldoorn, The Netherlands, 30, 35, 61

Higgins, Colin, Nine to Five, 30, 31
Hill, David: IBM NetVista X40i, 186; IBM ThinkPad 570, 187
Hobbes, Thomas, 19
Hochschild, Arlie Russell, 198
Holbrook, Richard: Levity Interaction Tower, 107
Hudson, Sofia Anna Varanka: Field Office, 152, 153
Hut, Thomas, 15
Hwang, Eunmee: Sprezuwing Jewel Maker Cabinet, 202

Idea Factory, 105
Ideation Group (Haworth), 105
iGo Design Team: Road Warrior International Access Pack AC and RJ 11 Bundle, 158
Illich, Ivan, 38

Jahns, Henner: Alumina, 88; Swell Station, options 1 and 3, 83
Jones, Andrew: Jack Flexible Workstation, 90
Jongerius, Hella: My Soft Office, 212
Joy, Bill, 10

Kaci, Yacine Aït: Écharpe Communicante (communicating scarf), 156, 157
Kaliber 10000 (screen shot), 13
Kalman, Tibor: Mystery Book, 170, 171; Paperweight, 174, 175
Kantor, Elizabeth Moss, 41
Kao, John, 105
Kersner, Scott, 56
Kitano, Hiroaki, 96; Symbiotic Systems Project Office: 14, 15
Knoll, Frances, 27
Knoll, Hans, 27
Knoll Design Team: The Calibre Collection, 81
Kohn, Martin: Spandrobe, 91
Kolatan, Sulan: Slices Furniture Line: Executive Table, 79; Slices Furniture Line: Junior Table, 78
Koronyo, Eliron: Ground Zero: Privacy in Public Space, 139
Krolopp, Rudolph: Pageboy Pagers, 138

Landa, Manuel de, 41
Laviani, Ferruccio: Max Table, 110
Lazarus, Arnold, 24
Lazor, Charles: Stackable Files, 204; 2D: 3D Catch-All Tray, 204; 2D: 3D Desk Top CD Holder, 204; 2D: 3D Wall Mount Magazine Rack, 204
Ledbetter, Carl: Intellimouse Optical Mouse, 180
Lee, Jae Kyu: Piano Seduto, 209
Leino, Jouni: Link X Chair, 106; Web Table, 106
Lenskog, Anna: Le Tosh Working Snob, 160
Leonard, Brian: IBM NetVista X40i, 186
Lignano, Giuseppe: Inspiro-Tainer, 213

Lindberg, Ann, 158, 159
Linz, Frédéric: Euroquation Calculator, 193
Lloyd, Tom: Homer, 208
Löw, Glen Oliver: AC2 Chair, 120; Ad Hoc System, 84, 85; Axess, 118; T-Chair, 118
Lucchi, Michele de: Artjet 10 Bubble Ink-Jet Printer, 182; Artjet 20 Bubble Ink-Jet Printer, 182, 183
Luchetti, Robert, 32, 34, 35

MacColl, Ian: San Fran Furniture System, 82, 83
Mac Donald, William: Slices Furniture Line: Executive Table, 79; Slices Furniture Line: Junior Table, 78
McGregor, Douglas, 29
McKay, Donald: Meadow Call Center, 90
McKinsey & Company, 24-25
McLoone, Hugh: Intellimouse Optical Mouse, 180
Maeda, John: Atmosphere, 217
Mangurian, Robert: Cabinet Vest, 134; Portable Person, 132, 133
Mann, Steve, 132
Manufacturers Hanover Building; see Union Carbide
Mari, Enzo: In Attesa baskets, 179; Manhattan Letter Trays, 194; Set Salina Blu Desktop Accessories, 195; Suva Letter Tray, 189
Marianelli, Giorgio: Babele Letter Tray, 177
Martin, Heather: Double Deck Desk 2, version A, 74; Double Deck Desk 2, version B, 75; Double Deck Desk 4, version A, 74; Double Deck Desk 5, version F and Digital Display, 74
Maslow, Abraham, 22
Massaud, Jean-Marie: Prima Calculator (LC 30), 193
Means, Bridget: Squiggle Mouse Pad, 181; Zago Folding Trash Cans, 178
Meda, Alberto: Meda 2 Chair, 121
Meda, Luca: Misura Office System, 72, 73
Mendini, Alessandro: Cioccolator Pad Calculator, 185
Menuez, Ross: CEF Table, 206
Mestaoui, Naziha: Écharpe Communicante (communicating scarf), 156, 157
Milder, Jonas: Workstation, 88
Miller, Jeff: Kiva Pebble Table, 87; Kiva Wing Table, 87; Red Spider Neck, 101
MIT Media Lab, Cambridge, Mass., 64, 96
Moeslinger, Sigi: IBM LifeNetwork InfoPortal, 197
Moggridge, Bill: Axis Hotel System, 82, 83
Morrison, Jasper: Tate Chairs, 128, 129
Motorola: advertisement, 12; Mobile Telephone System, 136
Myerson, Jeremy, 132

Nagele, Albert: Dyna Tac (cellular handset), 136; Star Tac Cellular Telephone, 137; V3620 Cellular Telephone, 137
Naisbitt, John, 18
Nelson, George, 29
Netherlands Design Institute, Amsterdam, 36, 37, 41, 42
Noguchi, Yukio, 16
Nokia Design International: Nokia 8850/8890 Digital Phone, 151; Nokia 9110 Digital Phone, 151; 3G Terminal Concept I, 150; 3G Terminal Concept III, 150
Ng, Hai: Mind'Space, 215

Opsvik, Peter: Capisco Chair, 123
Osgerby, Jay: Loop Desk, 201
Overthun, Thomas: Leap Chair, 112

Pakhale, Satyendra, 10
Paley, W. Bradford: Mind'Space, 215
Palm Company Design: Palm m100 Handheld and Cradle, 154
Paradiso, Joe: Atmosphere, 217
Pearson, Luke: Homer, 208
Pellone, Giovanni: Squiggle Mouse Pad, 181; Zago Folding Trash Cans, 178
Pesce, Gaetano: Chiat/Day offices, 15, 24, 34, 170
Pineus, Jennie: Cocoonchair, 162, 163; Headcocoons, 162
Plummer, Henry, 38
Prada Sport Design Team, 148, 149
Propst, Robert, 15, 29, 30, 32, 61; Action Office 2, 29

Quickbourner Group, 28, 35

Ray, Mary-Ann: Cabinet Vest, 134; Portable Person, 132, 133
Reddig, Ralph: Idea Factory Installation, version C, 104, 105; Idea Factory Installation, version E, 104, 105; Idea Factory Installation, version F, 105
Reuschel, Jeff: Mind'Space, 215; Sit-Stand Chair, 104
Reuter, Robert: Currents Office System, 73
Riccardi, Douglas: Mystery Book, 170, 171
Ritter, Thomas: MaxiMog Global Expedition Vehicle System, 168, 169
Roericht, Hans: Stitz 2 Stools, 124
Royal College of Art, Appliance Design Studio, London, 75
Rozier, Charles: Currents Office System, 73
Russell, Bertrand, 24

Saarinen, Eero, 8, 211
Sachs, Jane, 15
Sapper, Richard: IBM NetVista X40i, 186; IBM

ThinkPad 570, 187
Sarrazin, Laurence: Banana Bag, 184; Banana Wrist Pad, 184
Sawhney, Ravi: Lapstation, 142
Scheper, Robert: Please Chair, 122
Schudel, Paul: Wall Clock DK, 45
Scott, Caudill Rowlett, 30
Seifried, D, 38
Severen, Maarten van: Schraag Table, 110
Shubin, Russell: Alumina, 88
Siebert, Paul: The Personal Harbor® Workspace, 92, 93
Simons, George: Leap Chair, 112
Skidmore, Owings & Merrill (SOM): Connecticut General Life Insurance Company, 27; Lever House, 27, 28; Manufacturers Hanover Building, 27; Pepsi-Cola Building, 27; Union Carbide Building, 26, 29, 34
Sogabe, Takashi: Digital Blocks, 135
Sony Multiscan® N50PS Liquid Crystal Display, 196
Soren, Leon: Star Tac Cellular Telephone, 137
Starck, Philippe: Liberté and Pensées, 177
Steel, Fritz, 33
Steelcase Design and Engineering: Leap Chair, 112
Steelcase Design Team: Pathways, 76, 77
Stein, Mitch: IBMLife Network InfoPortal, 197
Stillion, Danny: IDEO 2010 Concepts, 166, 167
Stone, Phillip, 32
Struppler, Andreas: Werndl™ Emerge™ Desk, 99
Stumpf, William, 33; Aeron Office Chair, 108, 111
Swanke Hayden Connell: American Express Headquarters, NYC, 33
Swansey, John: IBM NetVista X40i, 186
Swatch Design: Net Invader, 141; Webmaster, 141
Syme, Paul: Rug, 90; Work Table, 91

Takahashi, Tomoyuki: IBM ThinkPad 570, 187
Tarabay, Pascal: Riding Desk, 209
Tati, Jacques: *Playtime*, 29
Tayar, Ali: Icon 20 Work Wall, 86
Taylor, Chuck: Jump Stuff Desktop Accessories, 176
Taylor, Frederick, 28, 44
Terho, Ikka: Netsurfer, 98
Thiel, Dieter: Figura 2000, 119
Thorp, Clarkson: Chunk Houses, 104; Eddy, 102, 103; Idea Factory Installation, version C, 104, 105; Idea Factory Installation, version E, 104, 105; Idea Factory Installation, version F, 105
Tingley, Michael: The Personal Harbor® Workspace, 92, 93
Tipp-Ex GmbH Design Team: Tipp-Ex Rapid Correction Fluid, 175
Tobon, Catalina: Riding Desk, 209
Toffler, Alvin, 44

Tolla, Ada: Inspiro-Tainer, 213
Tong, John: Rug, 90; Work Table, 91
Trium Company Design: Mondo Digital Mobile Phone, 165
Tsuge, Takahiro: Stereo Headphone SRF-H5, 189

Udagawa, Masamichi: IBM LifeNetwork InfoPortal, 197
Union Carbide Building (Bunshaft), 26, 27

Vidali, Zoe: Alumina, 88; Swell Station, options 1 and 3, 83
Vogtherr, Burkhard: Spin Chairs, 128

Wang, Wagon: Accompli A6188 63M Phone, 138
Weber, Max, 28
Whitelegg, John, 38
Wilder, Billy: *The Apartment*, 26, 35
Wilkinson, Clive, 34, 35; Nest, 106; TBWA Chiat/Day, 70, 71
Williams, Cecil B, 32
Winnicott, David, 38
Wright, Frank Lloyd, 20; Johnson Wax Headquarters, Racine, Wisconsin, 20, 27

Yahoo! advertisement, 14
Yamaji, Yasafumi: Caller ID Display TLID-10, 189
Yamanaka, Shunji: Tagtype Keyboard, 190, 191
Yamazaki, Kazuhiko: IBM ThinkPad 570, 187
Yousefi, Andre: IDEO 2010 Concepts, 166, 167

Zeller, Noel: Itty Bitty Booklight, 142; Long Reach Flexible Flashlight, 142, 143; Mouse Minder, 192